The Long Journey...

The Search Within

Jolene McCall

Volume One

The Long Journey... The Search Within
Copyright © 2012 by Hori-Son Press

Printed in the United States of America

Cover Art by Damon Edmonds

ISBN 978-1-938186-00-4

SAN 920-251X

Throughout this book, the name satan has deliberately not been capitalized. To capitalize a name would be proper grammar, and it also shows respect to that person. Since, I have no respect for satan or any demonic force of that nature, I choose to be grammatically incorrect and refrain from capitalizing his name.

Acknowledgements

To my Heavenly Father, Papa God, words alone cannot express my heartfelt love. You are my Alpha and Omega, my Beginning and my End. Your Words are a lamp unto my feet and a light unto my path. You have given me strength and encouragement. With every increase, it increases You; with every new revelation, it shows Your greatness; with every miracle, it makes known Your love. This journey of life has been extraordinary. All the revelation and insight into a deeper relationship with You has been the most rewarding experience in my life. I worship You and delight in serving You and Your people. May the world see how great You are, and may You be lifted on High as Your Words come to life within this book, Your book. Jesus, You are my Savior and my strength in times of trouble. You have led me to greener pastures, and my cup runneth over because of Your precious blood that covers my life daily. Holy Spirit, I welcome You into my life. You have brought me through many tests and trials and continue to do so. You have given me the power to overcome all obstacles that the enemy or world throws my way. May the Trinity be lifted up and exalted by everyone who receives the Truth, and may the Truth within this book set Your people free.

To my mentor, Sandy, with much love, I thank the Lord for sending you across my path and for your obedience. You will always be a huge part of my life. When I was down, you comforted me; when I was weak, you showed me strength, and when I desired growth, you fed me the Word of God. Great are those in the kingdom who are obedient to the calling of God. You touched my life for 10 long years, and because of your faithfulness to God, in leading me to still waters for His name's sake, I can rest in the love of my Heavenly Father. As I walk this path He has created specifically for me, I listen to the Holy Spirit's quiet voice, *"Jolene, go and give back all that was given to you."* You are truly an example of the virtuous woman spoken of in Proverbs. By the grace of God, I pray the anointing within this book will touch many lives, revealing our Savior in the same fashion shown to me many years ago. Your life was an example, which awakened within me a love I had never known, through Jesus Christ. As you were obedient to serving God's people, your compassion shown to me transformed my life to be the woman of God, He had predestined.

To my beloved grandchild, Jerrika, you are truly a blessing from God. Your timing into my life was absolutely perfect. A day never passes without your sweet little personality bringing laughter and tears at the same time to my eyes. God knew what He was doing when He blessed my life with such a wonderful gift. I am truly blessed to have the opportunity to enjoy that spark of life and love, which radiates within you. I thank the Lord for you daily, and I look to Him for instructions in raising you in His ways, in order that you live according to all which is written. Through you, God has revealed so much revelation, in observing the way you show compassion, forgiveness, and faith at such a young age. As you grow, know that God has placed a very great calling upon your life, and a legacy which will follow. Gammy loves you dearly!

To my daughter, Kristin Nicole, my miracle baby, God named you prior to conception which means "Christ Follower" and "Victorious People". He has given you a great calling. Through the pain and tragedies you have experienced at such a young age, God will continue to reveal your purpose in this life. Your Father in Heaven will wipe away every tear and restore you to be the daughter He created within. Everything the enemy has tried to use against you, God will turn those things around, in order that you rise up in victory and begin taking back that which has been taken. You have been blessed with many gifts and talents, and when you begin to line each of those up with the Word of God, you will be walking in the grace which has been bestowed upon your life. You are very much a leader among God's people, but continue daily to seek, knock, and ask. I am so very proud of you.

To my daughter, Karmin Michelle, my second miracle baby, whose name is a song and one who resembles God. The world may look at you as a mess-up, but God looks at you as the lovely and beautiful daughter He created. Baby girl, it does not matter what you have endured or where you have failed, you are created in the likeness and image of our Father in Heaven. God desires to use you greatly with such a magnificent calling upon your life, and you are seeing this as He continues to send young people across your path. Continue seeking His guidance and above all forgiveness, not from Him but yourself. God has forgiven you for everything you have done wrong, and it is time to see who you are in Christ. It is time to begin to trample over the enemy and bring down everything which exalts itself against the knowledge of Christ. It is time to take back all the enemy has taken from you. You shall be a warrior among His people, and nothing will hold you back. I am very proud to be your mother.

In memory of my daughter, Katrina Renae, meaning one who is pure, rebirth. Your life taught me many lessons, your death brought me redemption, your memory fuels me within to accomplish those things which you were able to see in me at a time I could not. I remember you writing a report in school, such a long time ago, about someone you wanted to be like when you grew up, and I remember that report was about me. I was always so proud to be your mother. Your beautiful smile is so very much missed. As I spend time giving of myself to others, I can see you smiling down upon me, happy that God gave you to me, even if it was for a little while. My beautiful daughter now in the Father's arms, safe and no longer in pain, we will be together again... one with the Trinity. I love you!

To my spiritual daughters, God has sent you across my path for reasons. As I continually pray for each of you, visions appear to me of a magnificent course in which God has designed for your lives. I am truly thankful that you have touched my life in such a powerful way. Prior to ever knowing you, God had given me visions of my daughters to come, and He continues to show me more girls suffering at the hands of the enemy which will cross my path. You may be reading this today and feel as though you know me, and perhaps, you do, perhaps, it is in a dream or vision. I will have many spiritual daughters whom I will love dearly, and I will lead each one to still waters to glorify my Father. Continue daily to seek His wisdom and knowledge into those things above and not of this world. As I have shared with each of you and will continue to do so, it is not about where you have been but about where you are going. Continue to focus on getting back up when the enemy knocks you down, and always remember that a soldier in battle never quits this walk of faith. Your endurance will pay off greatly in the end. Always be diligent, and may God continue to bless each of you as He draws you nearer to Him.

To my sisters in Christ, your friendship, your words, your encouragement, and your prayers have held my hand and strengthened my faith, in order to achieve those things within to bring me to the Cross at Calvary and share in the crucifixion with our Savior. My prayers and blessings remain always with each of you, knowing that our Father sees your faith, and He sees your heart, knowing all your desires. Through Him, we will triumph in our circumstances and victories together as one. I would not be here today without that strong, unique connection we have with each other. I love all of you dearly.

To my family and friends, those close at heart but perhaps far apart, even when we are not together, I pray for you often. I keep you close in my thoughts. As I have been diligent in my walk with my Father, He has been faithful in His promises to me. I know that God knows my heart and everything that is important to me. For the past two years, I have watched as God has been doing many works in the lives of those I love dearly and continues to do so. I pray that through God's Words, those I love will find comfort, answers to whatever circumstances they may be facing, and above all, that each of you will come to know God in the same way that I have come to know Him. I pray that each of you seek Truth for yourselves and your children, in order that you rise up to a place which brings genuine peace within your lives and a love that can only be found through our Savior, Jesus.

To my church family at Hope Alive, Pastor Bobby and Pastor Shannon, the dedication and determination to bringing the gospel in truth to this generation has been tremendous through such great leadership. My walk with God has ever increased due to the sacrifice of a body of believers, which walk out this journey of faith based on the whole principles and values as written in the Word of God. I am truly blessed to be a part of such a great ministry under such great leadership which not only leads, but opens doors for those coming into the fold to step out of their box and be all that God created them to be. I love all of you; you are my brothers and sisters in Christ and am honored that the path God planned uniquely for me crossed paths with the course this ministry is traveling. I thank you for your honesty and harshness when correction is needed; I thank you for your compassion and love when brokenness comes; I thank you for your humility and being real when seeking Truth in order to overcome personal obstacles. You have touched not only my life but made a huge impact in the lives of my daughters and grandbaby. My dedication to this ministry will never waver. I love you guys with all my heart.

Table of Contents

Introduction

In The Beginning

In the beginning, yes God created the Heavens and the Earth; however, in my beginning, God created a tiny seed which after conception and after a new birth – this seed began to grow and grow. And through this journey, God birthed within me, these words...

Through my journey, many things were encountered, many trials, and much tribulation. The search began with the desire to reach goals and obstacles which were only possible through my Father, only possible through His Son, and only possible with the Holy Spirit.

If you are reading this, look deep within yourself. If you are able to picture yourself in any of these characteristics, these words are for you. As you begin this journey to know the truth within, to perceive all which our Father desires for you, through the love of our heavenly Father, Jesus Christ, and the Holy Spirit – you can reach that destiny which has always been within. If you search deep, the seed is planted, and God is faithful to cultivate His desires within you.

It is written... God chooses those who the world despises. *(1 Corinthians 1:26-28)* Who does the world despise? To name a few: *prostitutes, those with no education, those on welfare, those in prison, those who have been in trouble with the law, those who do illegal drugs, those who murder, those who are weak, those who seem to be different...* but God has chosen you and desires to raise you above your circumstances. *If you fall in one of these categories – these words are for you...*

It is written... For it is by grace that you have been saved, through faith – and this not from yourselves, it is the gift of God – not by works. (Ephesians 2:8-9NIV) When we face judgment day, many will say they have done many works in His name. God will say, *"Depart from Me; I never knew you." (Matthew 7:22-24)* Many will try to enter the Kingdom of Heaven and will not be able. *(Luke 13:24)* Who will be excluded? There will be many who believe they are going to heaven, but these words will be spoken. *If you are unsure of your salvation – these words are for you...*

It is written... For those who live according to the flesh set their minds on the things of the flesh, but those who live according to the Spirit set their minds on the things of the Spirit. (Romans 8:5ESV) Ask yourself, *"What do you desire in life?"* Does your flesh line up with what God's Word says or does your flesh line up with the world? Who is your father? 1 John 3:10NIV says, *"This is how we know who the children of God are and who the children of the devil are: Anyone who does not do what is right is not a child of God; nor is anyone who does not love his brother."* Do you struggle with the temptations and desires of this world? Are you powerless to overcome those strong holds in your life? The Word says that the truth will set you free. *(John 8:32)* If you are *not sure of what God's Truth is – if you need that power to be able to overcome obstacles – these words are for you...*

It is written... Who is there to condemn us? Who shall ever separate us from Christ's Love? Shall suffering and affliction and tribulation? Or calamity and distress? Or persecution or hunger or destitution or peril or sword? Yet amid all these things we are more than conquerors and gain a surpassing victory through Him who loved us. For I am persuaded beyond doubt (am sure) that neither death nor life, nor angels nor principalities, nor things impending and threatening nor things to come, nor powers, nor height nor depth, nor anything else in all creation will be able to separate us from the love of God which is in Christ Jesus our Lord. (Romans 8:34-35, 37-39 Amp) Do you suffer from depression, from past hurts, from rape or incest, from physical or mental abuse, from loss? The Word says that nothing in this world from your past to your present and into your future will ever separate you from God's love. 1 Corinthians 13:7 says that love bears up under anything and everything; 1 Corinthians 13:8 says that love never fails. This is not love like the world knows and understands; this is God's love and God's love within us – His children. *If you desire healing in any areas of your life where there is great pain physically, mentally, or emotionally; if you desire to understand to a greater depth the power of that God-kind of love that the world does not know – these words are for you...*

It is written... If we have faith like a mustard seed, nothing will be impossible. *(Matthew 17:20)* Do you desire to walk in the same faith Jesus walked? Do you need healing in your body but you lack the faith to believe that God wants to heal you? Are there areas of your life that could use a great make-over? The Word says that whatever we ask in prayer, to believe and it will be given. *(Mark 11:24)* Do you question why your prayers are not answered? *If you desire to understand prayer, to understand faith – these words are for you...*

It is written... If you love Jesus, you will feed His sheep. *(John 21:17)* Are you prepared to feed His sheep? Are you ready to go forth with spiritual food and be a servant to God's children? Are you equipped as a Christian to serve? For even Jesus, came to serve and not to be served. *(Mark 10:45) If you are unsure of your calling, if you are unsure where you fit in to the body of believers, if you desire to seek God to a greater depth – these words are for you...*

We all have dreams. Do you ever wonder what it would actually be like to achieve those dreams? We need to realize that we have dreams deep within which we may think are unobtainable, but God has planted within you desires and dreams that only He can cultivate. God is not only the creator of the entire Universe and everything within, but He also planted deep within every one of His children the desire to be more than we could ever imagine. Those desires and dreams which we believe will never happen, can and will come to pass when we begin to see that God desires to manifest them in our lives. This will only happen His way not ours. When we begin to know God, He will begin to reveal His perfect plan. He has an absolutely remarkable course already designed and set in motion for each of our lives. Believing this and striving for this revelation, should make each of us excited to seek God daily in order to reach what we thought was unobtainable. Know that with God all is possible, with God we cannot go wrong, with God our lives will change in a way that we will never walk away from His love. *If you do not have this revelation, if you do not have this hunger for God in your life, and you feel that your walk with God has become stagnant, and you desire that energy, motivation, and excitement… these words are for you…*

1 The Journey through Self...

The Search for Salvation...

Where We Began

We all begin this life in different ways. Some of us may have been born into families who have very religious beliefs. Some may have been brought up in families that claim to be Christians, but what you see on the inside is not very Christ like. Others are born into families who do not believe there is a God, and there are some who have no religious or spiritual insight whatsoever. There are many who have different spiritual beliefs, and then we have those families who are Christians and try to conduct their lives according to the Word of God.

What brings someone to a book on Christianity? What is it that draws someone to a particular spiritual book? Many desire that growth, many are curious, some want to explore what they believe compared to what others believe, and still others are in search of answers. Whatever the reason, if you are in search of a closer relationship to God or if you are in search of knowing if there is a God, you will find your answers if you open your heart and begin to listen to the Holy Spirit.

As we begin this journey, we first will take a closer look within each of us. We will look at where we came from, where we are at today, what things we consider positive aspects to our character, and those things which we struggle with and would like to see changed within each of us. In order to search for the answers, we all have to come to a place where we are honest and desire something greater than what we have been able to achieve in our lives to present. The long journey is where we have all come from

1

and in order to change the course of our journey forward, we must stop, look within, and make decisions based on what needs to take place in order to bring about the changes we desire. This first chapter is a glimpse into our spiritual nature. This is where we look at our beliefs, what we know to be truth or fact, and what areas we are willing to be open-minded in order for God to reveal His nature within us.

Before beginning this search, write down the following:

1) I was raised in a home that believed

    _____

2) Today, I believe

    _____

3) Concerning salvation, I desire to know

    _____

My Testimony

I was raised in a family that had no spiritual belief whatsoever, and you never heard anyone speak of God unless it was used in vain. However, my journey with God really began at a very early age. You may ask how that could be. The answer is that I was chosen just like many of you and like many of you, I had no idea. My life growing up was a very painful time. I had a very painful childhood, adolescence, and into early adulthood. Being raised in a very dysfunctional family, deep within me was much pain; however, my God was with me even as a child. There was a seed planted within and even though I did not know God, He knew me. Did I believe there was a God? I did not believe or disbelieve. I did not know, did not ask, and did not search at that time. At some point, God had me look back to very early years, and I did. What did I see? At age 15, I overdosed on drugs and left my body. I could see my limp body lying on the floor lifeless. My spirit was being sucked into a dark hole, but the hole was not

2

empty. Within the hole were things which I did not understand, but I was terrified. I knew I had died, and the darkness which was consuming me was not heaven. Terrified, I cried out to God. Why would I do that? If I was not raised in a Christian or religious home, why would I cry out to God? If I had absolutely no influence in my life about God or no knowledge about who He was, why then would I cry out to a God I did not know? After crying out to God, my spirit immediately went back into my body with such force that it was very frightening to me, as well as my friend who was next to me.

At barely 17, my mother was on her death bed, and I found myself pregnant. I was trying to hide this fact from my family because they were all very worried about my mother. Finally, my mother died. I was frantic not knowing what I was going to do, but I knew the last thing I wanted was to hurt my dad or any of my family during this time of loss. I decided to try to abort the baby myself. I began to go into labor and doubled over in pain, I cried out again to God. Why? I did realize what I had done and that I did not want to kill my baby, but why would I cry out to a God that I did not know? What would have made me seek something or someone that I had no understanding of or no knowledge? Many years later, God began to show me these answers which will be shared in this book. At this time, I know that I was chosen; were you?

The Religious Family and Traditions

Many of you may say that you came from a family with many religious values which were instilled within you from a very early age. Many of you have carried on these values and traditions because of what you have been taught and what you know. We all have traditions in which we carry down from generation to

3

generation; however, all traditions may not necessarily be good. The word religion can mean the service and worship of God, and it can mean a personal set or institutionalized system of religious attitudes, beliefs, and practices. When we consider ourselves to be religious, this can be okay as long as the religion we practice lines up to what God's Word says. Far too often, our religion follows a personal or institutionalized system. Such systems many times have been handed down by a denomination that has set the practices on traditions, and often these traditions have been created by man many years ago. This is a fine line that you have to decide if your way of worshipping the "Most High God" is based on what the Word says or that of the world. Too often, the church has laid out the method in which the believers will follow in that particular denomination. There are many denominations in the world today, and I do believe that there are people in each denomination who may really be seeking God and desire to serve Him to greater depth. However, there are many who do not have that desire within them and may be lost up in a system which has turned into a social network. Those caught up in this system are in need of seeking and finding God in order to restore to the church what has been lost. We see that James, a servant of God, said if we think ourselves to be religious, we should keep ourselves unspotted and uncontaminated from the world.

James 1:26-27 (Amp) [26]If anyone thinks himself to be religious (piously observant of the external duties of his faith) and does not bridle his tongue but deludes his own heart, this person's religious service is worthless (futile, barren). [27]External religious worship [religion as it is expressed in outward acts] that is pure and unblemished in the sight of God the Father is this: to visit and help and care for the orphans and widows in their affliction and need, and to keep oneself unspotted and uncontaminated from the world.

Unspotted and uncontaminated from the world would be free from sin. I believe most of us would have to say that we have not done our share in caring for orphans and widows, according to verse 27. In reality, our outward acts should be focused on the afflictions and needs of others, those who cross our paths. If we all know of orphans and widows who have needs, by all means, that should be a focus in our life but is something that is not seen too often. This is an area that we do not want to acknowledge, but this is a great need in our country by far. On another note, uncontaminated from the world would also mean that we are not living according to the methods and beliefs of this world.

Romans 12:2 (Amp)[2]Do not be conformed to this world (this age), [fashioned after and adapted to its external, superficial customs], but be transformed (changed) by the [entire] renewal of your mind [by its new ideals and its new attitude], so that you may prove [for yourselves] what is the good and acceptable and perfect will of God, even the thing which is good and acceptable and perfect [in His sight for you].

So we see that we do not need to set our sights on the things of this world but renewing our minds on what is good, acceptable, and the perfect will of God. I have had many come to me for prayer and after asking a few questions, I would find that they go to church regularly and say they do not feel any different when they leave. I truly believe that if we are in a church where we feel the presence of God, we should be grounded and remain there. However, if you do not feel the presence of the Lord in the church you are a member, find a church where you can feel His presence. Jesus is the same today as He was yesterday; He never changes. When Jesus walked this earth, everywhere He went, people were stirred up. There were many miracles happening, and lives were changed. Men and women were so excited that they would leave all behind to follow Him, why should it be any different today?

Hebrews 13:8 (Amp) *⁸Jesus Christ (the Messiah) is [always] the same, yesterday, today, [yes] and forever (to the ages).*

Remember it is not religion that is bad, it is getting comfortable in doing things a certain way and forgetting that the Lord's House is just that – it is His House! As men and women of God, we should never forget that our time to come together as the body of Christ should be to honor and worship our Father in Heaven. Our fellowship within the walls of what we call our church home today is not for us to decide how God wants His time spent with His children to be conducted. If we walk into a church knowing that we spend 10 minutes to do this, 15 to do that, and we are walking out at exactly a certain time, how can we say that this is God's House? We have made it into something that man created in order to come together as a body of believers, but the whole concept of why we are really there has been lost to traditions.

Matthew 15:6 (Amp) *⁶So for the sake of your tradition (the rules handed down by your forefathers); you have set aside the Word of God [depriving it of force and authority and making it of no effect].*

This is nothing that is a new problem. This is something that has been passed down for many years, down from our forefathers. As children of God, are we not concerned with the concept of "just maybe" we have set aside the Word of God, as is written in Matthew? This was not written because it was not true. Everything in the Word of God is truth. We need to ask ourselves, *"Do we regularly go worship at a church service which is conducted according to a time schedule?"* Is it not true, many people today would not attend a church if they did not let out in

6

time for what they have planned in their personal lives that day? I know there are many men and women out there that desire more of God but we need to ask ourselves, are we willing to give up a little of our time to seek Him to a greater degree? Are we going to be upset with the pastor, priest, man, or woman of God, if they do not let the congregation go according to the traditions which have always been as long as we can remember? Does it really hurt our flesh so much that we cannot sit and endure a longer service in order to give time for God to move in our lives? Would a longer service be worth receiving the answers to life problems that we are seeking? God desires to bless His people to such a great degree, yet most lack in areas of their lives and do not understand why their prayers are not answered. I know there are those who are religious that would say, *"The bible also says everything should be done orderly." (1 Corinthians 14:40)* That is true, but I do not believe that orderly means we can only give God one or two hours. We need to go back and study the gospels to see how long Jesus ministered to the people who came from all over.

Matthew 14:12-16 (Amp) ¹²And John's disciples came and took up the body and buried it. Then they went and told Jesus. ¹³When Jesus heard it, He withdrew from there privately in a boat to a solitary place. But when the crowds heard of it, they followed Him [by land] on foot from the towns. ¹⁴When He went ashore and saw a great throng of people; He had compassion (pity and deep sympathy) for them and cured their sick. ¹⁵When evening came, the disciples came to Him and said, This is a remote and barren place, and the day is now over; send the throngs away into the villages to buy food for themselves. ¹⁶Jesus said, They do not need to go away; you give them something to eat.

This Scripture speaks of the death of John the Baptist, who was related to Mary the mother of Jesus. John was the one who prepared the way for Jesus' ministry. We make up so many

7

excuses to why we cannot even go to church and then while we are there, we complain if the service lasts too long. Do we see the love of Jesus in this Scripture? News came of John being killed because he stood up for his belief in Christ being the Son of God. When the news came, Jesus tried to slip away and go to a solitary place where He could be alone. Jesus was hurting over the death of one that He loved. Yet when he came ashore, compassion for the multitudes which had followed Him took over His emotions. It was no longer about what He felt at that moment. It was about Him serving the people. Even when the disciples wanted to send the people away, Jesus would not have it. Instead He multiplied the food and took care of everyone of them. Jesus gave of Himself throughout His ministry until the very end. We need to see the deep love in this for mankind and know that the little time we give during the service, does not even come close to the service that Jesus gave for us. Let's take a minute to focus on these questions and see where our heart is at this time.

1) Are you content with what you get out of your church service? _____
2) Do you desire to know God to a deeper degree, even if it means more of your time? _____
3) Have you questioned why God does not answer your prayers? _____
4) Are you open-minded enough to really listen to what the Word of God says? _____

Christian Families

We have many people today who claim to be Christians, but are they all Christians? Your walk with God will determine if your Christianity is real. Be honest and ask yourself, if someone were to ask those whom you are around on a daily basis, such as social contacts and business contacts, if they think you are a Christian, what would their reply be? Here is what I am getting at, many go to church on a regular basis or go on occasions, but they do not all "walk the walk" or "talk the talk." A great judge for this would be our children because they usually can see even those things you try to hide. I have ministered to many young people who have cried to me, and when I ask if they attend church regularly or if their family goes to church, too many times the response would be, *"Yes, they all go to church regularly."* However, it seems to end once they walk out of the doors of their church, playing church stops there. I have heard horror stories of families drinking heavily and even involved in drugs, but they are in church on a regular basis. Their children will tell you that church really means nothing to them; it is all about going for the image. Let's look at some of the false perceptions we face as Christians or as those who claim to be Christians today.

Once Saved ~ Always Saved

This question has been thrown out there many times from denomination to denomination, and I too have asked this same question many times. I believe there is great importance to us understanding what salvation is and what it means. So as Christians, we need to look deep within and make the assumption, were we really saved when we asked Jesus to come into our heart? We need to be sure that we know we are saved according to what is written in Scripture.

After becoming saved, I was very involved with the church for 10 years. I loved the Lord deeply, but I walked away from the church with the intentions of doing it alone. I felt that all I needed was just God and I. As I walked into the world away from the church or the body of believers that believed as I did, I made many mistakes. I made choices based on what I wanted not what God wanted for me. I never forgot God, and I still prayed but not daily. I still cried out to Him in times of trouble, and He still answered me – but not all the time. I still felt His presence in my life but not all the time. In fact, most of the time I felt I was walking my walk in the world by myself. I began to think like the world again, act like the world, and this life in the world began to consume me. I went through much pain and heartache, once again! If during this time someone would have asked me if I was saved, my reply would have been, *"Yes."* I knew that I had walked with God for 10 years; I knew that my relationship with Him those 10 years were wonderful and filled with revelation, wisdom, knowledge, miracles, peace, and victory. I knew that I was saved during that time, so my reply would have been, *"Yes, I was saved."* I knew that I was not living right, and I knew enough about the Word to know that I was not living according to what was commanded. I also knew that I had been saved and it was real. If someone would have asked me the question, *"If you die tomorrow would you go to heaven?",* my reply would have been something more like this, *"I just hope that if I die tomorrow that it isn't instantly, and I have time to make things right with God so that I am forgiven."* Or, my reply may have been something like this, *"I hope my time does not come until I have time to get my life back on track and have God be the priority in my life again."*

You may say that I was backslidden and some would say that I would have gone to heaven while others would say that I would have gone to hell. What matters here is that I know I was not right with God. I was not living right, and God was not first in my life. For that matter, He was not even second in my life. For me, I would have been scared to die knowing that I was not where I was supposed to be with God. My life was consumed in the world. I thought and acted like the world and for the most part, you would not have thought I had ever lived the life of a Christian because it did not show in my life. I did not want to die during this time. I

10

would have been scared to die. So the question to ask, was I saved? Is this salvation? Can we fall from grace? If that is salvation and all you have to do is get established living for God for so many years then go back into the world and live according to the desires of the flesh, that sounds pretty easy to be able to get into heaven. What God has shown me is that I was really saved, and I was backslidden. God also showed me that He knew I was coming back. However, I do not believe you can live according to the world doing whatever you want, living in sin, die, and go to heaven. I am sorry, but that is not what the Word says. However, God knows our heart. He knows who is His and who is not. God knew that I was coming back. He never gave up on me and knew that I was like the prodigal son, but I was coming home. I believe that God had His hands on my life to keep me safe until that day. Just like the prodigal son, he lived a life in the world full of sin, but He came home. God knew I was coming back; however, it was a risk to take. I do not believe if I had of died during those 15 years that I would have gone to heaven. I believe that I would have gone straight to hell; however, I know that my God knew I was His daughter. I know that He knew I was going through things, but I was coming home. So, do I believe that you can fall from grace? Let's look at what Paul said in Galatians...

Galatians 5:1 (NIV) [1]*It is for freedom that Christ has set us free. Stand firm, then, and do not let yourselves be burdened again by a yoke of slavery.*

In Christ, we are set free. Paul said to stand firm and not to let ourselves be burdened again by a yoke of slavery. He said, "Again." If we do not stand firm, we will fall into being slaves again, but slaves of what? We will become slaves of sin again and it goes on to say...

Galatians 5:4-5 (NIV) *⁴You who are trying to be justified by law have been alienated from Christ; you have fallen away from grace. ⁵But by faith we eagerly await through the Spirit the righteousness for which we hope.*

If we are not living by faith in Christ, we will be judged according to the law and have fallen away from grace. We can fall from grace, and when we do, we are no longer living by faith through Christ. We have chosen to walk in this world without Christ and have condemned ourselves to the law of sin and death.

Romans 8:1-2 (NIV) *¹Therefore, there is now no condemnation for those who are in Christ Jesus, ²because through Christ Jesus the law of the Spirit of life set me free from the law of sin and death.*

Paul goes on to say in Galatians...

Galatians 5:7-8 (NIV) *⁷You were running a good race. Who cut in on you and kept you from obeying the Truth? ⁸That kind of persuasion does not come from the one who calls you.*

You were once running a good race. Notice that it says, "You were running." At one time, you were walking with Christ running the same race that other Christians are running. You fell from grace, and who cut in on you? Who kept you from running the race? It is clear that when we fall from grace, it is not the Father or Jesus that cut in on us and caused us to fall. No, it is the enemy who has deceived us with words or deeds to make us begin to question God's words of wisdom and truth that has set us free. When we listen to the enemy and begin meditating on those thoughts, we will begin to question those things of God. If we continue to absorb what is not truth, we will be persuaded to do it our way and not God's way. It may be very subtle that the enemy comes in with a lie that we believe. It does not matter how it happens but it will happen. We can and will fall from grace if we are not walking on a daily basis with the "One" who called us! So, did I fall from grace? Absolutely! Did I listen to a lie? Absolutely! What did it cost me? It cost me 15 years of struggling trying to have that same peace and assurance of my salvation that I once had. It cost me pain and suffering, and the lie continued for 15 years before I was able to see the truth. It was 15 years before I even realized how I had stumbled and fallen from grace.

The Purpose of the Church

The Lord gave me great revelation when I came back home, to the church. One thing I know is that any time we walk away from the church, the body of believers which share our faith, we are going to stumble and fall from grace! I was running a good race; I was very involved in the ministry; I was raising my children in the ways of the Lord. I was strong but it did not matter. I opened a door for the enemy to convince me that I did not need the church to walk this walk with God. How many of us have said, *"It is not the church that gets us to heaven?"* I have said those exact words, and you are absolutely right. The church will not get you to heaven. Your own personal relationship with the Father, with Jesus is what gets you to heaven. In Ephesians it says that we fit together for a purpose with other believers, with the body of Christ.

Ephesians 4:16 (Amp) [16]*For because of Him the whole body (the church, in all its various parts), closely joined and firmly knit together by the joints and ligaments with which it is supplied, when each part [with power adapted to its need] is working properly [in all its functions], grows to full maturity, building itself up in love.*

We see that because of Jesus, we are closely joined together and this is how we work properly. Apart we do not work; apart we do not grow to full maturity. However, together we build in love. In 1 Corinthians 12, Paul informed us concerning the different gifts that are bestowed upon the believers. Paul went on to explain, we each are given individually as God chooses, but not all of us are given the same thing. Why is this and why is it important that we remain together as one?

1 Corinthians 12:14-22(Amp) [14]For the body does not consist of one limb or organ but of many. [15]If the foot should say, Because I am not the hand, I do not belong to the body, would it be therefore not [a part] of the body? [16]If the ear should say, Because I am not the eye, I do not belong to the body, would it be therefore not [a part] of the body? [17]If the whole body were an eye, where [would be the sense of] hearing? If the whole body were an ear, where [would be the sense of] smell? [18]But as it is, God has placed and arranged the limbs and organs in the body, each [particular one] of them, just as He wished and saw fit and with the best adaptation. [19]But if [the whole] were all a single organ, where would the body be? [20]And now there are [certainly] many limbs and organs, but a single body. [21]And the eye is not able to say to the hand, I have no need of you, nor again the head to the feet, I have no need of you. [22]But instead, there is [absolute] necessity for the parts of the body that are considered the more weak.

Paul used this to show how important it is for every single limb and every single organ within the body to work together, this is an example of the body of Christ. We all work together as one not apart but together. We find our strength in numbers. I cannot do what someone else can do, and they cannot do what I can do. When Christians get this revelation within them, they will begin to see the importance of not forsaking the body of Christ, and we are the body of Christ. It goes on to say in *Corinthians*...

25So that there should be no division or discord or lack of adaptation [of the parts of the body to each other], but the members all alike should have a mutual interest in and care for one another. 26And if one member suffers, all the parts [share] the suffering; if one member is honored, all the members [share in] the enjoyment of it. 27Now you [collectively] are Christ's body and [individually] you are members of it, each part severally and distinct [each with his own place and function].

How can we care for the other believers if we have walked away from the church or if we have cut off fellowship with those who have mutual interests? If we are suffering, how will the body know if we are no longer in association with them? We each have our own place and function within the body of Christ; however, if we have walked away then how are we going to do what we are called to do? I know when I walked away, I cut off all contact. I went as far back into the world as I could get and would avoid any of my former Christian friends when and if they tried to contact me. It is no wonder when we get out of church that we fall from grace. Why in the world would we believe that we can do this alone when we are called to be joined together with the other believers for a purpose? If we are not walking in the first thing that God called us to do, we are in it alone. I say this because when I minister to those who are new Christians, they want to know what they need to do next. A new Christian most of the time knows very little, other than the salvation message. In order to grow and walk with the Lord, they must be fed. Therefore, I tell them that it is God who will look at the overall picture of their life and begin to make changes. The changes that will occur in anyone's life will be in God's order. However, I can get them started on their walk with God. I let them know that they need to begin by seeking God and

15

this has to be done by daily setting aside a time to pray, read His Word, but above all they must be fed. In order to be fed, you have to be connected to a body. We have to be involved in a church and this is according to God's Word. We are expected to work together for the good of Christ, and it cannot be done alone. I listened to a lie from the enemy and thought that I could walk this alone. God distinctly said we are meant to share in this whole Christian walk with all of His other children. There is a reason for this. It was not written just to let us know we can do it this way or our own way. It has to be done God's way because His way is perfected. I believe we all know that we could use a little perfection in our lives, and that is only going to come when we look to the only source that is perfect.

James 5:16 (Amp) ¹⁶*Confess to one another therefore your faults (your slips, your false steps, your offenses, your sins) and pray [also] for one another, that you may be healed and restored [to a spiritual tone of mind and heart]. The earnest (heartfelt, continued) prayer of a righteous man makes tremendous power available [dynamic in its working].*

According to this Scripture, we are to confess to one another our faults and pray for one another. Who is praying for us if we are not walking with the body? Hopefully they still have you in their prayers, but do they really know what is going on in your life to pray effectively? We begin living in the world and seeking the wisdom of the world. We find ourselves back to old habits of running to friends, who are as lost as we are, and pouring out our problems. We somehow believe our lost friends are going to cause some miracle to happen which will make our circumstances change. We think if we seek wisdom or guidance through man that everything will somehow just fix itself, but the only truth that is going to line up your life to bring victory is found in the Word of God. By seeking godly wisdom and truth, we will be set free from the bondages that we are in. Our true freedom will never come from the wisdom of man.

John 8:32 (Amp) [32]*And you will know the Truth, and the Truth will set you free.*

In the book of Matthew below, Jesus said He is in the midst of those who are gathered together by two or three. Strength in numbers, we need to get this on the inside of us and stop living with pride believing that we can do anything we set our minds to. We need to stop assuming that our strength comes through our own accomplishments and through those things we have learned in the world, we are capable of mastering anything. We will fall when we look to ourselves for the solutions. Jesus is the solution; He is the only way. Many of us were taught as a small child to be strong in ourselves. We may have been taught that we do not need anybody or anything to be successful. We believe that we are capable of doing everything within ourselves. What happens when we walk in this concept and believe this? When misfortune happens and things do not go as we had planned, then we become disappointed and begin to feel that we have failed. God did not make failures; we can be all those things that we desire. The truth of the matter is that we have to know we can only do those things through Christ. We must realize when we are gathered in numbers, with those who believe as we do, we are much stronger. Why would anyone want to go to battle alone? We are in constant battle in the spiritual realm as long as we are living in these earthly bodies. I know I do not want to face the enemy every single day alone. I want the church in battle with me, the body of believers. I have yet to meet anyone who has said they did not want my prayers. In fact, many times when I see people passing and stop to say a few words, they always inform me to continue praying for them. So if we want others to

17

remember us in their prayers, why would we not want those who are on the winning side walking beside us?

Matthew 18:20 (Amp) [20]*For wherever two or three are gathered (drawn together as My followers) in (into) My name, there I AM in the midst of them.*

When we come together as believers, Jesus is with us. We need to know and realize that He is right there; He is knocking on that door for us to tear down those walls we have built. He desires to be a part of your life in order to make it better. He desires for your life to be more prosperous and more rewarding. Most of the time during my walk in the world, I did not feel the presence of God like I had during those years with the church. I had to come to a place where I knew that in order to get back to where I had been with my Father, I needed the body of believers. I needed to be connected. In Hebrews, it shows the importance of being together as one.

Hebrews 10:24-25 (Amp) [24]*And let us consider and give attentive, continuous care to watching over one another, studying how we may stir up (stimulate and incite) to love and helpful deeds and noble activities,* [25]*Not forsaking or neglecting to assemble together [as believers], as is the habit of some people, but admonishing (warning, urging, and encouraging) one another, and all the more faithfully as you see the day approaching.*

We are to give continuous care to watching over one another. We are to help each other to incite love, helpful deeds, and noble activities. There are times in our Christian walk where we may become discouraged. There may be times when we feel like giving up and maybe our faith seems to be wavering. Whatever we are going through in our lives, if we are connected, the body of believers will be there to help us walk through victoriously. When you are down, someone who is on fire and full of faith should be there by your side to pray for you, to lift you up, and to correct you, if need be. You may say no one knows what you are feeling, but if that be the case, it can only be your fault. If you are not sharing what you are feeling with a leader at your church or someone you trust who will give you godly counsel, there is always the alter call. You may come to church because you really needed something from God. You may feel that unction to go forward at the end of service for prayer, and this is the purpose of the alter call at many churches. If you do not feel that you received what you needed entirely from the service, then go forward on the altar call and let someone pray for you. How can they pray for your needs and minister to you if you do not make that step forward? How can anyone help you if you do not make the effort to share what you are going through? If we have walked away from the church because we were offended or wounded and back into the world, it does not matter at this point the reasons. It states clearly in *Hebrews 10:25* that we are not to forsake or neglect assembling together as believers. We are to warn, urge, and encourage one another faithfully. I know even with my walk now, I cannot do it alone. There are times I know the answer to my situation, but I will call one of my faithful ladies and tell them that I just need to hear it said to me. I no longer want to call those friends that are going to tell me what I want to hear; I call those friends that are going to be honest with me and give me God's Word. There comes a time when we are no longer satisfied with just milk, and milk alone will not give us all the nutrients we need to grow. Just as our physical bodies need to be fed meat or protein, our spiritual bodies also need something with more substance in order to be strong.

19

Hebrews 5:14 (KJV) [14]*But strong meat belongeth to them that are of full age, even those who by reason of use have their senses exercised to discern both good and evil.*

So before we can even begin to seek God to a deeper level, we must first take a deeper look inside each of us, into our hearts. Before we can even begin to know God or to understand God, we need to be sure of our salvation. God cannot even begin to start to bless us until we are His children and until we begin to share in the crucifixion of Christ. So ask yourself these questions and be honest with your answers.

1) Do you attend church regularly? _____
2) Have you become offended or wounded at church? _____
3) Does your Christian walk show outside of church? _____
4) What drives you to attend church? _____

Greater Depth to Knowing Salvation

When I meet people and begin to minister to them, one of the first things I ask is if they are saved. Surprisingly, most hesitate to answer the question but claim to be saved. If I dig a bit deeper, I find that they really do not even understand the meaning of salvation. As believers, we need to go deeper into salvation in order to know that we are saved. Let's first begin with what salvation is not. It is not an easy ticket into heaven! Salvation is not some ritual that is performed according to the traditions of man; it is not a prayer that we recite and it stops there; it is not something that you can do with good works in order to achieve eternal life. Many who are saved may never even attend church, just as I did for 15 years. I knew I was saved, but I seldom attended a church and never got involved if I did. This does not necessarily mean that you are not saved just because you are not in church. However, it does mean that you either are backslidden or you have never received revelation to the truth about what God's Word says concerning being joined with a body of believers. Of course, you may also be a new Christian and have not developed the discipline that it takes to serve God and begin to grow.

We have looked in depth about backslidden, and at this point, we should all understand that someone who is backslidden is basically back in the world, acting and thinking like those in the world. We have learned that when we walk away from the church back into the world, our growth with God stops right there. We will not live a victorious life in Christ. Instead, we will be defeated as a Christian as long as we continue to listen to whatever lie that caused us to stop running the race that was set before us. When I walked back into the world, I did not live any different than the world. I was not living a Christian life; therefore, I basically was living in sin. I had felt that my salvation and my relationship with God, was between me and Him. I had believed that it was no one else's business if I went to church. However, I was defeated and was no longer living a victorious life with Christ as I did the 10 years I walked with Him. From my own experience, I learned the hard way. If we are not being fed anything but the wisdom and knowledge of the world, we will surely die. We see in 1 Corinthians that Paul said...

1 Corinthians 2:6 (Amp) *6Yet when we are among the full-grown (spiritually mature Christians who are ripe in understanding), we do impart a [higher] wisdom (the knowledge of the divine plan previously hidden); but it is indeed not a wisdom of this present age or of this world nor of the leaders and rulers of this age, who are being brought to nothing and are doomed to pass away.*

Paul said it is those who are full-grown in the wisdom of God, not in the wisdom of the world, who will impart that higher wisdom and understanding which is of God. It goes on to say that those in this world who depend on the wisdom of the world, will be brought to nothing and are doomed to pass away. The Word also says that we must be different than the world, continually renewing our minds to that which is God.

Romans 12:2 (Amp) ²Do not be conformed to this world (this age), [fashioned after and adapted to its external, superficial customs], but be transformed (changed) by the [entire] renewal of your mind [by its new ideals and its new attitude], so that you may prove [for yourselves] what is the good and acceptable and perfect will of God, even the thing which is good and acceptable and perfect [in His sight for you].

We should continually be renewing our minds to that which is God, not that of the world. We begin by getting connected to a body. If, at some point, you question your salvation or feel that you have not given your life to God entirely, then you need to look further into what the Word says about salvation. So how can we be assured that we are one of God's children?

Salvation the Real Thing

John 1:12 (NIV) ¹²Yet to all who received him, to those who believed in his name, he gave the right to become children of God—

This was for all who believed. Jesus gave the right for all who believed on His name to become children of God. After getting back into church, did I go forward and get saved again? No, I did not. However, I did rededicate my life to God again, between me and God. I made a commitment and gave my life to Him. I chose to die to self that day. God has given me revelation that many times people go forward and say the salvation prayer in order to receive salvation. It is not the words that we speak which brings salvation. Salvation is what we believe in our heart, what we feel deep within. If we say the prayer of salvation and our life does not begin to gradually change, it is not heartfelt. If we feel no different after asking Jesus to be our Lord and Savior, it is not on the inside of us. Even if it is heartfelt, we will still miss it at times. Just because we are saved does not mean we will never stumble or fall. As we begin to draw closer to God and begin to walk in the Word and not the world, there will be trials and tribulation that we need to understand to a greater degree so that we do not give up and fall back into the world. These trials we will have to walk through will be discussed in greater detail through this series.

John 3:16 (Amp)[16]For God so greatly loved and dearly prized the world that He [even] gave up His only begotten (unique) Son, so that whoever believes in (trusts in, clings to, relies on) Him shall not perish (come to destruction, be lost) but have eternal (everlasting) life.

So who is salvation for? *John 3:16* says that whoever believes in Him should not perish but have eternal life. When we say we believe in Him, do we really mean that deep within our heart? Let's look at this deeper. What does it mean to believe something deep within our heart? Can we tell the difference when we say it with our minds and when we say it with our heart? Is it "mind-felt" or "heartfelt"?

If you have ever given birth to a baby, you have experienced that feeling of being in love. What about when we first met that person that we believed to be our soul mate? We know in our heart what that experience feels like to be in love for the first time, and there is no greater feeling than to hold our children in our arms. These experiences are heartfelt. Let's go a step further.

23

We understand how we feel that deep love within our heart for another person. What about when we believe in that special someone or our children? In order to believe in someone, we have to really know that person. As our children grow or someone we are close to, we begin to know them. We get to know their inner person, their heart, the way they think, the way they act, what makes them happy, and what makes them sad. We begin to learn about their emotions and feelings. We watch our children or that special person in our lives grow in areas. A child, we watch them grow into beautiful resemblances of ourselves; we watch them begin to learn and develop their own personalities. Whereas, a spouse, we will grow together as a couple. We will see that person many times make changes in order for the relationship to be nurturing in a positive way. So regardless, if we are watching our child grow or any other relationship grow, we begin to really know the person as we begin to see all their special tributes to life. We begin to believe in them in special ways, knowing they are capable of doing things at one time we were not seeing. So this person grows before our eyes, and we begin believing in them to greater depths. What happened? We allowed ourselves as people to trust, to love, to seek, and to search for those things within someone that at one time were not possible. Because we believed in them, we began to be open and anxious in learning more about them. At some point, we become more involved in their world. We get to a place where we are so excited to be around them and never become tired of spending those moments together. The same goes with God if we will just let go and begin to trust. If we take the benefit of the doubt and begin to seek and search the Scriptures for our answers, we will begin to know God. As we pursue those things that may not have seemed possible at one time, we will begin to know God to a greater depth. As the relationship is nurtured by us doing our part, we will begin to see wonderful things happen. We will begin to believe that Jesus is really the Son of God and that He really did die for us. We will begin to see that the love of the Father is the greatest love we will ever know.

Everything we just discussed is an action. We did not just get married one day and our spouse was the most wonderful thing ever. We soon learned their faults and shortcomings, but because of our deep love for them, we had faith enough to believe that this relationship would work. We even began to believe our relationship could go to greater depths. With our children, when they first came into the world, we soon found out that they were not the perfect little angels we had perceived. As they grew and we watched their lives unfold, we soon discovered that we had to put forth efforts of discipline in order to shape their character. As our children began to develop personalities, we were still in love with them and had faith to believe in them regardless if they did not turn out exactly the way we had dreamed. Sometimes we may want to give up as parents but when we persevere to the end, it can be worth it. Just the same with God, He does not give up on us, and when we seek and search the Scriptures, we will begin to get a greater image of whom God is and Jesus is. So it is not necessarily the words which we profess to be saved, but it has to be what we believe in our heart. We know when something is heartfelt. So in the same sense, we will feel it deep within our heart that Jesus is the Son of God. We will know He died on the cross for us and paid the price for our sins, in order that we have eternal life. We will believe in our heart that God looks upon us as His child, created in His image, just as we have looked upon our own children. We will feel deep within something different that we cannot explain, and that feeling is the presence of God the Father, God the Son, and God the Holy Spirit.

If all we ever do is just go to church, walk out of church, and go back into living like the world, we will be missing out on a wonderful experience of knowing that we are secure in the Father's love. We will miss out on understanding that He is all about our life here on earth. You may know Christians that everything seems to just go perfect in their life, and you may wonder if it is really as great as they make it out to be. This is something you will never know yourself, unless you make the decision to experience what they have. We have to come to the conclusion that we are tired of playing church and want the real thing. Our walk with God has to be something that we feel within our heart if it is ever going to be real. It is not a religious belief that we must recite a certain prayer or certain words in order to be saved. Receiving salvation is something that happens within our heart and it is something shared with our Father. If we do not have something deep down inside of us, it is merely words. Someone you deeply care about can tell you that they love you, but you are not going to just believe the words. We know that if someone really loves us, we feel it deep within our heart. In the same sense, God knows our heart. He knows if we are merely reciting words. Love is an action and our actions will speak much louder than words. If it is not heartfelt, our walk with God will continue to be nothing more than trying to make ourselves feel and look good by attending a church service. If it is not felt within our heart, we know it is not real, and there is something lacking in our walk with God. We know when we walk out of church if we are living the life of a Christian or if we forget about God until the next service. If our walk does not become real, there will be nothing in our life that illustrates we are Christians living for God. Without a manifestation within our lives, there will be no fruit. When we asked Jesus into our heart, we know if it was really sincere because if it was, it will be deep within us. We will have a desire to want to seek God, go to church, study the Word, and to pray in order to grow.

You may say that you do love God, and you were sincere when you asked Jesus into your heart. You may say that the desires and motivation are just not there to be committed to attending a church service each week. Perhaps you would say your life is too involved, and you do not have the time to devote to the church. I can only say that if you want something bad enough, you will find a way. We all have desires, and there are things that motivate each of us. It may be our children or perhaps it is our job for that paycheck. Maybe our time is spent with our spouse or with those we love. It may be spent with that particular hobby or sport. Whatever motivates us, we find time for it. This is where we are not getting that revelation. How can we love God, if we do not understand who God really is? How can we love God, if we are not even sure He exists? We cannot just all of a sudden believe that there is some supreme being that is offering us eternal life, and we will never make the choice to love Him and give up our other life if we do not really know Him. At some point when you get to a certain place in your life, you will have to make that decision. Do you believe there is a supreme being that is over the whole Universe? If you are not sure, then do you think that you are smart enough to figure all this out by yourself? Suppose the church is right and everything that you know about the bible is really accurate? If it is, would you not begin to think about just how much this "God" person really loves you? I mean, look at your life, many of us only our mothers could have put up with and loved. Many of us, our lives have been a total mess but suppose God really exists. Suppose everything about the Word of God is true. God really would have to love us a whole lot to let His Son die and go through the torture He went through for people who are selfish, inconsiderate, ungrateful, etc. I know He exists. I have that personal relationship with Him; therefore, I challenge any who are reading this to cry out to God. Cry out for Him to reveal Himself to you. You may be surprised what happens if you give Him a chance. Your eyes may be opened to reveal areas satan has you blinded. Now if you do believe and you look at just how much God loves you, the Word says that we love Him because He first loved us.

1 John 4:19 (KJV) [19]We love him, because he first loved us.

Think about this because it is how we first loved our own parents. They loved us, and we grew up knowing that they loved us. We loved and respected them because they were our parents. God is our parent. We have to understand how great that love is that He has for us. His love is so great that He sent His Son to die for each of us. When you get this revelation down on the inside of you, you will begin to feel this love. When you understand just how great God's love is for you, you will begin to feel it. When you can get to that place and cry out for God to forgive you of your sins and you realize that you can do nothing without Him, it will be heartfelt. When you can acknowledge that Jesus is the Son of God and that He died for you, then when you pray and receive Jesus as your own Savior, you will know true salvation. You will then feel the presence of God move in your life. Do not be like many who take one Scripture and profess it over their lives then continue living like the world. If that is where you are, you should question your salvation. We do not need to base our salvation on what some man has told us. We do not need to base our salvation on what a book, preacher, minister, or evangelist has said. We need to search the Scriptures of the Word of God and know within our hearts that we know we are saved. Why would anyone want to base their salvation on what someone besides God told them? This is life or death. We will wake up in heaven, or we will wake up in hell. Only you can decide your fate! Jesus had asked Peter who he said He was in Matthew 16. Peter had replied that Jesus was the Christ, the Son of the Living God. What was Jesus' reply?

Matthew 16:16-18 (NIV) [16]Simon Peter answered, "You are the Christ, the Son of the living God." [17]Jesus replied, "Blessed are you, Simon son of Jonah, for this was not revealed to you by man, but by my Father in heaven."

Jesus replied to Peter that man has not revealed this to you but His Father in heaven. Who has revealed to you that Jesus is the Son of God? Who has assured you of your salvation?

How to Become Saved

We know that salvation is for all who believe that Jesus is the Son of God, and we understand that what we believe must be felt within our heart. We must know who God is and how great His love for us is. We must also realize that we need Jesus in our life. We need salvation in order to not only have eternal life but also to have a victorious life here on earth. So let's look at some of the Scriptures pertaining to salvation.

Luke 23:42-43 (NLT) [42] Then he said, "Jesus, remember me when you come into your Kingdom." [43] And Jesus replied, "I assure you, today you will be with me in paradise."

Jesus was on the cross along with two other men being crucified, one on each side. One of the men spoke to Jesus and asked that He remember him when He comes into His Kingdom. What was Jesus' reply? He assured him that he would be with Him in paradise. This man did not ask for Jesus to come into his

29

heart; he did not say some kind of ritual prayer. This man merely spoke words to Jesus which told Him that he believed He was the Son of God! We know that our heart has to be right and it has to be heartfelt because if it is not, God knows our heart! We cannot pretend or go through the motions. God knows if it is heartfelt or not. This man on the cross, he did not say some kind of ritual, and he did not recite a certain prayer. It was merely what was in his heart, and Jesus knew he believed. Therefore, we can recite a prayer every week in church; we can go through rituals; we can do according to man's teachings, but if it is not in our heart, we are no more saved than when we walked into church. On judgment day, we will be one of those who say, *"But Father, I did all these things in Your name,"* and God will say to us, *"Depart from me, for I never knew you!"*

Matthew 7:22-24 (Amp) *[22]Many will say to Me on that day, Lord, Lord, have we not prophesied in Your name and driven out demons in Your name and done many mighty works in Your name? [23]And then I will say to them openly (publicly), I never knew you; depart from Me, you who act wickedly [disregarding My commands]. [24]So everyone who hears these words of Mine and acts upon them [obeying them] will be like a sensible (prudent, practical, wise) man who built his house upon the rock.*

The sad truth is that hell will be full of good people. It will be full of many who thought they were saved. We need to be assured that our salvation is real. We need to be assured that our salvation comes from our heart, and it is not something we believe because a preacher, a priest, or anyone else standing before us have taught a sermon based on salvation. I know it is not necessarily what someone has taught, but sometimes it is how we perceive what has been taught. The main concept to a salvation message needs to be emphasized that it is not merely the words we speak but what we feel within. I have had some people say that they do not know for sure if they are going to heaven. If you do not know for sure, you probably are not saved. Those who are living and walking in the Word, they know they are saved and are doing the will of God. Those who are saved know they have that personal heartfelt relationship with the Father, the Son, and the Holy Spirit.

1 John 4:15 (Amp) [15]Anyone who confesses (acknowledges, owns) that Jesus is the Son of God, God abides (lives, makes His home) in him and he [abides, lives, makes his home] in God.

In 1 John, the Scripture says that anyone who confesses Jesus is the Son of God... but note, when the man who hung on the cross asked Jesus to remember him in paradise, in that man's heart Jesus knew that he acknowledged He was the Son of God. That man knew that Jesus was going to be with the Father in heaven. The man did not have to say, *"I believe You are the Son of God."* No, in his heart, he knew Jesus was the Son of God. This man's heart was right. Words are meaningless to God unless it is heartfelt or unless it is action. On the same note, we should confess this because it is speaking faith. Speaking forth and professing that you believe is acknowledging this to ourselves, the world, and above all to our Father in Heaven that we do believe Jesus is the Son of God.

Why should we confess that Jesus is the Son of God? We see below in Romans, with the heart a person believes. So it is not what comes forth out of our mouth, but with the mouth, one confesses, why? That is faith, believing those things that you cannot see. When we proclaim this openly, we are by faith declaring that even though we cannot see God, we cannot see Jesus, we cannot see those things that have not happened yet, we believe. We cannot see that we will someday be in heaven, yet by faith, we believe that Jesus died for us. He died for you and if for no one else, it was for you! This is an open declaration that we realize just how much God loves us because He sent His son for all who believe.

Romans 10:10 (Amp) [10]For with the heart a person believes (adheres to, trusts in, and relies on Christ) and so is justified (declared righteous, acceptable to God), and with the mouth he confesses (declares openly and speaks out freely his faith) and confirms [his] salvation.

The New Christian

If you recently gave your life to Jesus and are just beginning your walk with the Lord, as a new babe in Christ, your growth will depend on how much effort you put forth. Take a newborn baby, they are all unique and grow at different rates. They develop physically and mentally at a different pace. It is not to judge how fast or how slow you are growing and learning. Do not base it on how spiritual you may think someone else is. Your new walk with Jesus should be a really exciting and fascinating experience. You are like a new born baby. You should enjoy time spent with your Father by getting to know Him and His love for you. Chapter 2 will begin a new journey that will lead you into many fascinating truths and healing in order to deepen that relationship with God.

2 The Journey through the New Birth...

The Search for Life after Salvation...

What is life after salvation? Does it just stop there? When we become saved, we feel a difference within our heart. We begin to acknowledge sin in our life but what next?

2 Corinthians 5:17 (NIV) *[17]Therefore, if anyone is in Christ, he is a new creation; the old has gone, the new has come!*

The New Beginning

We need to look at two walks with Christ. The first walk we will look at is that of the new babe in Christ. The second walk we need to focus on is the Christian who knows that they have not been living right, and because of conviction in their life, they are ready to begin that walk fresh with a rededication to the Lord. However, both of these walks need to begin as a new babe in Christ. The difference between the two, the Christian, who has rededicated their life, may know much more about the bible than the new babe in Christ. Yet, those who are coming back to the Lord need to realize there are many areas they do not have revelation. In receiving revelation in areas where we are weak, we will become strong. This should be an exciting beginning in your life because from this point forward, you should no longer be going backwards. Beginning today, it is no longer messing up and feeling the guilt, the shame, or the condemnation. You will begin a walk with the Lord knowing you will be able to overcome your shortcomings and failings. You will begin a walk which is forward, and you need only to look back to receive the necessary healing and revelations of your past in order to draw strength for victory to your future!

33

You may or may not know anything about the bible as a new babe in Christ; however, that is not your focus point. Your focus is to know, with Jesus, you will begin to receive the truth and revelation will come. In doing so, you will be set free in order to walk a victorious life with Christ. I was about 25 years old before I began my walk with God. Looking back to my past, it was easier for me to believe anything God's Word said because I was not dealing with years of being programmed wrong, so to speak. When we are raised in a Christian or Religious home, we may have also been raised in traditions which have been passed down from generation to generation. In fact, many times our traditions are contrary to what God's Word says. I am not saying every Christian home has traditions which are not biblical; however, I am saying many of the traditions of man are not of God. When you are a small child, you have no choice but to believe what you are taught. We come into this world eager and hungry to learn, but we do not always have a decision in what we are being taught. If the American families were being taught godly principles, we would not see so much crime, poverty, sickness, and defeat in our nation. By no means is this intended to put condemnation on anyone but to bring truth to a world which is destined to suffering, in hopes of setting this generation free from sin and death. The majority of families today are living exactly like the world because they know no difference. Through our Lord and Savior, we no longer have to live not knowing what God's Word says about our situation. We no longer have to live in a world filled with defeat because we have the tools it takes to rise above our situations. This is your new beginning, a beginning into a life which will be rewarding and dynamic.

If you have rededicated your life to Christ, it is going to be uphill from this point. I know if I am capable of overcoming all the obstacles in which satan has used to try and destroy my life, anyone is capable of doing the same. My God is your God. He is powerful and loves you the same as He loves me. When I rededicated my life, God put within my heart the unction to "Go!" His words to me have been powerful. I am called to rise and go forth. I am called to give back everything He has given me to those who need revelation in order to be successful, victorious Christians today. He put this on my heart because He loves you the same as He loves me. We should never think anyone else is greater than we are to God because He desires to use each of us in great ways. God is no respecter of persons. However, we are all nothing except through Jesus, and God desires for you to be what He created you to be. God does not make things which are useless or of no value, and He did not create His children to barely get by. He did not create His children to merely survive. On the contrary, God has this wonderful course of life for you to follow. In this path, you will be able to reach all those godly dreams and desires in which He planted deep within. Why would you want to follow a path you had laid out when the All Mighty God, who created the Universe, has a course created just for you? It is designed according to His thoughts, His might, His strength, and His wisdom. God sees you walking this course, and He sees you finding that joy and peace which can only be found through Him. My image of myself was so distorted, due to what I had been told growing up, that I believed I was a "nobody." I absolutely had no confidence that I would ever be anything. In fact, I was the child who would take an "F" in school before I would ever get up in front of the class to give an oral report. If someone would had told me that I would be doing some of the things I have done today, I would have said, *"Not me, you will never see me do that!"* However, God did see me doing those things and much more. God planted within me great things. He had confidence in knowing I would rise above my circumstances and overcome

35

those fears. Today, I know none of my desires could have ever been accomplished in me.

Pain Still Abounds

It does not matter if you are a new Christian or have just rededicated your life to Christ, pain still abounds within you. God wants to set you free from all the pain, set you free from being bound, and heal you from all the suffering within. When I walked away from the church, I was wounded like many today who find themselves backslidden. satan used that opportunity to attack me and drag me down. Did I stop loving God? No, absolutely not and God never stopped believing in or loving me. In fact, the Holy Spirit continued to convict me on a daily basis that I needed to come home and get my life in order. Why? God was not going to just let me go and walk away that easy. God is not going to simply let you fall back into the world either. God will fight to awaken you from the place you are at currently, in hopes you surrender totally to Him. You have decided to read this book because of something deep within that will not let you go. Something continually pushes you to surrender everything to God. Today is your day to be set free from your past. Any and all circumstances, satan has used to try and destroy your life, God will begin to turn around in order for victory to reign.

I knew I was not where I needed to be all those years. The longer I stayed away, the more I was sucked into the world deeper and deeper. However, I know God knew my heart and was with me all those years. When I did come home, God knew I was coming back stronger than ever. I would not have been able to return and become strong if I had not given all the pain and defeat to Him. Through my determination and persevering, God began to give me so much revelation in order that I would be able to

36

sustain the temptations of falling away again. With this revelation, He has spoken to me and said, *"Jolene, go – share what I have given you!"* God sees His people hurting and sees the pain within. He desires all of His children will come to a place of surrender. This is in hopes that He can wipe away every tear and make each of us whole. I have shared the revelation of the importance of staying connected to the body of believers, but there is more we need to see in order to draw strength to endure.

Why We Do The Things We Do

Do you ever wonder why we sometimes continually make the same mistakes? *"Why do I always choose the wrong people?"* *"What is the matter with me?"* I too have asked God questions like these. After coming home, I began to ask Him many more questions. I wanted to see the whole picture. I wanted God to reveal to me why I did certain things in my past. After all the miracles and signs, how could I have been so easily persuaded to walk away from the truth and believe a lie? During the 10 years of my walk with God, I thought I was grounded enough in His love and all He had brought me through that I could never have fallen away. I would have never thought I could have turned a complete 360° and become so much like the world again, but through the revelation I have received, God has shown me many of His people have not let go of their pain and allowed Him to heal them. Many today have not forgiven themselves. Others have quit believing in themselves as well as God. Many of us quit believing because of circumstances that have become too great to bear. Let's first begin to understand why we do some of the things we do. As I began to look into my past, God began to show me where we originated.

37

Exodus 14:21-28(NIV) ²¹ Then Moses stretched out his hand over the sea, and all that night the LORD drove the sea back with a strong east wind and turned it into dry land. The waters were divided, ²² and the Israelites went through the sea on dry ground, with a wall of water on their right and on their left. ²³ The Egyptians pursued them, and all Pharaoh's horses and chariots and horsemen followed them into the sea. ²⁴ During the last watch of the night the LORD looked down from the pillar of fire and cloud at the Egyptian army and threw it into confusion. ²⁵ He made the wheels of their chariots come off so that they had difficulty driving. And the Egyptians said, "Let's get away from the Israelites! The LORD is fighting for them against Egypt." ²⁶ Then the LORD said to Moses, "Stretch out your hand over the sea so that the waters may flow back over the Egyptians and their chariots and horsemen." ²⁷ Moses stretched out his hand over the sea, and at daybreak the sea went back to its place. The Egyptians were fleeing toward it, and the LORD swept them into the sea. ²⁸ The water flowed back and covered the chariots and horsemen—the entire army of Pharaoh that had followed the Israelites into the sea. Not one of them survived.

This is an incredible miracle God performed to set His people free. Can you even imagine being able to see anything remotely close to what the Israelites walked through and those things they witnessed? As the Scriptures go on, we see even after such a great victory, the Israelites complained.

Exodus 16:1-3(NIV) ¹ The whole Israelite community set out from Elim and came to the Desert of Sin, which is between Elim and Sinai, on the fifteenth day of the second month after they had come out of Egypt. ² In the desert the whole community grumbled against Moses and Aaron. ³ The Israelites said to them, "If only we had died by the LORD's hand in Egypt! There we sat around pots of meat and ate all the food we *wanted, but you have brought us out into this desert to starve this entire assembly to death."*

Can we not see ourselves in this? God blesses us with such a great miracle in our life and many times, we do not even acknowledge God was in the midst of our circumstances. We seldom give credit where credit is due. I can remember back in my self-centered life, when things went according to MY plans, I was content. I seldom even thought about anyone else being responsible for my good fortune other than myself. Remember the saying, *"Watch out for you because no one else will"?* We grow up in this self-centered world being taught that it is all about us. It is no wonder our lives are such a mess. When you begin to walk this walk with the Lord, you will recognize everything good comes from above.

James 1:17 (NLT)[17] Whatever is good and perfect comes down to us from God our Father, who created all the lights in the heavens. He never changes or casts a shifting shadow.

You may say, *"But how do you know God did this; how do you know that it was not just by chance?"* My response to you is, *"How do you know it was not God?"* Do you believe in Karma? Karma means actions or deeds. It is a theory used in Buddhism, Hinduism, and Jainism. The meaning is much like that of the "Law of Cause and Effect." When we do things which are evil or wrong, we will face hardships in life. When we do those things which are good, we will have good fortune. How most people see Karma, it is payback. You do something good; good will come. You do something bad; bad will come. Karma is nothing new and actually dates back to the beginning of time. Man or religion *(eastern religions)* wanted to give it the name Karma; however, God thought of it first but does not get the credit. It amazes me how many times I can minister about how we reap what we sow whether good or bad, and people have a puzzled look on their face. When I use the word "Karma," they understand.

Galatians 6:7 (NIV) [7]*Do not be deceived: God cannot be mocked. A man reaps what he sows.*

We give, and we will receive. We hold back, and it is held back from us. We do good; good will come to us. We do evil; we will reap evil. What you sow from your natural man or your flesh will reap destruction. What you sow spiritually will reap for eternal.

Galatians 6:8 (NIV) [8]*The one who sows to please his sinful nature, from that nature will reap destruction; the one who sows to please the Spirit, from the Spirit will reap eternal life.*

We know in the Scriptures, the children of Israel were thankful for the victory of being led out of captivity. After just a short time, they were complaining. We are no different. God will answer our prayers maybe in an area we have been seeking and praying about. We believe God for a miracle or a door to open in our life that we thought impossible, and it comes to pass. We then become hungry just like the Israelites. We feel we do not have enough or lack in material things we want. What do we do? We begin to complain just like the Israelites. God led His people out of Egypt after many signs and wonders. The Israelites saw things that to our mind are unbelievable. When they became dissatisfied because of their lack, why did they not believe God would provide for them? God was big enough to part the red sea and bring plague after plague on Egypt. All of a sudden, He was not big enough to provide them with food.

If you have walked with the Lord in your past and fell back into the world, was it because of disappointment? Was it because of a lack of faith to believe how great and powerful God is? In my walk with God, I became discouraged because of an attack on my family by the enemy. This attack was greater than I could bear alone. When I went to the church for guidance, I was let down. Instead of looking to God for direction, I ran back into the world. I became angry at the church and began the blame game. How many of us have played the blame game? When things did not go as you planned or you did not get what you wanted, then the blame begins. If someone told you wrong or led you down a wrong path, then it was not your fault and you begin to point your finger at someone else. We play the blame game because we do not want to take responsibility for choices we may have made. During my fall, I had this thought, *"If I had not listened to the church which gave me the wrong direction, I would not have spent all those wasted years trying to walk a walk which ended in such a great defeat!"* That was how I felt! I blamed the church for wasted years. Were my years really wasted? No! Anything we go through in life, God can turn around for His glory. I would not be writing this book today if I had not endured the test of that time. It may take a while before we get through something, but time is all we have while waiting for Jesus' return. We will get through as long as we persevere. Today, I am stronger and endured the hardship. In receiving all the revelation in which God has given me, I have surrendered to be used according to His perfect plan for my life.

James 1:12 (NIV) [12]*Blessed is the man who perseveres under trial, because when he has stood the test, he will receive the crown of life that God has promised to those who love him.*

This is not to say I have received the crown of life. There will be a crown awaiting every one of God's children as He has promised to those who love him. Throughout this book, you will be able to witness the great miracles God has performed in my life. You may question why I trusted God for some things but not for everything. If God was capable of doing the great signs and wonders in my life, how could I have become discouraged? There are many reasons we fall. If we look at the circumstances and take our eyes off of the source, which is Jesus, we will fall. Today, we are no different than the Israelites and no different than Adam and Eve. What did God do after the Israelites complained?

Exodus 16:4-5(NIV) [4] *Then the LORD said to Moses, "I will rain down bread from heaven for you. The people are to go out each day and gather enough for that day. In this way I will test them and see whether they will follow my instructions.* [5] *On the sixth day they are to prepare what they bring in, and that is to be twice as much as they gather on the other days."*

The Israelites continued to complain and walk in unbelief. There was little to no trust, yet what did God do? He provided food for them. When our own children begin to complain and not be satisfied, many times we make the decision they will do without until their attitude changes. But God did not withhold food from them. He gave them what they needed but also instructions to follow. Why were they given instructions? God knows we have not arrived at the place He desires us to be. He will continue to take steps to try to teach us in order that we do grow stronger. God wants us to realize that we cannot do it without Him. He wants us to understand we must turn to Him. He is the solution and the answer. Why can we not get the principle down that we just need to ask and not complain? If things do not turn out the way we planned, why can we not accept that it is likely for a reason? Think back when you were a teenager or think about your own children, if you have been blessed to raise adolescents. We all know these are the years where young people think they have already arrived and sometimes are not teachable. At this age, teens totally disagree with their parents who are only trying to provide for them. I know there are times I have asked my girls a simple question and their response back was one that was very bitter. Many times our bitterness is a result of hidden anger which has not been dealt with. Many times my girls would be apologetic because they realized my question was just a simple question of concern, nothing more and nothing less. However, there are many adults today that have not grown past the adolescent stage. We have to stop being bitter for circumstances in our lives whether past or present. If we are not satisfied with where we are, we need to step up and make the decision that we are willing to go forward with God. We must allow Him to change our lives. God is not against us but the world is.

Romans 8:31 (NIV) [31]*What, then, shall we say in response to this? If God is for us, who can be against us?*

Therefore, we need to put our trust in His decisions for our lives. If we will only surrender to God, we will begin to see that He has His hands on those things which concern us. If we are His children, He is going to take care of us. Now what was God trying to teach the Israelites? God wants a people who are willing to trust Him. He wants a people willing to follow and obey. God is continually seeking those men and women out there that are hungry for Him. When His children finally make the decision to walk with Him, He will then begin changing their lives. He will teach them to trust, to follow and not to lead. If you are a willing body, God is there to turn your situations and circumstances around.

43

The Beginning of Healing Our Wounds

We know from the beginning of time, man has always complained and frequently finds dissatisfaction in never having enough. We have all complained about something. Maybe we feel we do not have enough money. Perhaps we feel that we are not pretty enough or popular enough. We may feel that we are not smart enough. I know I have wondered how the children of Israel could have seen all the signs and wonders and still have doubted God. Do you ever think that if you had lived during biblical days and witnessed the awesome power of God, you would have trusted and not complained as they did? What about Adam and Eve, I have heard people criticize them saying, *"If it were not for them, we would not be living as we are today."* However, we can see we really are no different today than they were yesterday! I am thankful I live in a day where we have the blood of Jesus to cover our transgressions. We do not have to sacrifice animals hoping we are covered as they did. Today our faith has to rest in the fact that we never saw Jesus and never witnessed those unexplained miracles. We did not see the parting of the Red Sea or the plagues in Egypt. We did not walk with God in the Garden of Eden; therefore, we have to believe what has been passed down by our ancestors but not entirely. You will get to a place where there will be signs and miracles, and then you will be able to start believing in those things you cannot see. You will get to a place where God the Father, the Son, and the Holy Spirit are revealed to you in various ways. To begin our healing, we have to do something different. We have to get the revelation down deep inside of us that no matter what, we are not going to be a complaining generation. We are going to trust God with our walk, no matter what the circumstances look like. The end result, if it is God, will be worth it.

44

It has been human nature from the beginning of time to complain and be unsatisfied. We continually look at what we have had to endure in life. We look at how our life in the present is not where we want it to be. We look at others and wish we had what they have. Many of us have been wounded and carry this baggage around just like men and women in biblical days. If we have not dealt with the pain in our lives, then our wounds are still festering. We need to recognize the source. Nothing in our lives will change until we come to that place where we are tired of being beat down. To begin this healing process, let's think back to our childhood, adolescence, and into our adult hood. Make a list of everyone or any circumstances which have caused pain in your life in order to deal with your wounds. Take a minute right now and compose your list.

My List of Wounds: *(Use additional paper if necessary)*

1) _____

2) _____

3) _____

4) _____

After making your list, write a letter to every person who wounded you in any way. I remember being in counseling, as a young adult, and a counselor telling me to do this. My response was, *"I have done this my whole life."* Did you know this is self therapy? It is getting the ugly stuff within – out! We can only begin to heal those wounds when we open up and get them out. When I say to write a letter to those who have wounded you, I do not mean to give them the letter. Of course, if you feel led by the Holy Spirit to do so, then that is between you and God.

Otherwise, there is no reason to open up old wounds and hurt others. As a Christian, it is time to let go and heal those pains within us. It is time to forgive those who may have caused those hurts. The letter is merely to get the pain out of you and let go of those things which have kept you bound.

We can see by the circumstances of the children of Israel there were many wounds in their lives. They lived in captivity as slaves for many years. They had physical scars as well as emotional wounds. Even though God led them out of captivity, they still operated in the same way they always had because of the wounds they carried with them. Today, new Christians as well as those who continually fall back into the world continue to walk around on a daily basis with open wounds. Our first step is to get the wounds on the inside – out! The next step is to present them to the Lord by reading each one of those letters out loud. God knows what those wounds are, but you need to voice it openly. This will allow you to hear your spirit within releasing those things to God. In prayer or time with God, we need to take every letter or wound and give them over to Him once and for all. God will then begin the healing process and wipe away every tear. When we are wounded and carry this baggage around with us, it limits what God can do with us. Let me emphasize this one more time – God is limited on what He can do with your life as long as you hold on to the pain within. We must let go and let God! When we have open wounds, it is easier to walk away and become discouraged. It is easier to quit believing God is really working in our lives when we are wounded, and it is easier to stop believing we are capable of being something unimaginable. This is where we trust in His Word, *"... all things are possible for those who believe."*

Mark 9:23 (Amp)[23]*And Jesus said, [You say to Me], If You can do anything? [Why,] all things can be (are possible) to him who believes!*

After we first become saved, we walk back into the world after that wonderful experience of knowing Jesus died on the cross for us. After the Father has revealed how much He loves us, we walk back into the same situations and circumstances prior to our conversion. Furthermore, nothing immediately will change in your life. When you walk back into your world, all those issues which may have led you to find God will still be there. However, the difference is that now you have a Savior who will begin to clean up your life in order that those issues do dissipate.

As God begins to work in our lives, through the Holy Spirit, there will be a focus on pain in our lives. Most of the pain in our lives is due to things from our past, which have not been healed. Once those areas have been dealt with, we will walk away free. There may have been things which happened to us many years ago or even recent things, which caused us to give up hope. Whatever the case may be, once we put our trust in the Lord, He will show us a completely different way of making things happen in our lives. The part of your life that has changed after becoming saved will be the realization of knowing you have a God who loves you, a Savior who died for you, and the Holy Spirit who desires to walk with you daily. Your salvation is a new beginning, but like with any new beginning, it takes time. There will be a process of growth that must take place.

Take the addition of a new baby being born into your family for the first time; will you know prior how this will affect your life? You may have some kind of sense as to what life is going to be like, but you absolutely do not know how much it is going to change your life until you walk in it. It does not matter what others have told you about how a child changes your life; you will not experience it to the degree of reality until you have walked in it. In the same sense, when you become saved, you may perceive your life is going to go from a total mess to absolute victory over night. This is not going to happen just like that. Perhaps you are more realistic and believe because you are saved, things are up hill from this day forward. Therefore, you may believe that Jesus is going to just miraculously turn your life around within the near future. What I want to clarify here is that your life can and will begin to turn around for the better; however, being saved does not provide some magical solution to your current life. You cannot all of a sudden wake up one day, and everything is just great. Many people today go to church regularly and still cry out to God saying, *"Lord, why is my life so miserable when I go to church every Sunday, and still, I am constantly faced with problems?"* These same people will try and try, and some will eventually give up on God or give up on the church. Many times they will give up on believing God truly wants to bless them. Why is this? Because they feel nothing has changed; their problems still remain and so what is the use in trying.

With God, there is nothing negative. God only operates in positive ways. When we begin to think like Jesus, we too will operate in positive ways. Being negative has never and will never get anything accomplished; however, having a positive attitude and positive words will accomplish everything we set out to do. For those who get saved and never waver or fall, their childhood may have been full of all that was needed to grow healthy and strong not just physically but mentally, as well. They may have been raised by parents who set examples of what it means to be committed and dedicated to things of importance. However, many of us have lacked in the general purpose of families and unity. We may not have had that solid foundation. There may not have been any structure in our lives from those we looked up to and perhaps very little outwardly love. However, God is the ultimate Father and desires to nurture us in the love and admonition which we may have dreamed of as a child and never received. As a little girl, there were times I would think about what it would have been like to have had a mother and father like "Father Knows Best" or one of the other sitcoms which seemed to have loving, nurturing parents. I felt as an adolescent, I was cheated of something others had, and it was not fair. Thankfully, my Father in Heaven knew me even then and had great plans for my life. Those plans included healing to transpire in order for me to be satisfied with who I was and to no longer have the desires to complain like the children of Israel.

The Fall From Grace

There are many steps we must take in order to begin to walk without the afflictions from our past and in order to prevent falling from grace. Receiving healing from our past wounds is only the first step to having that close relationship with the Father. In our walk with the Lord, everything must become new. We not only become new beings but we are also renewed in the way we think, the way we act, the way we look at things, and the way we feel. This renewing also involves a complete make-over of becoming more and more like Jesus in every aspect.

When I fell back into the world, there were several areas or strong holds in which satan had on me. As discussed previously, we do have to recognize the pain in our lives. We also have to be able to see those walls which we have constructed. Everything in our walk with God is a process. When I walked with God for 10 years, I opened up and allowed Him to break down those walls I had built as a child in order to keep people from getting too close. I had built walls around myself from the time I was a small child to keep people at a distance because if they could not get too close, they could not hurt me. God showed me during my walk with Him many years ago that I had indeed built these walls. Remember, the Truth will set us free. *(John 8:32)* I knew those walls were there. It did not take a lot to convince me; however, I had not been able to see how those very walls I had built to protect me had actually hindered me from being able to be everything God had created me to be. The process began by me opening up and allowing God to heal those hurts. For the most part, my past was behind me where it needed to be. In fact, during those 10 years, my life was very blessed. God was definitely present in my life along with Jesus and the Holy Spirit. My journey with God during those years was fascinating and miraculous. However, if there is left anything undone in our lives, it opens a door for the enemy. When that door was open in my life, satan spent 15 years trying to destroy not only me but my whole family.

Many years have passed since those first days of my walk with the Lord. After coming home and rededicating my life, I asked God what happened. He began to show me the areas in which I had not received the revelation needed to endure to the end. The deception first began with an open door. The enemy is constantly seeking whom he may devour.

1 Peter 5:8 (Amp)⁸Be well balanced (temperate, sober of mind), be vigilant and cautious at all times; for that enemy of yours, the devil, roams around like a lion roaring [in fierce hunger], seeking someone to seize upon and devour.

I was walking with God, involved in the ministry, and He had healed me from my childhood pain in order for me to let go of the past. I moved ahead and was doing great. So what happened? satan brought sin in through a loved one during this time. If you do not have an open door, satan will then go to someone you are close to in order to bring them down. satan will use them in hopes

50

that you will take your eyes off of Jesus. We open a door for the enemy to walk into our lives when we take our eyes off of our foundation, and we look at the circumstances. satan was able to get to my loved one, and in doing so, I took my eyes off of the Lord. At that point, the rest was history. I began looking at the consequences of what the sin committed had produced in our family and how it affected my children. In not looking to Jesus, I began feeling betrayed and allowed the sin to destroy my family and everything God had built to that point in my life. My dreams were gone. My desires were no longer present and with this, sin walked right in and began destruction within my family. No matter what our circumstances, if we look to the problem and not to God, we will fall.

Once satan gets in through an open door, he begins to attack you in areas that are familiar. These are familiar spirits, which come into our lives once again and will be discussed in greater depth through another series. When the enemy slips in, we never see it coming. We are usually too busy focusing on the tragedy or problems which are occurring in our life or that of a loved one. That is why Jesus told His disciples to stay awake while He went to pray in the Garden of Gethsemane. We are to always be on guard, watch and pray in order that satan cannot come in to devour us. We need to know everything in the Word of God was written to give us instructions on how to endure until the end times. In doing so, we will live an abundant life.

Mark 14:38 (NIV) [38]"Watch and pray so that you will not fall into temptation. The spirit is willing, but the body is weak."

If we are going to walk this walk and be victorious, then we have to do according to all that is written in the Scriptures. When I fell, I fell into temptation in which satan had set out for me in areas

51

which were familiar. So what is familiar? Those areas in which you were weak in prior to beginning this walk with the Lord. satan hit me in the same areas and once again those same feelings and thoughts began to resurface in my life.

As a little girl, when someone wounded my heart, I retreated. I would go back into my shell, which was safe. As an adult, when someone wounded me, instead of speaking up or instead of going to Jesus for healing, I would retreat. When someone says something to you in which you take offensively, do you ever pretend it did not bother you? Do those words seem to play over and over again in your mind? Days go by, and you cannot seem to shake those words spoken to you. This is a seed the enemy would love to see destroy your self-worth or the way you see yourself. If all the enemy has to do is send someone across your path to speak something over you and you literally accept what was said, then satan has you where he wants you. If you cannot get the words spoken over you out of your head, then you are having a hard time believing that it is not true. In other words, you are accepting those words and images. So here I was again, many years later after much healing in my life, rebuilding those walls in which God had already broken through. satan used the same tactic in which he had when I was a little girl. Now as a grown woman, I took my eyes off of Jesus and looked to the problem. I opened a door, was deceived, and all those feelings began to resurface that had kept me bound for many years prior to being saved.

I began to question the church and feel betrayed. I began to doubt God really wanted to bless me, and all this was because I looked away from my source of direction. I spent 15 years back in the world trying to figure out what happened. I knew, during those years, I had missed it and several times tried to find my way back home but unsuccessfully. After making the decision to come home, I determined to stand firm regardless of how I felt. I knew I was coming back and would not leave the church until God spoke to me. After many months, God did speak to me. He began to reveal many things in order that I would be grounded and not fall again.

Sometimes we are faced with something tragic and may be walking close to the Lord. If we are wounded or a loved one, do we then begin to stop believing in those dreams and visions in which God has given us? Our human nature begins to reason that if God really desires for His children to be blessed, then why did this happen to me or to my family. This of course is taking our eyes off of Jesus to bring us through our circumstances. What we fail to see here is the big picture. Our minds do not think like God. No matter how much of His wisdom and knowledge we acquire over the years, we cannot always see the big picture. Therefore, our faith needs to be nurtured daily. We have to be grounded on the rock totally placing our trust in the Lord. If we know we are a child of God, then we should also know it does not matter what the circumstances say. He will bring us through. We do not always know why things happen the way they do because we cannot see the whole picture. Our eyes can only see that which is around us. However, when we trust in God, He can and will reveal to us in His timing why certain things may have happened. Today, I can look back and see many reasons why my daughter died in 2000. I can see many reasons why I lived through many of the tragedies I have in my lifetime. I am able to see who I am because of circumstances along with revelation God has given me. I am also able to see how God is capable of using me due to my past circumstances. I could have allowed satan to bring me down, but my choice was to go with God and walk this walk to the end.

We may not always understand why things happen the way they do, and we should learn from this. Our focus does not need to be on "why" but on just obeying and following. Anyone can claim to be a Christian, but only those who actually walk the walk and talk the talk are successful at it. Many Christians may desire to be more like those whom they see walking with the Lord victoriously. We may be able to see God continually increasing those who are walking this walk, not just in a financial sense but in the happiness and peace which emanates their existence. However, we need to realize, God wants all of us to know we are capable of being in that place.

I believe a piece of the puzzle in which God revealed to me that has the deepest meaning is being able to see the "Big Picture." We will understand why we fall and how to prevent that fall when we can grasp what the "Big Picture" is, which is what I call it. Before we look at the "Big Picture," we need to first look at the tests and trials we endure. We all face painful situations and some more than others. When faced with these trials, many times they seem too great to endure. These tests are what makes most people fall from grace because they do not know how to walk through them. Even today, I face tests. Yet my life is quite different than it was yesterday. Today, there is greater revelation to keep me grounded on the rock. After coming back to the Lord and rededicating my life, I faced many situations and continue even now to go through test after test. Why would I go through tests and trials if I am walking with God, and what is the difference today for me to walk through these tests victoriously? I have received the revelation to know when we are faced with something no matter how great or small, we are to look at it as a test. Everything we go through, if we endure and come out on the other side, we will be stronger. Does that mean God is the one responsible for what we are going through? No, it does not mean that. Many times we do not know why we are faced with what we are faced with. But we do know as long as we live on this earth, in this time-frame, and in these earthly bodies, we will face hardship. Jesus warned us of such.

John 16:33 (NIV) [33]*"I have told you these things, so that in me you may have peace. In this world you will have trouble. But take heart! I have overcome the world."*

Jesus overcame the world for us, but we will still face trouble. In studying the whole context of the Word of God, we learn how to walk through these times. The great men and women of the bible faced hardships; however, God brought them through miraculously. You may be saying, *"Why should I walk with God if my life is going to be no different than walking in the world, and I am still going to endure hardship, why make the effort?"* Here is why – I know for every test and trial I endure, I grow stronger. I know for everything I am going through, I am not walking it alone. I know through Jesus and the Holy Spirit, I am given the power along with everything else I need to triumph through my test victoriously. God gives us the wisdom and knowledge of how to endure hardships. Jesus endured hardships; however, He also had the power of the Holy Spirit to increase Him with wisdom, knowledge, and power from above. Were all Jesus' needs met during His walk on earth, and did He triumph over the enemy time and time again? Were scholars, who were known for their intelligence, baffled by His wisdom? The answer to these questions is *"Yes,"* and our life as a Christian is different than that of the world. Until you walk in this, you will never know. Those who have a deep and personal relationship with the Lord will tell you they could not imagine life without Jesus. Today, I have been given the revelation of how to walk through a battle. Does that mean all my battles are easy to endure? No, not all my battles are easy. However, when I stop looking at the circumstances and focus on the Lord, it does become easier. When we are right in the middle of our battle, there is usually some kind of pain or stress associated with what we are walking through. During these times, it is easy to look at the problem instead of focusing on Jesus. When we get still enough to hear the voice of the Lord, it becomes a different story. We then begin to know, we have the same power Jesus had in order to overcome our circumstances. We begin to look at the situation with a different perspective and a different attitude. Our way of thinking says, *"Thank you Lord with this test, I will be stronger. I count it all joy just like James said for every trial I go through."* Do you hear what I just said – "go through." We do not remain there – we go through it! When we are faced with pain, we must endure it and go through the pain! I was told many years ago when I was faced with my daughter's death, *"Jolene, you must go through the pain."* We cannot go around it, go over it, or under it. We must go through it. Going through it is facing it head on with the attitude, *"I will endure this, and for whatever reason, there will be something I will learn from it."* This is the attitude of a soldier. When a soldier is faced with danger, what do they do? They do not retreat, and as a Christian soldier, we should never retreat. We should go forth head on and face danger bravely knowing that God is on our side. The battle has already been won.

1 John 4:4 (Amp) [4]Little children, you are of God [you belong to Him] and have [already] defeated and overcome them [the agents of the antichrist], because He Who lives in you is greater (mightier) than he who is in the world.

After you endure or walk through the pain, you will begin to come out on the other side. You will come to a place knowing that the pain has lightened, and the days become easier to endure.

This is coming out of your pain. Once on the other side, you will realize that you have gained wisdom, knowledge, and revelation. We cannot endure something and receive nothing. There are always lessons to be learned and experience gained. It does not matter why you are faced with your particular situation. It does not matter if satan is behind this or if it is something which occurred because of your past or present. Sometimes God will test you because He desires to increase you. We may not know if it is a test from God, but if it is, He is trying to do a work in us in order to increase us. With every test, we should count it all joy knowing we are going to be increased one way or another if we endure. Being increased does not necessarily mean financially. God also increases us with wisdom, knowledge, revelation, and with spiritual blessings. Whatever our test may be, we will gain knowledge in that particular area to win that battle. Once we gain wisdom in that area, we will triumph through it easier if faced again with the same situation. As we walk in greater knowledge, we will have insight on going through that particular test in order to help others get through the same things.

During these times of battle, we may struggle and cry out, *"Why Lord; why me?"* We seek God, and we seek others. We cry, stress, and we worry. We have trouble sleeping. So why is this happening and how are we supposed to get through this? We are only looking at what we can see with our natural eyes. God, on the other hand, sees a much bigger picture. He sees what the outcome is going to be. We waver in our walk with Him, become weak, and feel faint. We begin thinking we will not be able to endure. We begin thinking this test is greater than we are capable of handling, but let's look more closely at what James had to say about trials and temptations.

James 1:2-3 (Amp) *²Consider it wholly joyful, my brethren, whenever you are enveloped in or encounter trials of any sort or fall into various temptations. ³Be assured and understand that the trial and proving of your faith bring out endurance and steadfastness and patience.*

We need to look deeply into this Scripture. We know we should count it all joy when we come out on the other side because we have been strengthened, but there is more. When we walk through the pain correctly, we achieve greater faith, endurance, steadfastness, and patience. You may be asking, *"How are we supposed to walk through the pain?"* First, let's look at what we gain by going through the pain before answering that question. How many of us would love to have greater faith? Faith is believing those things in which we cannot see but believing that they are so. If we believe there is a God and we have never seen Him, then it is by faith we believe. If we believe Jesus is the Son of God and He died on the cross to redeem us, we believe this by faith. Faith is the substance of things hoped for, the evidence of things not seen.

Hebrews 11:1(AMP) *¹NOW FAITH is the assurance (the confirmation, the title deed) of the things [we] hope for, being the proof of things [we] do not see and the conviction of their reality [faith perceiving as real fact what is not revealed to the senses].*

The Word says it only takes faith the size of a mustard seed to move mountains in our lives. If we were capable of making things happen in our lives for the better but it took faith, would you not want more of it?

Matthew 17:20 (ESV) *²⁰He said to them, "Because of your little faith. For truly, I say to you, if you have faith like a grain of mustard seed, you will say to this mountain, 'Move from here to there,' and it will move, and nothing will be impossible for you."*

So we see by walking through our tests, we achieve greater faith. Why is this? When we are faced with a test, we do not really know what we need to do at that moment. If we knew, it would not be much of a test. Think about it this way, when we had to study in school to pass a test or perhaps a test of our skills and/or achievements for a job or career change, often we would stress. We lose sleep and anxiety kicks in because we are not sure we can conquer that test, but as we study and get the knowledge down on the inside of us, what happens? We become confident we are going to breeze through that particular test, and this is by faith. By faith, we believe we are going to pass that test. Therefore, what we thought to be too hard to conquer becomes easy. Being confident we will pass a test does not come by just memorizing the facts. It goes beyond that. We can memorize all we want, but unless we actually understand the theory or process, we do not get it down deep inside of us. Many things studied in school take memorizing, for example, history. This area of study, we did not see firsthand or will never walk in those days to know exactly what happened. Therefore, it is merely memorizing to pass that history test. When we walk through life, we make memories. Those memories which are the most transparent will remain in our minds because we have firsthand knowledge, we lived them. With memorizing, after many years, you will not remember most of what was learned unless you continually read about it or stay current with studying. However, subjects that require us to learn methods and formulas, like math, we never forget as we use them on a daily basis. These methods are deep within us, just like riding a bike. With history, someone who decides to major in this subject and go on to teach it, will spend a good percentage of their life continually going over and over all the details and accounts from day to day. This person has history deep within them and knows their subject front to back, but those students enrolled in the subject, years later will not remember all the details to the extent the history teacher does. This is what I am getting at, with every test that we face, if we walk through it and get it on the inside of us then we gain greater faith in knowing how to conquer that particular test. Can we then have faith enough to conquer any test or trial? Absolutely! The Word tells us faith comes by hearing and hearing by the Word of God.

Romans 10:17 (KJV) [17]So then faith cometh by hearing, and hearing by the word of God.

Just like the two tests we looked at, math is something we use every day, and we know it like riding a bike. On the other hand, something like history, we would have to continually stay current in our readings in order to obtain the knowledge needed to pass a test on this subject. Therefore, we should do two things to acquire the kind of faith the Word talks about in order to move mountains in our lives. One, we must continually study and get God's Word deep inside of us just like the history teacher has history deep within. Two, as we face any test, we need to look at it as such and learn to walk through it. We need to learn to face our tests with a positive attitude. Now, as we begin to look at all our circumstances and situations as tests in a positive sense, guess what happens? It becomes like that math test. It is a way of life because we naturally begin to look at everything through the eyes of God. It is something that becomes a daily walk of life in which we never lose. In knowing this revelation, our tests become not much of a test because we have learned to just breeze through them. In my past, if I would have known this technique, my first response would have been to focus on the situation as a test. After seeing it as such, I would have never taken my eyes off of

Jesus and would have prevailed through the circumstances victoriously.

Now to continue with what our faith will produce. The proving of our faith produces endurance, steadfastness, and patience. Why do we want to count it all joy to go through tests and trials? We know to increase our faith, but let's look at endurance. Endurance is the ability to withstand hardship, to sustain prolonged stressful effort or activity, and to endure suffering. Many times when we are faced with hard situations or tragedies, we crumble and fall. Our whole world is rocked. I know from losing my daughter, which was the most horrible thing I ever had to face, at some point I needed to pull it together to be there for my other girls. Was I okay myself? No, I did not know how to endure this kind of pain. I did not know how to help my girls during this time or how to hold my marriage together. I did not know how to continue life as if everything was okay. When we walk with God, He has the answers. If we do not learn how to endure the small things in life, how will we be able to rise up and be strong when we are faced with a tragedy? If our health fails and we are faced with a terminal illness, will we be able to stand on God's Word and believe for our healing? Many people today have been healed, and the doctors write it off as a miracle because there is no explanation. These people will tell you God intervened. I know I want to live my life believing and knowing my God will supply all the faith I need, in order to sustain any event that could occur. We must start with the small and learn how to walk through the pain in order to come out on the other side unscathed.

Walking through our tests also produces steadfastness. Steadfastness is not subject to change, firmly fixed in place, firm in belief, and determination. As we begin to learn to walk through

61

our pain, steadfastness will rise up in us with future tests being easier because we will stand firm on what we believe. After we have seen God move in our lives, we make it a practice to see things through God's eyes and not the world. When we do this, we will become patient when faced with a test knowing we are coming out on the other side victoriously. With each test, we will also begin seeing what is gained by facing them boldly, courageously, and joyfully.

So how are we to walk through our pain? We know the benefits of walking through these tests, but we may still be asking how do we do this? The answer of course is that first of all, we look at everything as a test of that time. Second, we must understand there are also other areas we need to see. We should realize if we are a child of God, we are not walking through anything alone. The world may struggle to endure tragedies and hardships, but we are not the world if, in fact, we are children of the Most High God. Therefore, as we look at our situations as tests, we need to speak forth faith: *"Father, I count it all joy for this test before me. I will face this test and walk through it knowing when I come out on the other side, and I will come out on the other side, I will gain greater wisdom and knowledge which is through Your revelation. I gain greater faith, knowing how to face similar situations in the future and help those who are faced with tests in which I have endured. I gain endurance, steadfastness, and patience. Amen!"* Your faith is tested by what comes forth out of your mouth from this point. If you want God to move in your life, you must believe what you just spoke, and you must face the pain head on. Plow through it knowing the victory has already been won for you, and you will walk out on the other side more victoriously than when you first faced this trial.

1 John 5:4 (Amp) ^{4}*For whatever is born of God is victorious over the world; and this is the victory that conquers the world, even our faith.*

If you have to repeat those words to God several times a day, do so! Whatever it takes to get it down on the inside of you where you can begin to believe it. Then patiently wait and watch God move in your life because He will. What will cause God to "not move" in your life? What will cause your tests to continue to a place where it seems the pain is never going to end? Murmuring and complaining just like the children of Israel. Remember, they were in the desert for forty years complaining before the Lord brought them out. Therefore, we need to face the pain. We need to go through it without fighting, and we should begin to count it all joy for every test we encounter. If we are doing this, we should not be complaining. Complaining will only make your tests take longer, and you will gain very little. When you murmur and complain, you will not learn what God may be trying to teach you or what that test will teach you in order to grow stronger as a Christian. Just like a woman in labor, she must face her pain. The reason doctors have women breathe deeply is that it lessens the pain and speeds up the delivery. So for those women who have done the technique properly, they can account for the fact this works. Having a child in the 70's and then again in the 80's, times had changed so much from those two periods. There were no techniques taught in the 70's to make your pain lessen. In the 80's, my labor and swiftness of delivery were nothing compared to what I went through "pain wise" in the 70's. You will get to a place where you are ready for the next test because you are ready for growth. Once you have walked through some trials victoriously and you hold God to His Word, you will anxiously await the next trial. God has to be faithful to His Word because He cannot lie.

John 3:33 (Amp) [33]*Whoever receives His testimony has set his seal of approval to this: God is true. [That man has definitely certified, acknowledged, declared once and for all, and is himself assured that it is divine truth that God cannot lie].*

He is true to His Word all the time. He never changes. He is the same yesterday, today, and forever. We see in Psalms it says those who sow in tears will reap in joy.

Psalm 126:5 (Amp) [5]*They who sow in tears shall reap in joy and singing.*

Even if what you are going through brings tears, count it all joy for God has said, *"Those who sow in tears will reap joy."* Remember, when we sow something, we will reap something. If we sow something bad, we reap something bad. In this Scripture, you reap joy. We all know that joy is something good. Therefore, this shows us tears are not bad but good. I know when my daughter died, I was told over and over again that tears bring healing, and they do. Tears make us feel better because it is getting what is on the inside – out. Remember, to heal we must get the bad stuff out. It is sad our society has taught young boys it is not manly to cry. We have looked at men to be weak if they cry. It takes a strong man to shed tears. We see throughout Scriptures, men of God did shed tears. In Psalm, the Psalmist David many times shed tears. If you study Job, He too poured out tears to God. Isaiah, Jeremiah, and I could go on and on of the accounts where these great men cried out to God. I look at the great men of God as strong men. They may have felt weak at times, but look at everything they walked through and came out victoriously. Of course, we know nothing could have been and will ever be accomplished victoriously if it is not done through Jesus today!

The Big Picture

Now let's look at the "Big Picture." God began to show me this in my walk some time ago. I have gone through many tragedies in my life, and finally one way or another, walked through them and faced the pain. We cannot heal without facing the pain once and for all. If we have never faced the pain, we still deal with those areas and cannot be used to the entirety God desires. Here, is what He showed me.

Yes, our eyes can only see so much. On the other hand, God sees far into our future. He sees far into where He desires to send us and what the outcome will be. There have been times in my life when I have asked, *"Why God?"* I'm sure all of us know of these times. After getting through many of the tragedies I have endured, God began to have me look at things in a much broader sense. Here, are some things to think on:

•Suppose all of God's children came from families like those sitcoms such as "Father Knows Best".
•Suppose all of God's children never made mistakes.
•Suppose all of God's children never faced desires which were sinful.
•Suppose all of God's children daily and faithfully walked the course God laid out for them.
•Suppose all of God's children never had tragedies happen in their life.
•Suppose all of God's children never faced tests and trials.

First of all, what would have been the logic in us needing Jesus? Second, who would God be able to send to those who are struggling and do not know God or know how to be set free? Who would God send to those who do not know how to walk in faith? What about those who do not know how to pray and mean it, who would teach them? Who would counsel those that satan is holding captive in bondage and sin? For this reason, we count it all joy because God sees the whole picture.

With this, I began to think back of the areas I have triumphed victoriously. Some of my trials have taken years, and some have been days or weeks. Once you succeed in any trial, no matter the length of time it took, you have allowed God to bring you to the place where you will be able to minister to others. Every single one of God's children has areas they can actually help others. I did walk through the pain of the loss of my daughter, and God began to show me how to use this to help others. Over the years, I have touched many lives, and there have been many sent across my path facing a similar loss. God has opened doors for me to help others in areas I have prevailed. As time goes on, I continue to triumph in my trials joyfully knowing there are people out there who need what God has given me.

So yes, even the loss of my daughter is justified. Did God take her? No, this is not what the Word says. We do not always know why things happen, but that is not to question. What we do know is the world is full of people with pain. Until God's children learn to walk through their pain, God will not be able to turn it around in order that they see victory. Until we walk through our pain, we will not be set free from those areas satan keeps us bound.

Areas Which Cause Us to Fall From Grace

When we have not given everything to God, we will still miss it and fall back into our sin to comfort the pain. Just like the person who will continue to drink or engage in premarital sex to numb the pain, we tend to have things in our lives that are destructive. We use these things in order that we do not focus on what is happening around us or to deal with pain from our past, but when

66

we accept Jesus into our heart, the next step is the growing stage. This stage does not come overnight. Growing is something that will not happen unless we draw closer to God. God will begin to heal those areas. As He does this, we begin noticing how we no longer have the desires to commit sin. We no longer do those things that were once comfortable to us, and we no longer engage in things destructive that we may not have even given much thought to in our past. However, as we begin to grow or even after we are well established, there are areas that can cause us to fall from grace.

Over a period of several months, God began to show me many areas in which His children are bound. In order to be set free, we need to get this revelation down on the inside of us, so we will grow stronger. We will be able to overcome that which satan will use to try and keep us from rising to the level God desires.

We will briefly look at each one of the areas which can cause us to fall, but further into this series, we will go into greater depth. The first area, which will be discussed, is not recognizing and finding the root to why we build walls due to pain. The second will be looking at those who do not believe God desires to heal their pain and increase them. The third area, we will be looking into those who feel they are not capable of being free from all their troubles in order to do what God may be calling them to do, and the fourth area will be having no motivation, desire, or energy. This fourth area will deal with those who are satisfied with where they are in life when it may not be God's best.

The Root to Our Pain

As discussed previously, when we have been wounded there is pain. We may have endured many years of pain and many more years building walls in which only God can bring down, but there is a process of healing that must take place in order to be set free. We do not need to become discouraged when in one week we are still faced with struggles of letting go. However, this is one area which causes many to fall away.

First, we must recognize the walls are there to begin with and then search deep within for the root to the afflictions. You may be in a dark place where you do not feel you are capable of healing. If that be the case, many times people have to seek counseling in order to achieve the healing needed to fell complete. Never feel you are weak or that this is something to be ashamed of. I went through counseling many times in my life and know there were lessons learned through each encounter. You also need to search for either a Christian based counseling center or find a church where you can go through the counseling you need, but never give up. A good place to start is by beginning to pray for God to intervene and open doors. God desires for you to be made whole and one area of being made whole is to renew your mind. Your mind will not be renewed until the bad inside gets out. When we neglect getting the healing we need to deal with afflictions from our past or present, many times we become discouraged. We may try to do according to what the Word of God says, but we struggle to do so within due to the pain which is still present. This leads many continually falling back into the world again and again.

Believing God Desires to Heal Our Pain

The second thing we need to look at, many of God's children really do not believe God desires to take away their pain. They do not believe that He desires to increase them. Many of us believe God is, but we do not all believe He desires to deliver us out of our troubles. God is the God of the whole Universe, and if we are going to believe any part of the Word of God, we should and must believe everything that is written. We cannot say we believe one thing and not something else. Either we believe, or we do not!

God has shown me that many of His children believe Jesus died on the cross for them and that they have eternal life, but it stops there. They do not believe that their salvation also makes them whole or complete. We will never be completely perfected until Jesus comes back for us. However, it is possible to walk as close to God as Abraham, Moses, and all the other great men and women in the bible. Those in biblical days, they understood something that we have to get deep within us. God desires to bless His children. God desires to set us free. God is the same today as He was yesterday, and He never changes. The great men of God had a personal relationship with our Father. Through the blood of Jesus today, we all have this opportunity to be as close to God as we desire.

Believing in Ourselves

God sees many of us are in dark places in our lives because we do not believe in ourselves. You will never have that God given desire to rise and make something happen, until you first heal your wounds and begin to believe what God's Word says about you. We may have had negative words spoken over us at some time in our lives which became negative images. This alone can make us not believe in ourselves. God knows that many of us

69

no longer believe in ourselves because of mistakes we have made in our lives or because of much failure. Perhaps, we feel that we no longer have the energy to rise and try again. We may believe we are incapable, and we may see ourselves as failures even before we try. We need to ask ourselves these questions and be honest:

1) How do you see yourself today? _____
2) Do you believe God has a great path designed just for you? _____
3) Do you sometimes look at others wishing you could be more like them? _____
4) Do you sometimes wonder why God blesses others and you feel He does not love you the same? _____

No Motivation

Do you know how to tell if you truly want something bad enough? Do you honestly want to walk the path God designed just for you? Do you really want to see yourself achieve those dreams which are deep within your being? The way to tell is by how much you are willing to do in order to gain what you are striving for. God expects us to put forth effort; He expects us to do our part.

There are many Christians out there today who have basically given up. They continue to go through the motions of trying to live a Christian life and walk with the Lord; however, you can tell by their walk they are defeated. I have ministered to several who fit this description. It did not matter what I said or what I did; it would not change them. There was no Word from God that would make them get up and change the way things were in their life. They continued to murmur and complain. They continued to see the negative in everything and continued to live defeated. When I would share a Word from God, they would get excited, and you

70

could see in their eyes they wanted this. However, when it called for them having to step out of their box to make the changes, they retreated. This is quite sad because many of these who fall in this group know a lot about the Word of God. Many may desire to grow, but when it comes to them having to commit to doing something out of the ordinary to make it happen, they prefer to stay in their box. God cannot and will not bless you if you fall in this category. God is a God of action and wants a people who are willing to rise and go when He says go.

3 The Journey through Emptiness...

The Search for Fulfillment...

In order for us to begin to see ourselves the way God sees us, there has to be a total transformation from the old man to the new man. In walking through all the obstacles which have continued to absorb our whole being, we will begin to look into every aspect of our lives which could be holding us back from receiving what is rightfully ours. We will look more in depth at the root causes of pain and begin to receive the revelation God desires for His children. In this process, we will come out on the other side of our pain and receive our healing.

Empty Inside

We first must realize that we all have things buried deep within and those things must come out. As God begins to work in your life, He will start with emptying out all the bad and replacing it with good. God does not want us to be empty inside. Many Christians still find themselves empty inside even though they may be serving the Lord and living according to His commandments. God never intended us to just attend church every time the doors are open, go home, practice the commandments, and do all the routine things we must do in order to survive. Christianity is much more than just being programmed to do certain things and not other things. When you are where you should be with God, your walk should be very exciting and on fire. If you are not in the place where you can say, *"Each day is a new day with my Father"* and look forward to time with Him, then you are missing out on the total concept of how God wants His people to live.

The process of emptying out all the bad in our lives is a course of action which coincides with healing. We will continue to look at the afflictions in our life while focusing on the root in order to let go of that bitterness which keeps us bound. You may feel you have dealt with your past and need no healing. However, we need to realize if we find ourselves always complaining about things and never being satisfied, there is pain in our lives. If you find yourself not being satisfied after walking with God for awhile and opening up for Him to begin the healing process, there are areas that have been over-looked. A person who is never satisfied always finds something wrong or continually looks at everything in a negative sense. This type of person has areas of their life which need healing. Maybe this is something you cannot see. However, those close to you can probably see this. If you are constantly noticing fault in others, there is fault in yourself, as well. This is not an area that should make you feel judged but should be an area where you can honestly say, *"Lord, if this is me, I do not want to be that person."* If we can only see ourselves as never doing anything wrong and it is always someone else, we need to look more closely. Happy people look at everything with a different perspective than those who are not happy. With unhappiness, you will always see murmuring and complaining just like the children of Israel. It is a normal human response to complain when people feel cheated, or life was not fair to them. However, when we allow God to take all the bad out and forgive every person or everything which caused us pain, from the time we came into this world, we should begin to look at life optimistically, not as a pessimist. We make choices every day when we climb out of bed, *"Lord, I choose to have a positive outlook on life; I choose to look at the good in everyone who crosses my path."*

Let's first begin with looking at the root to our wounds in order to release those things to God for healing and begin to get all the

74

bad out. I have said many times, we sometimes feel that life has dealt us a bad hand. I have also shared how God showed me that all of us could not have had what we call, the perfect upbringing or the perfect parents. Remember, if none of us had ever gone through tragedies or pain, who would God send to help those who are hurting and need a Word from God? We have to come to a place to be able to say, *"Lord, I am glad for the person I am and what I have gone through because it has made me who I am today."* If most Christians had never come to that place of desperation, they may never have cried out to God or sought to find something greater in their lives. Some of us may not have listened to someone share Jesus, if we were not facing the unknown. I know with most I have ministered to, they were eager to listen or were seeking God because of something they could not handle in their lives. They were at a place where they needed answers. If I had not gone through those tragedies in my life, I do not know if I would have thought I needed God. So I am thankful for the trials I endured knowing I did come out on the other side, and I am who I am today as a result of those tests and God's love.

It does not matter how bad your childhood was, if you are alive today, you have something to be thankful for. If you are of sound mind, you have something to be thankful for. If you are capable of learning, you have something to be thankful for. There may be some who have had extreme situations happen to them, but it does not matter. God is the God of the Universe, and there is nothing we go through that He cannot fix. God knows you better than you know yourself, and He has a plan just for you. Think about it this way, if you have endured much, great will be your ministry. If you have endured horrible tragedies, terrible situations, and great pain, greater will be your ministry. The more you have endured, the greater you can be in the kingdom if you can let go of the pain. Begin forgiving yourself and allowing God to do His perfect work in you. James said it this way…

James 1:4 (Amp) [4]*But let endurance and steadfastness and patience have full play and do a thorough work, so that you may be [people] perfectly and fully developed [with no defects], lacking in nothing.*

When we allow God to do His work in us, while we endure patiently, He will thoroughly begin changing us, and we will become fully developed lacking in nothing. This is truth for God's children. I believe we all would love to be in a place with God where we lack nothing; all our needs met. Realize that lacking in nothing means absolutely lacking nothing. We always think of this in a financial aspect, but James did not say that. He just said lacking in nothing, and I take that to mean what it says. I will not lack in wisdom, knowledge, finances, peace, health, etc.

Looking at our pain, we need to go all the way back to our childhood, the root. Many may say that their childhood was okay, and this could not be where the root is. However, if you operate in ways which are unhealthy, the root is somewhere in your past. Your pain that you have not been able to deal with may be something more recent, perhaps some kind of tragedy, but wherever the root lies, should be our primary focus. You may have had much suffering, but God sees your pain. Many have suffered through incest; some were molested by their own fathers or another family member, and others were raped or beaten. Maybe you went through horrible torture which left scars on your body. Perhaps you find yourself alone and abandoned by every man who ever told you that they loved you and would never leave you. Maybe you are sitting in a prison cell wondering how your life wound up this way. You may be at your last straw and have nowhere to turn. You may be at a place of desperation. Maybe your thoughts have gone back and forth to suicide. You may have buried a child or lost someone that you loved dearly. Perhaps you have picked this book up with the thought of trying one more thing. Whatever your pain is or whatever you may feel inside, my God and your God is big enough to heal and restore you completely. When God takes our pain away, He then replaces it with what we need. Perhaps you need a feeling of self-worth, self-respect, confidence, happiness, a new beginning, or a renewed sense of well-being in order to rise above the situation in your life that has occurred. When God begins to take the bad out, He will replace it with everything you need in order to feel good about yourself. God will bring about that new life and a new beginning with Him.

In my life, I dealt with emotional abuse, mental abuse, and abandonment. I was conceived by a mother who did not take care of herself while she carried me and a father who did not want any children. I was brought into the world from conception not really being wanted. Many of us feel pain all the way back to conception. Do not think a baby cannot sense this rejection. My life as I knew it was filled with violence, hurtful words tossed about on a daily basis, and a sense of total rejection. When we come into this world, our desire is to be loved. We were created for that purpose, and when it is not fulfilled, we continually search to find that acceptance and love.

Around the age of 13, I found myself basically on the streets searching for anyone and anything which could fulfill that emptiness inside. My life was surrounded by drugs and alcohol. I never thought about consequences to the choices I made daily. All I knew was that being numb from the drugs kept me from feeling the pain which was inside. I built walls around me and existed for one purpose, destruction. I did not care what the effect of the drugs had on me and did not care who I hurt in the process.

People who are hurting, they continually are tearing apart those who are close to them. They do not see their destruction because they live in a world of "not caring." My life consisted of getting high and staying that way. I over-dosed on more than one occasion; however, this did not seem to stop my destructive path in life. Inside my spirit was crying out, *"Stop the pain!"* However, no one seemed to notice which told me no one really cared. On one occasion, my mother asked me why I did drugs. My response was, *"Why do you drink?"* Seeing she could not answer my question, her next question was, *"Would you stop using drugs if I asked you to?"* At 15 years old, my response to her was, *"I'll make a deal, you quit drinking, and I'll quit drugs!"* At that point, she walked out of my room and never said anything else about my drug addiction again. These were words I never forgot to this day. That conversation told me that she did not love me enough to stop drinking. I was 15 and knew nothing about addiction. What we see here are two addictive behaviors. I had no desire to stop what I was doing, and my mother was unable to stop due to her addiction. My addiction was not that I could not quit; I saw no need to quit. The drugs kept me sedated enough that at 15, I did not have to deal with the rejection and longing, for the love I desired. On the other hand, my mother's addiction was passed down through genes which were prevalent on her side of the family. Of course, this is all generational curses which will be discussed later.

Years after my mother died and I was saved, God opened my eyes to see my mother's pain. She lived in torment from her past as a child, and it was passed down through generations. My mother never was in a place to see God's love and healing for her life. I was able to look at my mother through the eyes of God, a little girl who had never been able to heal from the pain which was caused in her life as a child. This pain was carried into her adulthood and passed down to her children. My mother loved me and my sister dearly but did not know how to show it because it had never been shown to her. Many of you who are reading this and can see yourself in either my mother or me, it is never too late for God to intervene and do a complete makeover in your life. God can heal any situation and restore the whole family.

Before I go further, many have lived the life that I lived above and have brought children into the world doing the same thing which was done to them. You may be dealing with guilt. It took me years to forgive my mother and years to undo the damage which was done to me. However, my healing never completely came until I gave it to the Lord. We may be able to seek counseling or find solace through another avenue; however, it may still be buried deep within. Until we have a complete transformation through our Savior, the healing is never complete. I too brought children into the world prior to being healed of my own afflictions. I raised children doing many things wrong prior to revelation which was needed to train my children up in the ways of the Lord. God knows we have made mistakes and that we will make more mistakes. That was the purpose of Jesus coming and redeeming us from our sins. If God can heal you of all your pain, He can also heal your children. God does not want you to spend years dwelling on the, "What if's?" God wants you to receive your healing today in order for you to go forward and begin to share His great love to your children, family, and friends. Remember, God can and will heal and restore them, as well. God will take care of your children; He loves them just as much as He loves you.

One thing I shared was that I was able to see my mother through the eyes of God. Whatever you are dealing with, God desires you to see it through His eyes. Looking at things the way the world does will never bring healing. Dealing with any root to any problem requires that we are able to look upon it the way God does. When this happens, we will see it in a totally different perspective. Compassion will come over us so we are able to heal from past pain and forgive others, as well as ourselves. When I share about my mother's life, it brings tears of compassion that envelopes me. It is almost as if I can be in my mother's shoes and feel what she did. Compassion will be discussed in another series, but when we begin to operate in the compassion of Christ, we will be able to feel and hurt for all those God sends across our path.

If you came out of a dysfunctional family, you may have said you wish you could have had a normal family, but what is normal? I have been told normal is what we perceive it to be. However, what is normal according to the world's standards? Normal to the world, pertaining to families would be those who live good lives, are assets to society, of sound mind, have goals, and we could go on and on, but what is not normal to the world? Not being normal to the world would be those whose lives are messed up due to drug and alcohol addictions, cannot keep a job, those who spend years in counseling, bad parenting, etc. Ask yourself, what is normal to God? We say we wish we could have had normal lives, but what were we expecting? I'm sure if we were able to look closer into the hidden lives of those the world considers to be normal, we would find a lot of sin. The world looks at those who commit horrible crimes such as murder, rape, and stealing, as definitely being messed us. However, God looks at those who the world sees as normal as also being messed up. Why? Those who claim to have normal lives, there is sin. The Word says that none are without sin.

Romans 3:23 (NIV) [23]for all have sinned and fall short of the glory of God,

80

So does God look at those who claim to have lived normal lives as normal? We need to ask, *"Is God normal?"* Absolutely not! In fact, many in the world look at those who live Christian lives as being radical or weird. God is anything but normal. Why would we want to be normal? God is different! He is unique and extraordinary, and His Word says if we are His people, we are peculiar!

Titus 2:14 (Amp) ¹⁴*Who gave Himself on our behalf that He might redeem us (purchase our freedom) from all iniquity and purify for Himself a people [to be peculiarly His own, people who are] eager and enthusiastic about [living a life that is good and filled with] beneficial deeds.*

Jesus gave Himself on our behalf so that we could become His peculiar people. As peculiar people, we should not only be eager to serve our Lord but also enthusiastic. Those who are His will live a life that is good. We all strive to live a good life but according to Paul, in order to live a good life, we must be hooked up with God. In Exodus, God spoke to Moses, and it tells us what we must do in order to be His possession. If we obey and keep His covenant, we will be His own peculiar possession and treasure. God considers us His treasure.

Exodus 19:5 (Amp) ⁵*Now therefore, if you will obey My voice in truth and keep My covenant, then you shall be My own peculiar possession and treasure from among and above all peoples; for all the earth is Mine.*

I have said the same thing many of you have, *"I just wish I could have had a normal life."* I have even asked God in my past, *"Why can't my life just be normal?"* No wonder He did not answer me because if I am one of His children, my life will never be normal. My life is different, and it is awesome! So instead of us seeking some kind of normalcy, we should be glad we are not normal and strive for what is different!

Let me share another situation about a lady I ministered to awhile back. This is an example of how our lives are messed up and need healing. This lady had been having an affair with a married man. She got saved and started trying to live for God. She then found herself involved once again with the same married man. She sought out the church for prayers, and in praying for her, you could see pain in her life. What was happening here? The lady was aware of sin because she had been saved, and she had been excited with her new life. However, she had a long way to go to be where she needed to be in order to not fall from God's grace. Sometimes coming to the church for prayer is not enough. Sometimes it takes more one on one with someone who is grounded on the rock of Jesus, and sometimes it takes seeking out counseling through a licensed counselor. If this woman never sought out for the healing that she needed, she probably fell back into the world. We must remember that it is not about just getting the healing we need, but we also need to find the root of the problem. If the healing does not come, you will begin to feel unworthy and feel that you are unable to walk this walk. Never become discouraged. Never feel you are a hindrance to those you seek out at church for counseling. Many people bear the impact of their pain by themselves because they feel they are a nuisance to continue needing prayer over and over again. satan is the one who makes you feel that way. satan tries to discourage you to give up with many techniques that he has been using since the beginning of time. You will have thoughts come to mind from the enemy such as:

•Look at you, you can't do this.

•You keep falling because maybe this walk just isn't for you.
•How many times are you going to run to the church for prayer; they probably feel that you are weak?

Whatever satan says to you, I'm telling you right now, *"Do not listen to the lies!"* If you feel that the person who is ministering to you at the church is tired of you bothering them, find a different person. If you feel the church is not helping you, find a different church, but do not give up. Those same people who are ministering to you have been exactly where you are, and we all go through pain differently. What may have worked for one person, may not work for you. How fast someone else healed, may not be your time frame. Do not compare your walk to anyone else or allow someone to do the same with your situation. We need to stop looking at how long this is taking us and focus on getting through our circumstances! This lady was a new Christian, and satan did not want her succeeding just like he does not want you succeeding either. satan knows what a threat you will be when you walk through to the other side, but we must stop saying, *"If I make it through,"* but rather focus on, *"When I make it through!"*

We all deal with things in our lives. It does not matter who you are, how old you are, what background you came from, and how much you have or do not have. We are not where we need to be with God until we totally surrender all to Him. We must allow Him to begin emptying our vessels and refilling it with more of Jesus. After you look back at your past and into your present, write down everything that you see. Many times we can begin to see why we operate the way we do based on the things which occurred in our lives. Many of us feel unworthy to come before God because of sin in our lives. Thankfully, God has given us everything through His Word to heal us at the root. As we begin to be healed, God will awaken us to a new level where we can begin to have a more personal relationship with Him.

From Nothing

Galatians 5:4 (Amp) *⁴If you seek to be justified and declared righteous and to be given a right standing with God through the Law, you are brought to nothing and so separated (severed) from Christ. You have fallen away from grace (from God's gracious favor and unmerited blessing).*

In *Galatians,* those who live according to the law are brought to nothing. If you are not saved or if you are backslidden, then you are being judged according to the law. This refers to the Law of Moses which is the 10 commandments. Even though, we are to live according to the commandments of God, that alone will never bring us into a right relationship with God. Therefore, Jesus died on the cross for us in order that we can be in right standing with God. It is by the Grace of God we are declared righteous. We are all born sinners and as long as we are in our fleshly bodies, we will miss it and fall short of the glory of God. If you are not saved, you are judged according to the law. Those who are not saved are brought to nothing, and they are separated from Christ. According to this Scripture, prior to being saved, we were nothing. Without Christ, we can do nothing. Many of God's people today still see themselves as nothing. We first need to be able to see, in our natural self, we will never be anything and never be able to do anything. However, many today are redeemed and fall under grace instead of the law, but they continue to see themselves as not being anything or being able to do anything. God desires His people to be set free from this wrong kind of thinking.

John 3:27 (Amp) *²⁷John answered, A man can receive nothing [he can claim nothing, he can take unto himself nothing] except as it has*

84

been granted to him from heaven. [A man must be content to receive the gift which is given him from heaven; there is no other source.]

According to John, not only is man nothing except through Christ, we will only receive that which is given to us from heaven. The Kingdom of Heaven is our only source; God is our only source, and Jesus is our only source. As children of God, we must realize no matter what gifts are given to us from heaven or what great things we do for the Kingdom of Heaven, we are only able to operate through Christ and no other way. We must be content and satisfied with our walk with God from the beginning, thankful for whatever gifts are bestowed upon us. If we cannot be thankful with little, God will never give us much.

Matthew 25:21 (Amp) [21]*His master said to him, Well done, you upright (honorable, admirable) and faithful servant! You have been faithful and trustworthy over a little; I will put you in charge of much. Enter into and share the joy (the delight, the blessedness) which your master enjoys.*

When we begin our walk with the Lord, it will be baby steps. A baby comes into this world eager to learn. We also should come into this new life, born again and eager to learn. With a baby, they begin their walk as being hungry; however, they begin learning early on what they need to do in order to be fed. We need to look at this closely. When a baby is hungry, they learn if they cry, someone will feed them. We should approach our new walk with hunger, and we should be observant to what will get us fed. However, maybe we should look at the opposite approach. If a baby was brought into this world and was not being fed, what would happen? We all know the answer to this; the baby would die. This is a terrible thing that happens in our world, and there are many countries in severe poverty. The reason this happens in

America many times is due to neglect. There may be various reasons for the neglect; however, this is not our focus. The point I am trying to make, if a baby is neglected by not being fed, the result would be death. In our case, as new Christians, our spirit within is hungry to be fed the Word of God. What is it that would keep us from being fed? The answer again of course is neglect. In this case, what would be the reason for the neglect? We are all capable of going to church. We are all capable of picking up our bible and reading. We are all capable of praying and seeking God. Therefore, what would be the root cause of the neglect to our spirit man? The answer is our flesh. When we begin our walk, we are fighting with our flesh.

*Romans 7:23 (Amp) *[23]*But I discern in my bodily members [in the sensitive appetites and wills of the flesh] a different law (rule of action) at war against the law of my mind (my reason) and making me a prisoner to the law of sin that dwells in my bodily organs [in the sensitive appetites and wills of the flesh].*

We are at war with our flesh, and if our flesh were to have its way, our spirit man would dry up and die. In order for us to understand the biblical principles, we must listen and learn just like a baby coming into the world. As they begin to grow, they begin to listen and learn. Their purpose is survival at this point. Our spirit man which has been awakened after being saved also has a purpose to survive. However, our spirit man is striving to overpower our flesh at the same time our flesh is trying to keep our spirit man in place. Have you ever cried out to God, *"Why is my life so messed up; why are my children giving me so much trouble?"* Your answer to those questions and probably many more is you! You are allowing your flesh to control your spirit man. For this reason, many of God's children cannot rise above their circumstances in order to begin to see themselves as something instead of nothing.

A baby becomes observant to what they need to do to get themselves fed. If we were to be observant to what we need to do in order to feed our spirit man, what would it be? It is not that hard to be fed, if you attend church or you are around other Christians whom seem to be living a victorious life with Christ. What are their habits? What does the man or woman of God continually preach that we are to do if we want to walk an abundant life? What is it the bible tells us that we must do? All these things are areas we need to be observant if we desire to rise above our circumstances and begin to see ourselves as something instead of nothing.

You may be saying you have tried the "God stuff" and it did not work. If that is you, you may have tried, but you never connected. When you find God and you get connected, it is not a means of trying, it just works! Perhaps many today have approached trying the "Christian thing" with a wrong or negative attitude or a wrong way of thinking. Too many people today see themselves as unworthy. Too many believe that if God exists, there is no way a great God could ever forgive them. I have ministered to those who have said, *"I have sinned for many years and have done horrible things, maybe God is not listening to me because I have done too much. Maybe God will not forgive me."* What did it say in *Luke 15:7*? There is more joy in heaven over one especially wicked person who repents. That does not sound like God is saying He will not forgive you if you have been too wicked. To God, sin is sin, that simple. Heaven will rejoice the day you repent and ask Jesus into your life. It does not matter if you have committed murder or have lied. God desires to use His children no matter what shoes they have walked in. God desires to forgive you and heal the pain that is trying to destroy you. Let's look at the prodigal son.

Luke 15:11-24(ESV) The Parable of the Prodigal Son

[11]And he said, "There was a man who had two sons. [12]And the younger of them said to his father, 'Father, give me the share of property that is coming to me.' And he divide] his property between them. [13]Not many days later, the younger son gathered all he had and took a journey into a far country, and there he squandered his property in reckless living. [14]And when he had spent everything, a severe famine arose in that country, and he began to be in need. [15]So he went and hired himself out to one of the citizens of that country, who sent him into his fields to feed pigs. [16]And he was longing to be fed with the pods that the pigs ate, and no one gave him anything. [17]"But when he came to himself, he said, 'How many of my father's hired servants have more than enough bread, but I perish here with hunger! [18]I will arise and go to my father, and I will say to him, "Father, I have sinned against heaven and before you. [19] I am no longer worthy to be called your son. Treat me as one of your hired servants."' [20]And he arose and came to his father. But while he was still a long way off, his father saw him and felt compassion, and ran and embraced him and kissed him. [21]And the son said to him, 'Father, I have sinned against heaven and before you. I am no longer worthy to be called your son.' [22]But the father said to his servants, 'Bring quickly the best robe, and put it on him, and put a ring on his hand, and shoes on his feet. [23]And bring the fattened calf and kill it, and let us eat and celebrate. [24]For this my son was dead, and is alive again; he was lost, and is found.' And they began to celebrate.

If you have ever backslidden, you have fallen from grace. If you once knew and walked with God, this parable should minister to you. This parable is where so many Christians today have been, or they are in this place currently. The prodigal son had been raised by a man of God, one who was devoted in serving the Lord. Like so many of us today, he decided, he did not want to follow in the footsteps of his father. He wanted to do things his way. He wanted his dad to give him his inheritance, what he felt was rightfully his. He wanted to spend his money his way and not God's way. The father gave his son his inheritance and let him go. How many times do we make decisions based on what we believe is best for us and not look to God for direction. We feel we know what is best, and what does it cost us? When I walked away from the church, did I seek God's direction on this? No! I had already made up my mind, I would just pack God and myself up, and we would walk away together. That seems funny today but was basically what I was saying. This is what you are saying too when you believe you do not need the church. Too many times I hear Christians say, *"I do not have to go to church to be close to God."* That is a lie from the enemy in order to keep you defeated. I spent 15 years defeated not seeing victory in my life. I lived through total destruction because I had made the decision I would just keep God at my home and that was it. God did not make that decision, I did. When we get to a place to realize we need God and He expects us to be connected, we have conquered one aspect of growing strong in our Christian walk.

We all know the prodigal son came to his senses and came home, but what had this taught him? When we are backslidden, we are struggling trying to do it in ourselves. When we finally come to our senses, what do we learn or what should it have taught us? The prodigal son teaches us something valuable. It is one thing to be backslidden and come home, halfway serving God as so many people do, but when things got tough with the prodigal son, he knew the path which led to righteousness. There was no straddling the fence as we see so many times in our churches today. The prodigal son learned from his mistakes. If we do not learn from our mistakes, we will wind up right back in the world again because we were not able to see the valuable lesson in making wrong choices. It is a lesson that time in the world taught the prodigal son. It was a lesson he would not forget. Time in the world also taught me a lesson I would not forget. During those 15 years, I ran back and forth from this church to that church which is what many today do. I call it church hopping. I expected something to just miraculously happen each time I found myself seeking God in church. I would struggle to try to get back close to the Lord, only to find myself falling away again and again. When I finally came back and became grounded, something different had taken place within me just like the prodigal son. The prodigal son had been humbled. He had hit a place on his course of the path he had chosen to walk where he realized he needed God. That simple! We may come to a place where we hit bottom. We may come to a place where we are no longer satisfied or we desire something different in life, which we cannot find in the world. Whatever place we come to, we are all in search of answers and solutions. We are in search of what it will take this time to change our circumstances and make us happy. Many have hopes of believing there has to be more to life than what they currently have.

I came to a place where life in the world no longer satisfied me. I wanted to, once again, live that vibrant life I had once lived with my Father, Jesus, and the Holy Spirit. Wherever you are at, once you come to a place where you humble yourself to know you need God in your life or you need God to a greater degree, then the door will be opened. The prodigal son had humbled himself to come home, and he looked at himself as unworthy saying, *"Father, I have sinned against You and Heaven."* This is powerful, when we walk away and fall from grace then we have sinned against our Father in Heaven and against Heaven itself. As a child of God, we bring shame to our Father when we sin and this also shames all of His Kingdom. He no longer felt worthy to be called his son. When we humble ourselves before the Lord, we have to realize we have sinned against our Father and His Kingdom. When we repent and show the Father our heart has been broken and our pain is real, we will understand that we do not deserve any better than a servant. What did the father do in this story? He rejoiced and celebrated just as our Father in Heaven will do over each of His children. When one sinner or one who is backslidden realizes he needs something greater and he repents, all of Heaven is rejoicing and celebrating that he has come home. *(Luke 15:7)* This is the place where we need to be, to know we are nothing until we repent and begin to get our life right with the Father. Then through Jesus, He makes us into something. It is only through the shed blood on Calvary that we become anything.

To Something

Many of God's children read the Word of God and still continue to speak negative over their lives. Many see themselves as the world may see them but not as God sees them. The world tends to look at the outward appearance, but God is not shallow like the world. God looks on your heart. Maybe you have spoken one or more of the following over yourself:

•I am not smart enough.
•I am not athletic enough.
•I do not look good enough.
•I am over-weight.
•I do not know how to be in charge.
•I do not know how to be bold.
•I do not believe people will listen to me.
•I am not assertive.
•I do not see myself as a leader.

91

•I do not see myself as being good at anything.
•I could never get up in front of a crowd and teach.
•I do not have enough knowledge to proclaim Jesus to the world.
•I cannot fix someone's problems, much less my own.

People see themselves according to the way they have been taught, and many were programmed to believe they could not succeed at anything. Many have come from families who barely got by and believe this is just the way it is. Many would be content, if God would just bless them with a little that would be good enough. God's children continue to proclaim negative statements such as the following when it comes to either speaking blessings over their lives or curses:

God is not going to bless me with more because...

•I do not have a good enough education.
•I do not have an out-going personality.
•I do not have nice enough clothes.
•If I can just make it to heaven that is all I need.

If you can just make it to heaven that is all you need; however, many who cannot rise above those beliefs will have a hard time persevering to the end to make it to heaven. On the other hand, those who learn to be soldiers will win the battle. We need to set ourselves apart from the world because according to Scripture, we are not of the world. We should not think or act like the world.

John 17:16-17 (Amp) [16]*They are not of the world (worldly, belonging to the world), [just] as I am not of the world.* [17]*Sanctify them [purify, consecrate, separate them for Yourself, make them holy] by the Truth; Your Word is Truth.*

While praying to the Father, this is what Jesus prayed for those who believe in Him. Just as, Jesus is not of this world, neither are we if we claim to be a child of God. We are to be sanctified and set apart from the world. This happens when we receive the Truth which is God's Word. Once we begin to see we have risen above being nothing, we need to begin to look at who we are supposed to be. According to the Word, those of the world are not concerned with things of God. The teachings on the cross and the teachings about God mean nothing to the world, but to God's children His Words are life!

1 Corinthians 1:18-19(ESV) [18]For the word of the cross is folly to those who are perishing, but to us who are being saved it is the power of God. [19]For it is written, "I will destroy the wisdom of the wise, and the discernment of the discerning I will thwart."

God said He will destroy the wisdom of the wise, those who think they are wise. This is the world, the people who are not concerned with things of God and believe they do not need Him. The point I am trying to make, we look at those in the world who have great educations and great jobs as being so wise. We find ourselves desiring to model our lives around others who are successful in the world. However, to God it is foolishness. When we quit comparing ourselves to the world and begin comparing ourselves to our walk according to the Word, then we will be able to see our true value. We will be able to see ourselves capable of rising to be something through the blood of Jesus.

1 Corinthians 1:20-25(ESV) [20] Where is the one who is wise? Where is the scribe? Where is the debater of this age? Has not God made foolish the wisdom of the world? [21]For since, in the wisdom of God, the world did not know God through wisdom, it pleased God through the folly of what we preach to save those who believe. [22]For Jews demand signs and Greeks seek wisdom, [23]but we preach Christ crucified, a stumbling block to Jews and folly to Gentiles, [24]but to those who are called, both Jews *and Greeks, Christ the power of God and the wisdom of God. ²⁵For the* — *foolishness of God is wiser than men, and the weakness of God is stronger than men.*

God said those who are wise are foolish. God made foolish the wisdom of the world. Do those in high worldly places think they are foolish? Those who live according to the world do not think they are foolish because they believe they already have all the answers and do not need God. What they do not know is He is very real. What they do not know is they are very foolish people. I am not implying everyone who has a degree or a great job is foolish and not wise. Many are in those places because God has blessed them. I am referring to the world that does not know Jesus; they rely on themselves for success, happiness, and prosperity. In the Word, it says the foolishness of God is wiser than men. So even if you know very little about the Word, if you believe, are saved, and are growing, what you know is even wiser than the wisdom of the world. Even those who feel they are weak are stronger than the world. The weakness of God is stronger than any man who does not have Jesus. If you are learning and growing in Christ, your weaknesses will be strengthened through Him who has called you.

2 Corinthians 12:10 (Amp) ¹⁰So for the sake of Christ, I am well pleased and take pleasure in infirmities, insults, hardships, persecutions, perplexities and distresses; for when I am weak [in human strength], then am I [truly] strong (able, powerful in divine strength).

We know if we are saved, in Jesus we are somebody. Do we believe God wants to really make us something great? Remember, I shared the more you have endured in hardships or tragedies, the greater your ministry could be if you line up with the Word. This is what Paul said in Corinthians…

1 Corinthians 1:26-31(ESV) [26]*For consider your calling, brothers: not many of you were wise according to worldly standards, not many were powerful, not many were of noble birth.* [27]*But God chose what is foolish in the world to shame the wise; God chose what is weak in the world to shame the strong;* [28]*God chose what is low and despised in the world, even things that are not, to bring to nothing things that are,* [29]*so that no human being might boast in the presence of God.* [30]*And because of him you are in Christ Jesus, who became to us wisdom from God, righteousness and sanctification and redemption,* [31]*so that, as it is written, "Let the one who boasts, boast in the Lord."*

Consider your calling, are you saved? Do you consider yourself a Christian? If you consider yourself a Christian, the Word says to consider your calling. God called you for a reason, for a purpose. God did not pick those who were wise according to worldly standards. God did not pick those who are powerful according to worldly standards. Are you of a noble birth, were your parent's royalty or were they in powerful positions? God picks those that the world considers to be foolish. He chooses those the world considers to be weak and not just physical weakness. We can have weaknesses in other areas. Maybe you are considered weak minded or someone who believes they cannot accomplish things. Maybe you are one that cannot see yourself as being great. Perhaps you have some weak character trait, and the world looks down on you. However, God will pick you up and take you to higher places. God chooses those that are the lowly of the world, those that the world despises. Who does the world despise? The world despises those who have criminal records, those who have committed adultery, those who have abused people, drug addicts, prostitutes, those who do not have an education, those on welfare, those who do not pay their child-support, and those who do not take care of their children to name a few. If you fit into one of these categories, despised by the world, God chose you to be one of His children. He chooses those over the ones who do not live for God. They may live productive lives. They may take care of their children and abstain from drug use, but that is not what God chooses. God takes those things the world looks at as nothing. He chooses the lowly of the world, and the uneducated. He chooses those who the world looks at as nothing, and He makes them into something. Why does God do this? The Word says, *"So that no one might boast,"* (*vrs.29*). Boasting is being proud or taking credit for something. God does not need that man who has a master's degree to bring Jesus to the world if that man cannot see himself as being lowly. We are all lowly, but those who have great educations and are successful may not perceive themselves as lowly. It is easier for those who have never had anything, or it is easier for those who have had to struggle and work hard for what they do have to be able to see themselves as nothing, except through Christ. Those who have been at the bottom know what it is like. They are able to see and recognize there is a greater power. They are able to see that it is not in them that they are where they are today. The glory goes to God. For those who are at the bottom and seeking God for wisdom to pull out, the Scriptures tell us if any lack wisdom, let him ask.

James 1:5 (ESV) [5] *If any of you lacks wisdom, let him ask God, who gives generously to all without reproach, and it will be given him.*

There are all kinds of agencies and organizations that try to help people. These agencies help reform them in order to show a different course that can lead to productive lives. Not all of these agencies are doing a bad thing, and many are using methods that are biblical, except God is left out of the equation. What happens when God is not in it? People seeking these agencies for help may develop some useful skills to help in life, but they will never overcome their difficulties entirely. Being able to overcome areas of your life totally cannot be done except through Christ. Many of these organizations get recognition for what a good job they are doing when, in fact, they are doing everything in themselves. No matter what they do or how much effort they put forth, it will never be good enough. If you take a man straight out of prison and put him in a half-way house, they will attempt to reform him before sending him back into the world. What happens? The statistics show 70% of all those released from prison will go back. This is not very good odds of rehabilitation. God does not need man's wisdom or the world's solutions to rehabilitate people. God has His own book of laws, and in His book, there is no error. If you have a past, then God has your future and is calling you. God wants to show the world that He can take something they looked at as nothing and put that person in a position or place no one would have ever thought possible.

I was not someone who the world saw as being successful. I have a past like many out there. It is a past of imperfection. I would have never in a million years have seen myself getting on stage talking to hundreds of people, but God saw me doing this. God has put me in those places. He has shown me that in Him, I can do all things because I'm not doing it in myself.

1 Corinthians 2:12-13(ESV) [12]Now we have received not the spirit of the world, but the Spirit who is from God, that we might understand the things freely given us by God. [13]And we impart this in words not taught by human wisdom but taught by the Spirit, interpreting spiritual truths to those who are spiritual.

We are not doing those things we are called to do in ourselves. You may not see the potential in yourself, but Moses did not either. It is not in yourself that the works God has sent you

97

to do are done. The Word says we have not received the spirit of the world but the Spirit who is from God. If you know you have accepted Jesus into your heart and know the Holy Spirit walks with you daily, do you doubt that God can use you mightily? It says we have received the Spirit who is from God in order for us to understand. We need to understand those things freely given to us are by God. When we go forth to do those things which He has called us to do, He also equips us with His wisdom, not ours or that of the world. Verse 13 says we impart this in words not taught by human wisdom but taught by the Spirit. As we begin to walk in our calling, the anointing is going to come upon us, and once that happens, we are going to soar like an eagle. You will begin to see that your growth with God will take off. You will be able to interpret things you never thought possible. You will have spiritual wisdom that passes all understanding. However, in order to get to this place or to get to any place with God depends on how much you are willing to give with your time and effort. If you want it bad enough, you will feed it. We feed our physical body daily in order to be strong and not weak. In the same sense, we must also feed our spiritual body the food it requires in order to rise and be strong in the things of God. If we are fed properly, we will not walk around beat down and weak. Daily if, we are being fed life, we will not walk around thinking we cannot do those tasks that He has called us to do. If we feel that way, we are starving our spirit man and it is crying out, *"Feed me!"* The more you feed it, the faster it will grow. The faster it grows, the sooner you will be walking in what God called you to do. Once this happens, spiritual blessings will also begin to come your way.

1 Corinthians 2:14-16(ESV) [14] *The natural person does not accept the things of the Spirit of God, for they are folly to him, and he is not able to understand them because they are spiritually discerned.* [15] *The spiritual person judges all things, but is himself to be judged by no one.* [16] *"For who has understood the mind of the Lord so as to instruct him?" But we have the mind of Christ.*

We will remain like the world, living to appease our natural man, if we do not accept the things of the Spirit of God. If we do not understand the spiritual things of God, it is because they are spiritually discerned. How are you going to learn something if you are not studying? No one ever received a degree by NOT spending time studying. If you want to be a successful Christian, you must spend time with God and in the Word of God. Your mind will only be transformed to the mind of Christ if you are diligently seeking the wisdom of God.

God created His children to rise above their circumstances and become everything He created them to be. God sees us as being successful, and we have to begin seeing ourselves through His eyes. We can all see according to Scripture, God desires us to be something. God desires for us to be free from all the bad within us and replace it with something good. God desires to take those who believe themselves to be nothing and make them into something. If we begin to see ourselves the way He sees us, we will begin to rise and take our place as His children, not as those in the world.

How Does God See You

You need to look deeply at just how God see you. If God is for us, who can be against us? *(Romans 8:31)* God desires for all of His children to be blessed, not just some of them. In order to begin receiving these blessings, we have to be able to see who we are in Christ. As parents, we do not want our own children to grow up and not be blessed. Why then would we think God wants

99

less for His children? We need to begin to grasp a reflection of who God is and why we were created.

Genesis 1:26 (NIV) [26] *Then God said, "Let us make man in our image, in our likeness, and let them rule over the fish of the sea and the birds of the air, over the livestock, over all the earth, and over all the creatures that move along the ground."*

We know according to Scripture, we were created in the likeness and image of God. We consist of our body, soul, and our spirit.

1 Thessalonians 5:23 (Amp) [23]*And may the God of peace Himself sanctify you through and through [separate you from profane things, make you pure and wholly consecrated to God]; and may your spirit and soul and body be preserved sound and complete [and found] blameless at the coming of our Lord Jesus Christ (the Messiah).*

If we were created in the image and likeness of God, then we know God also consists of a soul. What is our soul? In researching, our soul consists of the moral and emotional nature of human beings. It is the quality that arouses emotion and sentiment. This is where our emotions originate and our feelings. We are emotional beings created in the likeness of God. However, we also know that our emotions can get us into trouble, and we cannot go forth based on everything which we feel. Our decisions have to be based on not only what we feel but what we think. We get into trouble in both of these areas because our minds have to be renewed to thinking like God thinks. This only happens through time in the Word. This is what I am getting at, our emotions also desire. Man from the beginning of time has desired love, acceptance, approval, etc. If we are created in the likeness of God, we would assume God also desires these same

100

things. We know God is a jealous God according to Scripture. *(Exodus 20:5)* God also desires our love. He wants us to accept Him and come to know Him. We see from this, God desired to make man in His image to have someone He could love, shower blessings on, accept, and someone He could approve of. We desire those same things that God desires, and for this reason, we were created. We do not like to be alone. God too wants someone as a companion, and of course, He wanted someone that was like Him. We have children because we want someone that is in our likeness. God saw it was a good thing that He created man. We too see it as a good thing when we have a child.

Therefore, we know the reason why God created us, but let's go further to begin understanding more of who God is. After we begin to understand who God is, we will be able to understand more of who we are inside. Looking back on my walk with God and all He brought me through, I began to ask questions. Why it is so easy for some to get saved and walk away while others get saved and just jump right in never compromising with their walk. I have heard it said those who can easily walk away should question their salvation. If they were really saved, then that would not happen. I have to disagree. This may be the case with some; however, in my case that was not what happened. I asked God what needed to change in me in order for me to be grounded and not fall again. I believe the desire has to be there to want to know God to a deeper level because if that desire is not there, you will never seek. The Word tells us to seek, and we will find.

Luke 11:10 (NIV) [10]*For everyone who asks receives; he who seeks finds; and to him who knocks, the door will be opened.*

I came back eager and ready to find God to another degree. I came back determined to gain revelation from my mistakes. This has to take place if we truly desire to know God in depth. I have shared several of the areas in which God has shown me why His people are living defeated. After we take a deeper look into how God sees His children, this will help us in our walk in order to rise and take our place to do those things we are called to do. We will be able to see God desires to heal each of us in areas where we struggle with pain from our past. He desires to get close to each of His children in order that we have an intimate relationship with our Creator. If any walls are left undone and not torn down, we will not be set free from all those areas in which satan has kept us bound.

My God is your God, and Jesus died for all of us. God desires great things for you as much as any of His children. If you have children, you want good things for all of your children. You may have a child who grows up to be something really great according to the world's standards, and you may have a child which pursues a lifestyle that is very simple. Does it matter? No, as long as our children are content and happy, we love them the same. However, what is the ultimate that we desire for our children? I know I have said it did not matter what my children pursued in life. It does not matter to me who they marry, but I do not want my children to be in situations where there is pain in their lives. I want my children to be able to see themselves capable of doing whatever their heart desires. I want to see my children rising up to be everything they are capable of being. I want to see my children pursue life with a passion. I want them to experience love with a passion. I want them to have children that they can teach to pursue life with a passion, but if we look back over our own lives, have we pursued life with a passion? Have we found that happiness and succeeded with our deepest dreams? Most of us would say, *"No!"* More than likely, our children will follow the same course we walked unless we begin making drastic changes. This is where we have to let go and let God. We have to trust that the Creator of the Universe and of mankind knows exactly what we need in life, in order to find the passion and drive to rise and succeed with our deepest dreams. If there is a dream you have held on to for many years, God may have placed that dream there and if so, He will be faithful to bring it into play.

1 Corinthians 6:11 (Amp) [11]*And such some of you were [once]. But you were washed clean (purified by a complete atonement for sin and made free from the guilt of sin), and you were consecrated (set apart, hallowed), and you were justified [pronounced righteous, by trusting] in the name of the Lord Jesus Christ and in the [Holy] Spirit of our God.*

After we go before the Father and repent of our sins, the Word tells us that we are born again. Paul tells us in Corinthians, we are washed clean. We are purified and free from the guilt of sin. Many people today, after getting saved, continue to feel the guilt of all the things they have done wrong. Why is that? satan is going to be the first one to come in and say things such as:

• You are nothing.
• You really did not mean it when you asked Jesus into your heart.
• Look at your life, your sin is too great to just be forgiven like that.

satan does not want you to get saved. He does not want you coming back home if you have backslidden. He does not want you to be set free from all those lies he has led you to believe for many years, and he definitely does not want you strong!

Do not listen to the enemy and believe a lie. Just because, you have sinned or done horrible things, God will forgive you and love you. It is far from the truth to believe otherwise. If you are a parent, you know it does not matter what your children have done because you cannot stop loving them, and if you do not have any children, look at your own parents or those who have been the foundation for your life. Do they still love you when you do something wrong? Not all parents know how to show love, but when it comes down to it, who are they going to fight for? If you have any kind of past, if you have done horrible things, or lived through terrible tragedies, God will turn it around. Once those things begin to turn around where you are living for Christ, you will be great in the kingdom. satan also knows this and will do what he can to keep you from either returning or keep you from coming in as a new Christian.

Who are we in Christ? How does God see us? In Romans 8, we see that if we are led by the Holy Spirit, then we are the sons of God. If we are the sons of God, we are His children. Being led by the Holy Spirit is a gradual process of lining up your will with the Fathers. This is something God will begin working on after you get saved, but look at what else this Scripture says.

Romans 8:14-15(ESV) **¹⁴***For all who are led by the Spirit of God are sons of God.* **¹⁵***For you did not receive the spirit of slavery to fall back into fear, but you have received the Spirit of adoption as sons, by whom we cry, "Abba! Father!"*

We have not received the spirit of slavery to fall back into fear. Fear is not of God; it is from satan. When we come to God, we should never fear that we will never be able to walk this walk. God said we do not have the spirit of fear. We should be confident our life is going to change. We will not begin to see this until we begin to believe what God's Word says about us and every situation we face. As we draw close to God, we will also begin to learn how to recognize the voice of God and the voice which is satan. When we are bound in anything which is from satan, we are in bondage in that area, and not free. God desires us to be set free, and we are only free by the Truth. God's Word is Truth and shall set us free.

John 8:32 (NIV) [32]Then you will know the truth, and the truth will set you free."

In Romans, it continues to say the Spirit bears witness with our spirit. We are God's children and if His children, then what?

Romans 8:16-17(ESV) [16] The Spirit himself bears witness with our spirit that we are children of God, [17]and if children, then heirs—heirs of God and fellow heirs with Christ,

Yes, we are heirs of God and fellow heirs with Christ. Do you see yourself as an heir to the Most High God? As an heir, you are entitled to whatever belongs to your Father. God has everything we need to walk this walk, and in this book, you will begin to learn how. A good way to get the Word grounded in you in order to see yourself the way God sees you, is to take a Scripture like Romans or several Scriptures, and write them down. Take those Scriptures you have written and tape them somewhere where you will see them daily. Every time you are in front of those Scriptures, you need to read them out loud. Go a step further to say, *"Yes, I am an heir of the Most High God; I am your son or your daughter."* Saying these things not only helps you to believe it but it also says to our enemy to, *"Watch out, I am coming through, and nothing is going to stop me!"* Of course, this begins by believing God is who He says He is, and we can only please Him by believing those things which are written in His Word.

Hebrews 11:6 (NIV) *⁶And without faith it is impossible to please God, because anyone who comes to him must believe that he exists and that he rewards those who earnestly seek him.*

We will continue to operate the same way we did prior to being saved, even if we were saved many years ago. Nothing will change until we diligently seek Him out faithfully and allow that faith to rise up in us. When we do this and set aside that time needed to study and pray, then our way of thinking will begin to line up with the Word of God. We will begin to see according to His Word, He does desire not only to take away all the pain but to bless our lives, as well. God looks upon us like we look upon our own children or like our parents look upon us. God loves us, and He is for us just like our earthly parents are for us. He sees us rising to great levels, and in doing so, this glorifies Him. When we do well, our earthly parents are proud, and they brag to others about how great we are doing. God is also enjoying the glory that He is receiving because of a job well done.

Ephesians 3:20 (NIV) *²⁰Now to him who is able to do immeasurably more than all we ask or imagine, according to his power that is at work within us,*

God's power is continually at work within us. He is continually going before us. Prior to us rising each morning to begin our day, He has already set the stage for where we will be and what we will be doing.

Isaiah 64:4 (Amp) *⁴For from of old no one has heard nor perceived by the ear, nor has the eye seen a God besides You, Who works and shows Himself active on behalf of him who [earnestly] waits for Him.*

If you are a child of God, He has designed specifically and individually that course of life for you to travel. It will fit your personality, your desires, and your ambitions. I have had some say to me, *"I could never do what you are doing."* My response is, *"You are not supposed to do what I am doing; God has a plan for you individually."* We do not need to look at others with jealousy, and we do not need to feel that we are incapable of doing great things either. We need to realize that it takes all of us in what God called us to do in order to fit together perfectly for the body of Christ. We need to see that every calling is unique and important.

Ephesians 4:16 (Amp) [16]*For because of Him the whole body (the church, in all its various parts), closely joined and firmly knit together by the joints and ligaments with which it is supplied, when each part [with power adapted to its need] is working properly [in all its functions], grows to full maturity, building itself up in love.*

If you are called to care for the elderly, if you are called into ministry for children, or if you are called to be an Evangelist, each one of these areas can be an awesome calling. If you are doing what God called you to do, He will be looking at you with a great big smile because He will be pleased. Also, we should know that God is not going to call someone to be involved with a children's ministry if there is not some kind of passion for children. In the same sense, if there is not a passion to help the elderly, it will not be your calling. God takes those dreams and desires that are in your heart, and He cultivates them into a plan or a course of action just for you. Do not think it cannot become great. God is a God of increase. As He increases you, it increases Him. If you walk in your calling, God will make it great to a degree your mind would never have even fathomed. Yes, it will be as great as the TV Evangelist or as the Missionary. God is God! He is the creator of all. We do not need to think, God has to hire someone

107

with an Engineering Degree to help Him figure out how to make someone with a desire in the children's ministry great. Some may feel that a children's ministry would not be great, but for those who have a love for children, this is what they have been dreaming of. God only needs you! What I mean by that, God desires to see you be all He created you to be, not what you are capable of believing you can be. You can be all that His Wisdom and His Knowledge can see you as. Remember, He created you, and He knows every single thing about you including exactly how many hairs you have on your head. However, His Will for your life will never come to pass until you really desire it deep within your heart and begin believing God desires to make you into something great.

Luke 12:7 (Amp) [7]*But [even] the very hairs of your head are all numbered. Do not be struck with fear or seized with alarm; you are of greater worth than many [flocks] of sparrows.*

God sees us with great worth. If He did not, why did He bother to send Jesus? If He did not, why from the beginning of time has He tried to bless man? It is not God who has cut off those blessings; it is man who is continually disobeying God and in doing so, our blessings stop.

Jeremiah 5:25 (Amp) [25]*Your iniquities have turned these blessings away, and your sins have kept good [harvests] from you.*

Once we can begin to see just how much God loves us and desires to increase us, maybe then we will no longer do those things that disappoint Him. When we love someone with all our heart, we desperately try to please them. This is human nature; however, in ourselves, we always miss it and fall short. In Jesus, we can begin to line up to that which we strive to accomplish. As we begin to see just how much God loves us and we mess up, it will bother us to disappoint Him, and it should bother us. All God wants us to do when we miss it, is to repent. He wants us to mean it in our heart and then try again. Do not just assume that asking for repentance is some magical tool, which can be abused by doing whatever your flesh desires and then running to God to make things right. That is not a right heart attitude, and God can see through it.

In Right Standing

Are you in right-standing with God? Do you boldly go before the throne of grace with your prayers knowing you are right with the Father? There are many parables in the bible which are there as examples to teach us and instruct us in the ways of the Lord. God wanted us to have a book of His Words, so we can rise to different levels as we grow. We are not to be as the world and live defeated; we are to rise and take our place as children of the Most High God. When we study the parable of the prodigal son, we see a glimpse of what God is like as a father. We see how He forgives and how He loves.

At this point, we should all be familiar with the story of the prodigal son. When the son came home, what did his father do? The father called to bring his son the best robe, a ring on his finger, and the best calf. What do you think our Father in Heaven does when we come to the place where we wake up and make that right decision? When we cry out, *"Lord, it is all about You; it is not about me and I am nothing without You!"* God knows our heart; therefore, our heart has to get right with Him. How do we do this? We must come to a place where we humble ourselves and repent of doing things our way. We must come to the place where we cry out and say, *"Father, no longer my will be done, but*

109

yours." When we get to that place God desires for us, we will begin to experience the flow of blessings within our lives. Remember, Jesus told the parable about the prodigal son, and in the end, the father not only rejoiced and celebrated but he gave him the best of everything. Many people today can only believe God for barely getting by. I have known people who were sharing how they were barely making it, and in the next breath, they are thanking the Lord because they have seen harder times. Yes, I agree we should be thankful that God has brought us out of worse times; however, our God desires to give His children the best. After all, our God is over the whole Universe and everything within it. The best to our God is not hand-me downs; the best is not a second-hand car, and it is not food stamps. It is great that we are not greedy, but in order to begin to understand God, we have to know Him. In knowing Him, we have to understand His desires are to bless His people. The father of the prodigal son gave his son the best. He did not give him second best but the best. This story was for us to see inside the mind of God, how He thinks. Once we begin to please God, He desires us to walk with Him. God desires us to trust Him and to realize who we are because of the blood of Jesus. In doing so, we will realize that it is because of Jesus' blood which makes us in right-standing with our Father.

If you are a born again Christian, covered in the blood of Jesus, then Paul said in Romans, you are made upright and in right-standing with God.

Romans 5:17 (Amp)[17]For if because of one man's trespass (lapse, offense) death reigned through that one, much more surely will those who receive [God's] overflowing grace (unmerited favor) and the free gift of righteousness [putting them into right standing with Himself] reign as kings in life through the one Man Jesus Christ (the Messiah, the Anointed One).

Grace is a gift and with any gift, what do we do? We accept it! A gift is something given to us freely; we do not have to pay for it. In the same sense when we become saved, we accept the gift of grace. This gift of grace allows us to have favor with God, and we are made righteous in His sight because of the blood of Jesus. It does not matter how we see ourselves, what matters is how God sees us. Through studying God's Word, we will begin to see ourselves as He sees us. We will never be able to accomplish our goals and dreams God has planted deep within, if we see ourselves as defeated before we have ever begun. satan loves to keep God's children beat down in order that they never are able to reap that which God desires for them. If we were to all rise up and take our place, standing firm with Christ, we would begin to see a revival in our nation like never before. How then do we begin to stand up boldly and righteously knowing God is calling us for a great purpose? Let's first ask ourselves these questions:

1) Did you accept Jesus into your heart? _____
2) Are you a child of God? _____
3) Do you believe Jesus, not only died for you, but if you were the only person left on this earth, He would have made that sacrifice just for you? _____

You should have answered yes to at least the first two questions, if you are a born again Christian, but let's look deeper into the third question. If you were the only one, would God have sent His son just for you?

The majority of Christians today, do not see themselves as righteous before God. Instead, they believe because of their shortcomings, they are incapable of being who God has called them to be. We see in Romans that all, not some, are made upright and in right standing with God through the redemption of Jesus.

Romans 3:24 (Amp)[24][All] are justified and made upright and in right standing with God, freely and gratuitously by His grace (His unmerited favor and mercy), through the redemption which is [provided] in Christ Jesus,

In Luke, this is a parable in which Jesus shared in order to show the people God sent Him for those who were sinners.

Luke 15:3-7 (ESV) The Parable of the Lost Sheep [3]So he told them this parable: [4] "What man of you, having a hundred sheep, if he has lost one of them, does not leave the ninety-nine in the open country, and go after the one that is lost, until he finds it? [5]And when he has found it, he lays it on his shoulders, rejoicing. [6]And when he comes home, he calls together his friends and his neighbors, saying to them, 'Rejoice with me, for I have found my sheep that was lost.' [7]Just so, I tell you, there will be more joy in heaven over one sinner who repents than over ninety-nine righteous persons who need no repentance.

God sent Jesus for those who feel inadequate and those who feel they are nothing. God knows His children. He knows how we have suffered and how many have so much pain within. The good news is that God sent His Son, not only to save us but to restore us, so that we become who He created us to be. If it were only for one sinner, just like the one sheep, God still would have sent Jesus to die just for you. Here again, we see another parable in which Jesus shared.

Luke 15:8-10(ESV) The Parable of the Lost Coin [8]"Or what woman, having ten silver coins, if she loses one coin, does not light a lamp and sweep the house and seek diligently until she finds it? [9]And when she has found it, she calls together her friends and neighbors, saying, 'Rejoice

with me, for I have found the coin that I had lost.' ¹⁰Just so, I tell you,
there is joy before the angels of God over one sinner who repents."

We see by both of these parables that heaven rejoices when just one of us repents. As Christians, we need to think about this Scripture, do not just read it. This is the God of the Universe who sent His only begotten Son to die for you and me. When you come before God to repent of your sins, and you ask Jesus into your heart, heaven is rejoicing. Can you imagine someone in high authority, in our nation, coming to your birthday party and celebrating with you? For most of us, we could not imagine that happening. There is not a person on earth today who is worthy enough to hold a candlestick for the God of the Universe that created all, but the day you were saved, that day became your new birthday. When we are saved, the bible tells us that we are born again. This is our birthday into our new family, and God was right there along with all of heaven celebrating our birthday of being born into the Kingdom of Heaven. To God, you are that special, and you need to begin to see yourself that way.

Luke 15:7(Amp)⁷Thus, I tell you, there will be more joy in heaven over one [especially] wicked person who repents (changes his mind, abhorring his errors and misdeeds, and determines to enter upon a better course of life) than over ninety-nine righteous persons who have no need of repentance.

We need to see how God looks on sin compared to how He sees those who are righteous. We know to be righteous is through the blood of Jesus; however, in the Old Testament times, those who were in right standing with God had to sacrifice innocent blood through the means of animals. In Genesis, we see a conversation between Abraham and God.

113

Genesis 18:23 (Amp)[23]And Abraham came close and said, Will You destroy the righteous (those upright and in right standing with God) together with the wicked?

Abraham was pleading to God on behalf of the people in Sodom and Gomorrah because he did not want any who were in right standing to perish. God began to agree He would spare the city if, in fact, there were 50 righteous among them. As the conversation went further, God finally agreed to spare Sodom and Gomorrah if there were only 10 righteous.

Genesis 18:32 (Amp)[32]And he said, Oh, let not the Lord be angry, and I will speak again only this once. Suppose ten [righteous people] shall be found there. And [the Lord] said, I will not destroy it for ten's sake.

At the end of this story, we see Lot was the only righteous man among Sodom and Gomorrah. God had angels lead not only Lot out of the city but any of his family members that would go with him. This story shows just how much God loves His children. God did not spare the city, but because of one righteous man, He led him out of the city and away from destruction. We need to see something else here. Because of the great love God has for just one righteous man, he also allowed Lot to gather up his family to take with him. God desires not only to save one of His children from destruction but his family, as well. Our family has favor with the Lord because of us. This is something that will be discussed further when we get deeper into prayer and standing in the gap for those we love. Another thing we need to see in this Scripture is God desires for His people to be free from destruction. God led Lot out of the midst of his destruction, out of the midst of sin and evil. We know God is the same today as He was yesterday *(Hebrews 13:8)* and desires His children are free from destruction and sin.

114

2Peter 2:7 (ESV)[7]and if he rescued righteous Lot, greatly distressed by the sensual conduct of the wicked [8](for as that righteous man lived among them day after day, he was tormenting his righteous soul over their lawless deeds that he saw and heard); [9]then the Lord knows how to rescue the godly from trials, and to keep the unrighteous under punishment until the day of judgment, [10]and especially those who indulge in the lust of defiling passion and despise authority.

What does this mean for us today? Today think about your life, think about all those things that keep trying to pull you down and destroy you and your family. God desires for you to rise above all of your circumstances. He desires this for you and those you love. I have ministered to those who will not make that step toward God because they do not want to go it alone. They want their spouse or another loved one to go with them. We need to realize, our loved ones will have favor if we step on board and come to God once and for all giving it everything we have. As we begin to see ourselves as righteous because of the blood of Jesus and we begin to look to God and not the world, He will lead us out of the path of destruction. Do you want your children to be free from destruction? Do you want your loved ones set free? You may be the key to making that happen.

Today, Christians all over the world are defeated because they fail to have the revelation within about what the shed blood on Calvary has done for them. We may think we could never be righteous like the men in the Old Testament in which we have read about; however, because of the shed blood on Calvary, we need to realize it is much easier for us to be in right standing with God today than it was yesterday. We no longer have to go before a priest to be sprinkled with blood for sanctification, and a priest is not the only one who can go into the Holy of Holies for intercession on behalf of God's children. The Word says we can come before the throne with confidence.

Hebrews 10:19 (Amp)[19]Therefore, brethren, since we have full freedom and confidence to enter into the [Holy of] Holies [by the power and virtue] in the blood of Jesus,

If we have repented of our sins, God is just to forgive us of our sins. We are righteous because of the blood of Jesus. We are able to come before the throne ourselves and present our prayers to the Most High God. I am glad I live in a day and time after Jesus and not before. Do you realize if you are in right standing with God, you are actually able to go before the throne, before the Almighty God who created the heavens and the earth? In the Old Testament, there was only one who could go into the Holy of Holies, and there were all kinds of rituals which had to be performed prior to him entering the Most Holy Place. Aaron the brother of Moses and his sons were appointed by God along with Moses to attend to the altar. Anyone else who even came close to it would die. This was how sacred the place was. Only one could actually enter into the Holy of Holies which was within the veil.

Numbers 18:7 (Amp) [7]Therefore you and your sons with you shall attend to your priesthood for everything of the altar [of burnt offering and the altar of incense] and [of the Holy of Holies] within the veil, and you shall serve. I give you your priesthood as a service of gift. And the stranger [anyone other than Moses or your sons, Aaron] who comes near shall be put to death.

Because of the shed blood of Jesus, there is no longer a veil to separate us from God. When we repent to the Lord and

116

become saved, what happens? That veil is stripped off; it is gone. There is nothing to separate us from the Most High God.

2 Corinthians 3:16 (Amp) *16But whenever a person turns [in repentance] to the Lord, the veil is stripped off and taken away.*

It is only through Christ the veil is removed. If we have not repented of our sins, that veil still separates us from God. We can cry out to God and pray day after day; however, if we have not repented of our sins, our prayers are just words which have no meaning. We have to understand in order to move God, we have to allow ourselves to be broken or our hearts to be broken. If your heart has not been broken, then it is hardened. God cannot move in someone whose heart is hard and cold. We have to come to the place that we realize there is a greater power. There is an Almighty God who has power over all the earth and all the heavens. He has power to move in our lives. When this happens, you will never be the same.

2 Corinthians 3:14 (Amp) *14In fact, their minds were grown hard and calloused [they had become dull and had lost the power of understanding]; for until this present day, when the Old Testament (the old covenant) is being read, that same veil still lies [on their hearts], not being lifted [to reveal] that in Christ it is made void and done away.*

We know once we get to this place, being a child of God has certain privileges just as we have certain privileges in our earthly families. Once saved, we have favor with our new family. One privilege in our new family is that we can now go boldly with confidence to the Holy of Holies. We can now come to the throne and present our prayers and petitions before our Father who has the power to move in our lives. If you do not see yourself as righteous, it is not because God cannot see you that way. When we fail to see ourselves as righteous, it is a battle within our own minds. Ask yourself these questions:

1) Can you see yourself as being a great man or woman of God like those during Old Testament times? _____
2) Do you believe you have God given talents? _____
3) Do you believe God desires to give you spiritual gifts in order to excel in this life here on earth? _____

Filling the Emptiness

When we get to the place where we are ready to submit to God, He then can begin to empty us totally. We need to understand, God desires to fill us back up with more of Him. In order for this to happen, we must begin to desire to be grounded on the rock, which is Jesus. To be grounded takes determination! I finally came to a place where I said to God, *"I will not leave or walk away from this church until I feel you again in my life, and I do not care how long it takes!"* It was 3 long months before I began to feel God working again in my life; however, I was determined. I stood on God's Word, *"Lord, You said You would never leave me or forsake me; I know even if I do not feel You, You are there!"*

Joshua 1:5 (NIV) [5] No one will be able to stand up against you all the days of your life. As I was with Moses, so I will be with you; I will never leave you nor forsake you.

We already discussed getting all the bad stuff on the inside of us out. This is merely giving all those things which have caused pain in our life to God for healing. However, there is more to emptying ourselves; we must also replace it with good. Our walk with the Lord should be a gradual process of becoming more and more like Jesus every day. In order to do this, we have to realize there are more things on the inside of us that need to come out.

Many times, our worst enemy can be ourselves. Self is what will bring us to a place of defeat time and time again. Walking with God should be a rewarding experience where you would never want to go back. It becomes rewarding as we become more and more like Jesus every day. Why is this? We know we are created in the likeness of God, but we also know we are far from being little Jesus' walking around. In 1 Corinthians, Paul said that he dies to self daily.

1 Corinthians 15:31 (Amp) [31]*[I assure you] by the pride which I have in you in [your fellowship and union with] Christ Jesus our Lord, that I die daily [I face death every day and die to self].*

In dying to self, we begin to let go of exactly what it says – self! Self and all of its ways, for example, begin with the letter "I". *"I want to do it this way; I am not going to do that; I do not like that; I am going to do this on Saturday; I want one like she has."* We can see the selfishness and sometimes we can see it better in others than in ourselves, but filling the emptiness will begin as we decrease and God increases within us. In order to do this, we have to be honest with ourselves and answer these questions. If we cannot be honest, God cannot do a work in us. If we cannot be honest, we will never see the blessings of God, and if we cannot be honest, our dreams and visions will never come to pass.

1) Before you begin a project, do you ever ask God if this is something you should be doing? _____
2) When you get invited to do something really exciting, do you automatically say yes before even consulting anyone else? _____
3) Do you ever not show up somewhere you committed to be without so much as a phone call because you were too busy doing something else? _____

4) When you pray, are your prayers more about God doing a miracle in your life or about God intervening for someone other than yourself? _____

5) How often do you do things for someone else?

_____

6) How often do you do things for a complete stranger?

_____

Being filled with more of God is a process. We take more of us out and replace it with more of God. We have to realize we need God to be in charge. When you realize your life has been such a mess because you have been doing it alone, you should also realize, in order for your life to change, you have to let go of you and look to God.

I said our walk with God should be rewarding because as we become more and more like Jesus, we will also act, think, and say those things Jesus did. When this happens, we will begin to see God move in our lives. We must know in order to get there, that our walk with God should be selfless. This means less of us and more of Him. As we are filled with more of Jesus, our way of thinking will be for others and not ourselves. Our way of thinking will be more for those things above and not of the world as we line up to the Word. There are times we may not understand something until it is explained in a different way. I like to use the phrase, "a light-bulb turning on" to explain how something all of a sudden becomes clear. When you begin to get the concept of thinking more like God by receiving more of His wisdom and knowledge, it becomes like that light bulb. All of a sudden, our life becomes clear.

I remember in college, I was once again taking English which I dreaded during high school and struggled in this area. I could not believe I had to learn nouns, pronouns, adjectives, and all the grammatical rules again. However, I applied myself right because

I wanted to do well. In doing so, one day when the teacher asked me a question and began to show me something, it was amazing how everything clicked. I all of a sudden understood the process. From that day forward, I excelled in English and actually loved it. I could not believe I had even struggled with it in high school. The same is with the wisdom and knowledge of God. When we begin to understand and get the process of why we have to put more of Him in and less of us, that light begins to turn on in our mind. At that point, you will love reading and studying God's Word because more wisdom and knowledge will begin to fill you. It is truly exciting when your walk begins to blossom.

I remember when I came back and pressed in, I was determined to wait on the Lord no matter how long it took. I made a decision to do something I had not done before. I decided I was going to praise Him even if I could not feel His presence. Normally, in my past when I was at church, if I did not feel like praising God, I did not praise Him. This time when I stepped out of the box and did something that was not normal, I was showing God it did not matter if I felt His presence or not. I wanted to show God I loved Him and desperately wanted Him back in my life. Those 3 months seemed forever, but it was worth it! Once God begins to move in your life, you will begin to see changes. These changes will occur not only within you but also all around you. It will become so exciting seeing the power of God work in your life to the point of saying, *"I'm back, satan move over because here I come!"* This reminds me of a saying, *"I want to be the kind of woman that when I awake in the morning and my feet hit the floor, satan is saying, 'Oh crap, she's up.'"*

We do not walk this alone. Like I said, God never leaves us and the Holy Spirit walks with us. Do you desire to take charge of what happens to you and around you? God will give you the desires to take charge and to rise up and be the child He created you to be. God will hook you up with the Holy Spirit who will walk you through your circumstances.

Romans 8:10-11 (ESV) ¹⁰But if Christ is in you, although the body is dead because of sin, the Spirit is life because of righteousness. ¹¹If the Spirit of him who raised Jesus from the dead dwells in you, he who raised Christ Jesus from the dead will also give life to your mortal bodies through his Spirit who dwells in you.

Through the Holy Spirit who dwells in you, your spirit man will awaken and rise up to be and do all which God has called you to do. Remember, we are not doing any of this alone and God never called us to do this alone. God knows we need His power just as Jesus also needed the anointing and power of the Holy Spirit when He walked in an earthly body.

Mark 1:9-13 (Amp) ⁹In those days Jesus came from Nazareth of Galilee and was baptized by John in the Jordan. ¹⁰And when He came up out of the water, at once he [John] saw the heavens torn open and the [Holy] Spirit like a dove coming down [to enter] into Him. ¹¹And there came a voice out from within heaven, You are My Beloved Son; in You I am well pleased. ¹²Immediately the [Holy] Spirit [from within] drove Him out into the wilderness (desert), ¹³And He stayed in the wilderness (desert) forty days, being tempted [all the while] by Satan; and He was with the wild beasts, and the angels ministered to Him [continually].

It was not until Jesus was baptized that the Holy Spirit came upon Him. At this point is when He was led by the Holy Spirit into the desert where He then faced temptation, but God did not send Him alone. Jesus had the Holy Spirit with Him which is power from above. Jesus went through a horrible forty days of being tempted while He was hungry and had not eaten through this whole ordeal. How many times do we think our situation is never going to end? However, Jesus was not alone. Besides the Holy Spirit, angels continually were ministering to Jesus. We are not alone; God equips us with whatever it takes to walk through our situations. Therefore as a child of God, we need to realize, we have a purpose. As God begins to fill us with more and more of Him, we will have a deep desire to share our God with the world. As we are obedient by sharing the gospel, we will become full of power and wisdom from above.

Romans 8:27-30(ESV) [27]And he who searches hearts knows what is the mind of the Spirit, because the Spirit intercedes for the saints according to the will of God. [28]And we know that for those who love God all things work together for good, for those who are called according to his purpose. [29]For those whom he foreknew he also predestined to be conformed to the image of his Son, in order that he might be the firstborn among many brothers. [30]And those whom he predestined he also called, and those whom he called he also justified, and those whom he justified he also glorified.

If we love God, all things work together for good. If you are a child of God, you are called for a purpose. Every one of God's children has a purpose. You may not know what your purpose is yet, but you do have a purpose. We not only have a purpose, but we were also predestined to be conformed into the image of Christ. Therefore, we see that we are to be more and more like Jesus. After becoming saved, the next step is growing in the Word in order to begin to be more like our Savior. Never think you cannot walk this walk because if you are a child of God, God knew you before you were even born. God knew you before you knew Him, and if He knows you, He also knows what you are capable of doing.

Let me share something God showed me a while back. I have shared that I was raised in a home where there was no God. Later in life after finding God, I would question, *"Why did I have to be born into a family that did not know you; why did I have to go through all the horrible things I went through?"* God began to show me something very amazing. He began to have me look back into my past, not just to the days I remembered. He also had me look into days in which I was in my mother's womb and days when I was just a toddler. Many of those things I only knew because someone had told me, and there have been a few of those incidents I had dwelt on over the years. I was conceived during the years no one really knew the dangers to drinking and smoking during pregnancy. There were several women over the years, who knew my mother very well, tell me that they were all surprised I even made it due to the amount of alcohol she consumed while carrying me. My youngest years, that I remember, were times my mother would be asleep in my room and fall out of bed on the floor. I was probably around 4 or 5. After trying to awaken my mother, I would go wake my father because I did not want my mother on the floor. My father would tell me to go back to bed. I can remember at this early age not understanding why my father would not come and take care of my mother. What I did not know was that she was passed out from drinking excessively. My dad had come to a place where he did not approve of her drinking anymore. Another incident in which I had been told when I was older that somewhere between 2 and 3 years old, for some reason I had stopped breathing. In those days, ambulances were just for transporting because they did not have life support. All I knew was that I was told an ambulance came and picked up me and my dad. I was taken to the hospital where a doctor worked on me and brought me back. God had me think back to those days. This is what I am trying to bring to light, if you are one of His, you have a purpose. God showed me that

He was with me during all those times and made sure I was born into this world despite my mother's drinking. He made sure I did not die when I quit breathing. I could go on into my past because there are more times I should have died; however, the point I am trying to make is that God has you here for a purpose. God desires for you to rise and surrender all of you to Him. He desires you to decrease in order that He can increase and then your life will begin to fulfill its purpose.

God gave His only begotten Son to give us life. He did this in order to take back everything satan had stolen. satan has been stealing from God's children long enough. He has been stealing your peace, your finances, your family, your joy, your health. We need to see it is time for us to surrender all in order that God can begin showing us a different life, a better life. As we begin to be transformed into the image of Christ, we will begin to love like Jesus did, forgive those who offended us, show the world how to be humble and not boastful, enjoy giving instead of receiving, etc. We all know the golden rule, to do unto others like you would have them do unto you. As we walk in this manner, we will see blessings follow us wherever we go and with all we come in contact. God's desire is for us to be more like Jesus in order that we show reverence and honor unto Him, in order that we glorify and magnify Him, and in order that our main focus and love of our life is our God. God is a jealous God and desires our love and affection.

Deuteronomy 4:24 (Amp) [24]For the Lord your God is a consuming fire, a jealous God.

When we begin to seek God because we desire to be more like Him, our path He has designed specifically for us will begin to be revealed. In Romans it says, those whom He called, He also

125

justified. He has made you in right standing with Him because of the blood of Jesus. It continues in Romans with those He justified, He also glorified. God sees you as being much greater than you can see yourself. We need to step out of our boxes and allow God to take control over our lives and see if our dreams and visions do not begin to materialize.

Our way of thinking is totally opposite of God's way until we begin to be transformed. Many times this is because we were raised in families or situations where we acquired bad habits and habits do not just break over night. Therefore, even though we may have come to the Lord, we will go back into the world doing the same things and reasoning in our minds the same way because we were programmed to be like the world. Until our minds are renewed, our circumstances will never change. In other words, we do the same things expecting different results only to wind up again alone and without. satan at this point will try to tell you that God is not true to His Word; however, that is only a lie to discourage you. Never become discouraged because with God, old things have passed away and every day can be a new beginning.

2 Corinthians 5:17 (Amp) ¹⁷Therefore if any person is [ingrafted] in Christ (the Messiah) he is a new creation (a new creature altogether); the old [previous moral and spiritual condition] has passed away. Behold, the fresh and new has come!

Walking with the Lord may be a way that you have never tried, or you never really knew how. However, the end result will be well worth the effort you put forth. We must first begin to believe not only that God desires for our lives to be rewarding, but He also rewards those who diligently seek Him.

Hebrews 11:6 (Amp) *⁶But without faith it is impossible to please and be satisfactory to Him. For whoever would come near to God must [necessarily] believe that God exists and that He is the rewarder of those who earnestly and diligently seek Him [out].*

Today make the decision, *"Lord, I want more of you and less of me!"* Then begin by giving God your best. Begin each day by spending time praying, studying, seeking, asking, talking, crying, reading, and above all – listening!

4 *The Journey through Negative Images...*
The Search for Christ's Reflection...

How Do You See Yourself

In this chapter, we will look deeper within to begin to see ourselves in a new light, as a new creation in Christ. We will go in greater depth and look at those areas which have held us in captivity, beginning at conception and carried through to where we are today. In order to rise to the level God desires for your life, you must put to rest the following beliefs:

1) The concept, you will never be good enough.
2) The belief, you will never be able to succeed.
3) The idea, you will never be able to live in complete and total happiness.

In other words, that way of thinking has to cease, and the new way of thinking must line up with what God's Word says. If we are going to believe any of the Word, we must believe it all. Through God's Word, we will learn we are good enough because of the blood of Jesus. We will learn that we are capable of succeeding and living fulfilled in total happiness. However, all these things are only possible through Jesus, not through us. As for living in total happiness, we will find that happiness is the state of mind which we choose. Total happiness can be ours because as we awaken each day, we make that choice to either be happy or be a complaining and murmuring generation like the children of Israel. We will grow to the place where we change on the inside; therefore, things around us begin to change. Our outlook cannot be, *"I need to change him"* or *"If she would only act right, my life would be better."* Happiness is not about changing those around us to make our life better. Happiness is about changing ourselves

129

on the inside to exceed the limitations we have placed in our lives. As this happens, people around us will automatically begin to change.

Is it hard for us to see ourselves as good enough because of sin? In the Word, we see it says because of the blood of Jesus, our sins have been forgiven. Once our sins are forgiven, we are able to come with confidence before the throne of God.

Hebrews 10:18-19 (Amp) [18]*Now where there is absolute remission (forgiveness and cancellation of the penalty) of these [sins and lawbreaking], there is no longer any offering made to atone for sin.* [19]*Therefore, brethren, since we have full freedom and confidence to enter into the [Holy of] Holies [by the power and virtue] in the blood of Jesus,*

In Hebrews 4, it says to draw near to the throne of grace boldly.

Hebrews 4:16 (Amp) [16]*Let us then fearlessly and confidently and boldly draw near to the throne of grace (the throne of God's unmerited favor to us sinners), that we may receive mercy [for our failures] and find grace to help in good time for every need [appropriate help and well-timed help, coming just when we need it].*

When we approach the throne with confidence, we should go boldly. I always think about Star Trek, *"To boldly go where no man has gone!"* In a sense, that is what it means. No man in himself has ever been able to go before the throne of God. However, because of Jesus we can now go boldly to our Father not fearing, not hesitating, and not thinking we are not good enough. We are sons and daughters of the Most High God because of the blood that Jesus shed. We can see this to be truth according to the Word, but when it comes to getting it inside of us that we are His children, it is a different story. The reason is because of sin in our lives. We will still miss it and commit sin as long as we are walking in our earthly bodies. We will be faced with temptations, tests, and trials, and there will be times we will just simply mess up. We also know Jesus' blood was once and for all sacrificed in order that we are sanctified. His blood was the ultimate atonement for our sins. The price has been paid. Think about it this way, it was hard to face your own parents during your childhood/adolescent years when you did something wrong and even harder to look them in the eye. The reasons were not necessarily because you feared they were going to strike you down, especially if you were raised by loving parents. The reasons were because you felt that guilt of your sin. You were ashamed to face them, ashamed of rejection, and ashamed of the disappointment which emanated from your parents. This is the same reason we have a hard time going boldly to the throne of grace, but that was the purpose for Jesus dying on the cross. It is not because of anything we have done to make ourselves righteous but because of the blood. We are consecrated and set apart. We are made righteous in the sight of God today because of Jesus paying the price for our sin. Therefore, knowing the blood has already been shed, by faith we should cover ourselves and our families with His blood. This is how we boldly go before the throne, covered in the blood. We are able to do this daily, not because of anything we have done but because of Jesus.

In order to be sure God hears my prayers, daily I repent in case there are any areas I have missed it. I then plead the blood of Jesus over myself for sanctification. At that moment, I know by faith that I am in right standing with God. I know that I am able to go before the throne of grace, and He hears my prayers.

In Leviticus, Moses is preparing Adam and his sons by sanctifying them with the blood of a ram. This was done prior to Adam and his sons going into the Holy Place. There were many sacrifices they had to do in order to go into the Holy Places and before the Lord. These accounts can all be read throughout Exodus and Leviticus. However, the point I am trying to make is that we must prepare to go before God.

Leviticus 8:22-23 (Amp) [22]*And he brought the other ram, the ram of consecration and ordination, and Aaron and his sons laid their hands upon the head of the ram.* [23]*And Moses killed it and took some of its blood and put it on the tip of Aaron's right ear, and on the thumb of his right hand, and on the great toe of his right foot.*

We do not have to kill an innocent animal in this era, but how are we preparing? God does not look upon sin and as long as we are in these earthly bodies, there will be sin. We prepare by repenting and applying the blood. This is something that should be done daily. Let's look at two different scenarios because it absolutely means nothing to God if our attitude and our hearts are not right. In the first scenario, we have someone who goes to church and regularly pleads Jesus' blood for their atonement. Then they walk out of the church and live no different than the world. This person believes as long as they repent, they can continue living in their sin. This person feels that since we are going to miss it, living in our earthly bodies anyway, they might as well enjoy life their way. They continue living according to their own appetites and enjoying the sensual things which satisfy their flesh. On the other hand, we have someone who desires to walk closer to God, and they desire to obtain the full benefits that we are entitled to as a child of God. They desire within their heart for God to walk with them and teach them what they must do in order to get their life right. This person may miss it time and time again, but there is a difference, this person recognizes their weaknesses and seeks the truth. This person allows the Holy Spirit to begin to awaken and change them, even if it means giving up those things they once thought they could not live without. This person desires to know God to the fullest and desires that intimate relationship with God. What will each of these obtain? The first person will go through life enjoying the lusts of the flesh and may feel that their life is good, but there will come a day when they realize those things of the world will be their destruction. This person invested their whole life in storing treasures on earth and not in heaven, unlike the second person. This second person will face tests and trials just like the world, but they will soon realize there is a greater power leading them. Their journey will be filled with excitement and amazement at how they once were so connected to this world but found something far greater. As time goes on, they will no longer be blinded to truth like that of the world. In fact, their way of thinking, acting, and every aspect of their being, will have risen to a level of wisdom and knowledge unknown to the world. Who will have a fuller life? Who will find true happiness? Who will find satisfaction? Who will find peace? We see according to Peter, the eyes of the Lord are on those who are righteous. This is for those who are sanctified because of the blood. Those who are in right standing with God know in their heart that there are things which need to change. They desire to listen and grow in order to obtain the abundant life.

1 Peter 3:12 (Amp) [12]For the eyes of the Lord are upon the righteous (those who are upright and in right standing with God), and His ears are attentive to their prayer. But the face of the Lord is against those who practice evil [to oppose them, to frustrate, and defeat them].

The eyes of the Lord are continually on those who are in right standing, and that of course is through Jesus. God hears our prayers. He will lead and guide us through life. You may be saying it is not necessary to plead the blood of Jesus over yourself on a daily basis. You may believe because the blood was shed once and for all on Calvary this is not necessary, but Jesus said in Luke, we should take up our cross daily and follow Him.

Luke 9:23 (NIV) [23]Then he said to them all: "If anyone would come after me, he must deny himself and take up his cross daily and follow me."

Paul said it another way; we should die daily.

1 Corinthians 15:31 (Amp) [31][I assure you] by the pride which I have in you in [your fellowship and union with] Christ Jesus our Lord, that I die daily [I face death every day and die to self].

This is to die to self, and how do we do that? When we cover ourselves with the blood of Jesus, we are a new creation. We have died to self, died to the flesh and it is Christ who lives in us.

Galatians 2:20 (ESV) [20]I have been crucified with Christ. It is no longer I who live, but Christ who lives in me. And the life I now live in the flesh I live by faith in the Son of God, who loved me and gave himself for me.

If we believe by faith, we are covered with the blood of Jesus and His blood sanctifies us, then it is by faith we should look upon ourselves the way God sees us. This kind of faith is no different from when we asked Jesus into our hearts. Did you believe that you were saved? Did you believe Jesus died for you? Did you believe He forgave your sins at that point? If so, then you have eternal salvation, and you are righteous in the sight of the Lord. However, by daily pleading the blood over yourself, you can remain in right standing with God even when you miss it. If we do not see ourselves as righteous, then we are not walking according to what God's Word says. We are not walking by faith. Remember, faith is when we believe those things that are not, as though they were. *(Hebrews 11:1)* This is how God operates. God knows our heart; He knows if we truly desire to be more like Jesus. He knows if we desire to walk with Him to a degree that we can only imagine. God will meet us if we make that step forward. He will be there to begin to change you from the inside out. God sees you as righteous in His sight. By faith, if we plead His blood over us and envision in the spiritual realm that Jesus' blood is flowing over our whole body, guess what? We are righteous; we are sanctified; we are forgiven. God not only forgives us of our sins, but they are forgotten.

Hebrews 8:12 (Amp) *[12]For I will be merciful and gracious toward their sins and I will remember their deeds of unrighteousness no more.*

Sometimes, we are our worst enemy. God says He forgives us, but many times, we do not forgive ourselves. That is the hard part, letting go and forgiving ourselves. Many times, there are areas in our past where we may have made mistakes and not forgiven ourselves for things we have done or faults we may have. What has to take place? As we spend time in the Word and prayer, we will begin to know our Father to a greater degree. Our mind will gradually begin to be transformed to seeing things according to the Word and not the world. Prior to this, pleading the blood of Jesus daily over ourselves, by no means, is meant to be a "Free get out of jail card." Our heart has to be right. In our heart, we must have the desire to walk with God. It does not matter if you keep missing it. It does not matter if you have sin in your life. What matters is that you are basically saying, *"God, I want to be more like Jesus; I recognize that I am not right; I* recognize my heart wants to do one thing, but my flesh/mind wants to do another; I struggle with what is right and what is wrong."

Romans 7:18 (ESV) ¹⁸For I know that nothing good dwells in me, that is, in my flesh. For I have the desire to do what is right, but not the ability to carry it out.

Paul also battled with the flesh. God knows we cannot do this in ourselves, and that is why, the Holy Spirit is with us. Jesus said it is better for Him to go in order that the Comforter, which is the Holy Spirit, would come and dwell with us.

John 16:7 (Amp) ⁷However, I am telling you nothing but the truth when I say it is profitable (good, expedient, advantageous) for you that I go away. Because if I do not go away, the Comforter (Counselor, Helper, Advocate, Intercessor, Strengthener, Standby) will not come to you [into close fellowship with you]; but if I go away, I will send Him to you [to be in close fellowship with you].

We can see that the Holy Spirit is all things to us; He is our counselor, helper, intercessor, advocate, strengthener, standby, and He will teach us all things.

John 14:26 (Amp) ²⁶But the Comforter (Counselor, Helper, Intercessor, Advocate, Strengthener, Standby), the Holy Spirit, Whom the Father will send in My name [in My place, to represent Me and act on My behalf], He will teach you all things. And He will cause you to recall (will remind you of, bring to your remembrance) everything I have told you.

Therefore, we are incapable of doing what is right without the blood of Jesus. We are incapable of making the right choices without the Holy Spirit walking with us, and we also have to have a right heart attitude. You can plead the blood over yourself and go before the throne; however, if your heart is not right, God knows it. God knows when you desire to do those things which are right, and gradually, He will transform you into being more and more like Jesus. Jesus died on the cross for sinners, not for those who believe they are righteous. He died for those who know they have missed it. Jesus died for those who want a different life, but they just do not know how to get there. With this book and your diligence in seeking the Father, your life will begin to change. Remember to God, sin is sin. There is no such thing as an exceedingly bad sinner and one who is just a little sinner. No, sin is sin! God desires for you to come to the throne not timidly but boldly. God wants you to know that Jesus paid a great price to give you this privilege.

Blessed Assurance

What is blessed assurance? Assurance is being certain in your mind, being confident. It is a guarantee or a pledge. When you are assured, you are free from self-doubt and self-confidence. Assurance inspires or tends to inspire the confidence you need. Blessed means held in reverence, honored in worship, enjoying happiness, contentment, and good fortune.

Hebrews 10:22 (Amp) [22]*Let us all come forward and draw near with true (honest and sincere) hearts in unqualified assurance and absolute conviction engendered by faith (by that leaning of the entire human personality on God in absolute trust and confidence in His power, wisdom, and goodness), having our hearts sprinkled and purified from a guilty (evil) conscience and our bodies cleansed with pure water.*

As we come forward to draw near to God, we have that assurance and confidence in knowing all things are possible for those who believe. *(Mark 9:23)* We are guaranteed our life will find happiness and good fortune. What is it that we desire in life? All of us desire happiness, but like I have said, we have been programmed to see things through the eyes of the world and it is a misconception. The world would tell us that in order to be happy that we must be successful and financially secure. In fact, the world would have us believe that if we have enough money, we will be happy. The world would say happiness can be found in marriage; it can be found in traveling to exotic places, or in just living the good life. The good life to the world would be, making money to the extremes that you can afford to go anywhere, buy anything, and do anything. However, we see this as a lie from the enemy because if such were the case, those in high places with great amounts of resources would not be plastered all over the media with their lives a total mess. True happiness will never come from what money can buy. True happiness will come when we expand our visions and beliefs beyond those things we imagine, and this is only done through Jesus. As it says in Hebrews, when our personalities lean and trust on God with confidence in His power, we are assured of what we thought impossible. Let me say being created in the likeness of God, if we have a personality, so does God. Every personality is unique, and it was created by God. When you begin to line up your own unique personality to God's Word, He will bring out that which is hidden. Have you ever found you were good at something that you would never have thought possible? When you begin walking with God and leaning on His understanding, things will come to light that you never expected. All of a sudden, you will begin to blossom in areas which were unfamiliar and in doing so, you will find areas you excel in beyond your imagination.

Another area in which the world seeks is peace. The world strives to find happiness and peace in their lives. Peace is something many would give anything to obtain. There is only one way to obtain that peace which passes all understanding and this would be through the Father.

Philippians 4:7 (ESV) ⁷And the peace of God, which surpasses all understanding, will guard your hearts and your minds in Christ Jesus.

In John, Jesus said to his disciples, *"My peace I give you."* This is not peace that the world understands.

John 14:27 (NIV) ²⁷Peace I leave with you; my peace I give you. I do not give to you as the world gives. Do not let your hearts be troubled and do not be afraid.

The world would have you believe it is not possible to have peace in your life continually. However, Jesus said that He left us His peace. The world does not understand this peace. The reason why the world does not have peace and cannot obtain it is because they try to find it in themselves. However, being a child of God, we have the assurance that peace will dwell with us. Jesus went on to say, *"Do not let your hearts be troubled and do not be afraid."* Why is this? In John 16, Jesus said to take heart for He has overcome the world.

John 16:33 (NIV) ³³"I have told you these things, so that in me you may have peace. In this world you will have trouble. But take heart! I have overcome the world."

Jesus said that we will have trouble, even though we are God's children. There will be tests and trials that will come upon us. However, Jesus gives us the assurance that it does not matter because He overcame the world for us. Through Him, we have that peace that the world will never know. The Apostle Paul said in Romans, since we are declared righteous through faith, we need to grasp the fact that we have the peace of reconciliation to hold and enjoy peace with God through Jesus.

Romans 5:1 (Amp) ¹THEREFORE, SINCE we are justified (acquitted, declared righteous, and given a right standing with God) through faith, let us [grasp the fact that we] have [the peace of reconciliation to hold and to enjoy] peace with God through our Lord Jesus Christ (the Messiah, the Anointed One).

In other words, we need to realize when we become saved that God has reconciled us to Him. We are in right standing with the Father; therefore, we need to see that we are His children. We are able to come before Him and able to hold on to that peace which He gives to His children. God's peace the world does not understand and this peace which is with us as God's children, guards our hearts and minds in Christ Jesus. Our minds can and will be renewed to a new way of thinking if we spend time in the Word.

Philippians 4:7 (ESV) ⁷And the peace of God, which surpasses all understanding, will guard your hearts and your minds in Christ Jesus.

Jesus said in John 14, for us to believe, adhere to, and trust on God.

John 14:1 (Amp) ¹DO NOT let your hearts be troubled (distressed, agitated). You believe in and adhere to and trust in and rely on God; believe in and adhere to and trust in and rely also on Me.

All we have to do is believe and trust. The Word has promised us peace which is something that is obtainable; however, we have to let go of our old way of thinking. We have to begin to see ourselves through God's eyes not our eyes or that of the world. As a Christian, God is going to lead you down a path which is filled with excitement and new beginnings. This is the time to put aside our old way of thinking and begin to realize old things have passed, all things become new.

2 Corinthians 5:17 (NIV) [17]*Therefore, if anyone is in Christ, he is a new creation; the old has gone, the new has come!*

God's Word gives us the assurance of happiness, good fortune, and peace. We go on to see in 1 John, we also have the assurance, once again, to go boldly before God. We have the assurance and confidence whatever we ask according to God's will, He listens and hears us. This will be discussed more in depth through this series; however, John said we are to be confident and bold.

1 John 5:14 (Amp) [14]*And this is the confidence (the assurance, the privilege of boldness) which we have in Him: [we are sure] that if we ask anything (make any request) according to His will (in agreement with His own plan), He listens to and hears us.*

As a child of God, there are privileges, and like with privileges you have with your earthly parents, you now have many great privileges with your heavenly Father. When you want something that your earthly dad has, what do you do? You simply ask. As we continue to grow, we have the assurance of those things in which the world strives for daily but cannot obtain. We know that as of now, if we are a child of God, by faith we have the blood of Jesus to apply over ourselves in order to be sanctified. We can then go boldly where no man has gone in themselves. We can ask our Father for that happiness and peace to infiltrate our lives. As we continue to grow, our way of thinking will line up to what the Word says and not what the world says. Our lives will radically begin to change at this point and blessings from on high will be poured out upon us.

Seeing Ourselves In A New Light

We have covered a lot of ground on who we are in Christ and how we are righteous because of the blood of Jesus, but we have become so used to seeing ourselves the way we are today, that we need to begin to look upon ourselves through faith. This will be seeing ourselves as God sees us even though it may not be so presently. By faith, we begin to see things according to what the Word says regardless of how it may look. In other words, you may say, *"I still do not have power over my flesh; I desire to do what is right, but my fleshly desires do not line up with God's Word."* So here is your homework…

1) Daily, look in the mirror and speak over yourself out loud claiming to be what you are not. *(Ex. I speak harshly to my children, and even though I try not to, I get upset and lose my temper).* You would say something to this effect, *"Thank you Father that I have the mind of Christ and hold the purposes in my heart. I do not speak harshly, but in every word which comes out of my mouth, I speak in love. I can control my temper and walk daily in Your Words, by the power of the blood of Jesus, Amen."*

2) Take the Scripture below in Romans or one Scripture on being in right-standing with God; write it on a piece of paper and tape it on your mirror in your bathroom or another place where you will see it daily. Every time you see this paper, repeat it out loud.

3) Daily speak these words out loud, *"I am created in the image of my Father in Heaven and am beautiful in body, soul, and spirit. I am not only a beautiful person, but God has also created me to increase in everything which He has given me, such as: my talents, my strengths, and my abilities. I know He will perfect each of these areas, through His Son Jesus, in order that it brings glory to Him and His Kingdom."*

Paul writes in Romans, if Jesus lives in us, our natural body is dead to sin and to guilt, and the Spirit is alive because of the righteousness Jesus puts in us.

Romans 8:10 (Amp)[10]But if Christ lives in you, [then although] your [natural] body is dead by reason of sin and guilt, the spirit is alive because of [the] righteousness [that He imputes to you].

It is not anything we have done which makes us righteous but only because of the blood that flows through us, the blood of Jesus. Paul said if Jesus is in us, our bodies are now dead to sin and dead to guilt. These are areas that keep us from being able to see ourselves in a new light. According to Scripture, these areas are dead in our lives. We get saved, and our natural bodies are now dead to sin and guilt, but how is that? The Spirit dwells with us as Christians and is alive within us. When we do become saved, we begin to look upon sin differently. All of a sudden things we used to do without even acknowledging it becomes evident. It begins to bother us to do those things which were wrong. This is the gradual process of the Holy Spirit within us beginning to transform our ways. We do not have to feel that guilt because we know God is working in us. If we desire to be all God created us to be, we must know as long as we are willing and do not fight God, He will have His perfect work in us. You may miss it, but it is the Holy Spirit's job to convict you. It then goes back on you to repent and try harder in that area. Does that mean we will

143

not ever sin again? No, but as we walk this walk, we will realize the significance of the power in Jesus' blood, and when we do miss it, we repent and plead that blood over us in order to stay in right standing with God. Then is it okay to sin? No, as Christians there should be a desire within us to continually, on a daily basis, strive for that excellence in which our Father desires for us. In Hebrews, it says we should throw aside any sin or anything which entangles us in order to be able to run the race.

Hebrews 12:1-3 (Amp) ¹*THEREFORE THEN, since we are surrounded by so great a cloud of witnesses [who have borne testimony to the Truth], let us strip off and throw aside every encumbrance (unnecessary weight) and that sin which so readily (deftly and cleverly) clings to and entangles us, and let us run with patient endurance and steady and active persistence the appointed course of the race that is set before us,* ²*Looking away [from all that will distract] to Jesus, Who is the Leader and the Source of our faith [giving the first incentive for our belief] and is also its Finisher [bringing it to maturity and perfection]. He, for the joy [of obtaining the prize] that was set before Him, endured the cross, despising and ignoring the shame, and is now seated at the right hand of the throne of God.* ³*Just think of Him Who endured from sinners such grievous opposition and bitter hostility against Himself [reckon up and consider it all in comparison with your trials], so that you may not grow weary or exhausted, losing heart and relaxing and fainting in your minds.*

Let me share an example in my own life of missing the mark. I was back walking with God daily growing and striving to do what He called me to do. I was faced with a test; however, I did not recognize it to be a test. I got upset with someone at the church because of an error which had been made concerning me not once but three times. At least it took three times before I got in the flesh and missed it; however, this was a test that God was trying to teach me something. After missing it, I could hear that small, quiet voice continually trying to tell me, I was wrong and missed it. I did not need the voice to tell me that I was wrong because I already knew that and did not want to hear it. But the Holy Spirit continued to convict me, and it took about two hours before I broke. I knew I was wrong when it happened two hours prior, but my flesh wanted to prevail. What happened? My spirit man is stronger because I feed it daily on the Word of God. Therefore, my natural man did not win in the long run because my spirit man rose up and over-powered the flesh. That is what it takes sometimes. That is what happens when we are big enough to admit we are wrong. When we put our flesh down and allow our spirit man to have precedence over our natural desires, we begin to grow. After feeling that conviction, I went and apologized to everyone I had missed it with in order to make things right. I repented to the Lord because I knew I was wrong, and after getting it right with God, He began to speak to me and give me the revelation of the purpose for that particular test. When the revelation began to come, it was absolutely awesome and a beginning of looking at my tests in a totally different light. This is where we come to when we obey God. God begins to open our eyes to things that the world cannot see.

Notice, I said my spirit man is strong. Our spirit man can be strong; however, this only happens when we spend time feeding it. If you desire that power over your flesh where you can begin to see yourself in a new light, this is done by meditating on those Scriptures which reveal what you need. Whatever areas you are weak in, to become strong, you must search out Scriptures that teach on your particular weaknesses. If you have a problem with anger, search for peace, forgiveness, love. If you have a problem with commitment, search for obedience, etc. The only way we will

145

get our minds thinking like God thinks is to renew them. This can only be done by reading the Word of God over and over again pertaining to areas we are weak, so we become strong. You can read something over and over again but in order to believe it, it has to be a continual process. With putting the new in, it must force the bad out. In order to keep the negative things out of our mind, we must not dwell on them and need to pull away from all which brings us down. You may daily read the Word of God and say it is not working; therefore, the questions below will help to find your answers.

1) How often do you watch television which is filled with filth of the world, such as: adultery, murder, sexual immorality, etc.? _____

2) Do you willingly associate with others who regularly conduct themselves in a manner like that of the world, such as: telling lies, cheating, slandering others, stealing, cussing, getting drunk, illegal drug use, adultery, etc.? _____

3) Do you spend countless hours on the internet for entertainment into a world of deceitfulness or reading and indulging in those things which are not godly? _____

If you answered yes to any of these questions, then your problem may simple be you are putting more of the world in than the Word of God. In order to renew your mind to begin to think like God, you must be putting more of the Word in you. This is not a hard process; however, it does take time and discipline. To begin this walk with God, by all means make a commitment to at least begin reading the Word a little each day. Do not try to read a book a day, just a small part. It is not a matter of quantity here but a matter of quality. We can get so caught up on thinking in our minds, *"If I read a book a day, God will be pleased."* However, what pleases God is when we learn of Him. We learn by simply studying and meditating not trying to absorb a whole book. It is

146

when you take a small part, read it, and think on it that you begin to learn. Then ask yourself what you see in that part or what meaning were you able to understand from what you just read? This is how you will begin to understand the Word of God, and you will begin to desire more and more. As God sees your faithfulness, He will begin to open your eyes to revelation that you never dreamed of.

Galatians 2:16 (Amp) [16]*Yet we know that a man is justified or reckoned righteous and in right standing with God not by works of the Law, but [only] through faith and [absolute] reliance on and adherence to and trust in Jesus Christ (the Messiah, the Anointed One). [Therefore] even we [ourselves] have believed on Christ Jesus, in order to be justified by faith in Christ and not by works of the Law [for we cannot be justified by any observance of the ritual of the Law given by Moses], because by keeping legal rituals and by works no human being can ever be justified (declared righteous and put in right standing with God).*

According to Galatians, there is nothing we can do that will make us in right standing with God. It is not by any reasoning in our minds such as – committing to praying a certain length of time each day, committing to reading a certain amount of the Word each day, or committing to doing a good deed each day for someone other than ourselves. These things are all good, but they are works, and works do not make us in right standing with God. It is not by our works, not by what we do with our hands, or what we do according to the Law of Moses, the commandments. Being in right standing with God is only through our faith of believing that Jesus is the Son of God, and it is His blood that justifies us. If we spend our whole life time trying to please God by good works, guess what? We will still die and come short of heaven. However, we should spend our life time with good works, but our desires should be to become more and more like Jesus.

147

We will come short and fail if we are not truly saved, and all those works we did for recognition will bring nothing. However, to those who live by faith and spend their lifetime seeking, will be those who truly find the answers to life. Those who seek and find will be the righteousness of our Father in Heaven. Without truly walking with Jesus, our works of righteousness will just be works.

1John 3:7(ESV) ⁷Little children, let no one deceive you. Whoever practices righteousness is righteous, as he is righteous.

In order for us to walk in the light and not darkness, we need to allow God to do a work in us. We need to commit to just spending time with Him, and we do not need to make it complicated because it is much better to have quality time instead of quantity. Too many people fall because they say they cannot do this walk. This walk is not what is hard, but it is those who make it hard because of continually trying to do it in themselves. If you are a new Christian or were backslidden and you are trying to get back in right standing with God, you are at the right place if you are striving to walk according to the Word. God knows your heart and knows if you truly desire to know Him to a greater degree. Do not feel you cannot be where you need to be, and do not listen to the enemy trying to tell you that you cannot do this. Remember, I too was backslidden for 15 years. I can remember during those years, walking back into many churches trying to get back right with the Lord. Each time I would fall away again and again after just a short time. Why? I know now I listened to the enemy when he would try to tell me various lies such as:

•God is not listening to you anymore.
•You cannot do this walk again.
•You have lost everything, and God is not going to give it back to you.

When I did not feel God moving in my life, it was hard not to believe what the enemy was telling me. But in all reality, I was trying each time to do it in myself. I was trying to tell myself to at least commit each day to praying a certain amount of time and reading a certain amount of the Word. However, I needed to go to my Father and just repent. I needed to cry out for Him to show me the way back home. I could not see this, so what changed for me? I came to a place where I knew the Word said my God would never leave me or forsake me, and I began to speak this over myself. I began to cancel out those thoughts from the enemy.

Hebrews 13:5 (ESV) 5Keep your life free from love of money, and be content with what you have, for he has said, "I will never leave you nor forsake you."

This was my starting place. I stood on that Word and decided, *"God, I know you are here even if I do not feel you in my life, and I am not going anywhere!"* That was Amen! In my mind, it was final – period! I made a small commitment and that was to stand on a part of the Word. I stood on believing that God was there with me even though I did not feel His presence. Sometimes we do not feel God because of sin in our lives. Many want to blame it on the church not flowing in the gifts or the pastor not giving a good message. However, it is not because of the church or because of a certain denomination, and it is not because of the speaker. The reason we may not feel God in our lives is because we have to repent and mean it.

When you get to the place that nothing matters but what the Word says about you, your vision will begin to change. We must know that it does not matter what the world or the enemy has to say about who we are. It does not matter what you may be feeling inside, the Word says something totally different about you and about what you are capable of being. When you make your stand on what the Word says, then God will begin to move. Remember to stand on the Word means that you are not moving until something happens. You are not moving until God moves you! If you are tired of what the world has to say, what your circumstances have to say, and what the enemy has to say, then find a Scripture and stand on it. Do not allow yourself to be moved unless it is God that moves you. God desires to bring you to that place above your current circumstances and has given you the power to overcome in the name of Jesus.

Overcoming Negative Images

We should have begun to understand who we are in Christ at this point, and we should see some of the benefits to being a child of God. However, in order for us to be raised to the level God desires, we must look at our attitudes and our disposition towards life in general, including looking at ourselves. To come to that place where we can see ourselves as capable of being all things and doing all things, our outlook on life must change. What causes most of us to be unsuccessful Christians is not the world, and it is not the enemy but rather it is ourselves. We can be our worst enemy. This is not to say the enemy will not attack us. However, with the revelation I have gained due to falling from grace, there are fewer areas the enemy can attack me. If you have fallen from grace, there will also be fewer areas the enemy will be able to attack once you get the revelation needed deep down. To explain, when we get to the place where the Holy Spirit is operating within us, doors will begin to open in order to bless us, but when we are doing those things the Father has called us to do, we must also realize there will be trials that will test our faith. As we deal with much of our past and walk through those tests, the enemy will have to come up with other strategies to try to move us, but even while the enemy strives to bring us down, we are continually growing stronger and stronger. Eventually, those tests will become easier and easier. However, before we can get to this place, we need to begin focusing on where we are at currently because most of the time we cannot move forward due to our own insecurities. What makes us not step out of the box? Why do we have such a hard time believing in ourselves?

As we begin to look back into our childhood, our focus should be to understand why we put up those walls in our lives in the first place. This of course, will be stepping back into those same shoes and reliving the pain, but this is important for our healing to take place. The root to every problem is the cure. If you smoke cigarettes, if you currently do not have health problems, there will be a time when you have either bronchitis or something more serious. Yes, you can treat the symptoms; however, until you address the root of the situation, there is no cure. Whatever your ailment, it will return again and again and eventually will be your death. If we have areas of our lives we cannot overcome, we have to stop doctoring the symptoms and instead address the root in order to be totally set free. You can go to counseling every day of your life to deal with marriage problems, addiction problems, etc.; however, until you look to see where these problems originated, you will never be set free. When walls are still present in our lives, we will not be able to see ourselves the way God sees us. Like I said earlier, we limit God from being able to use us. If you can see yourself in this, you are also limiting yourself from being able to break free from areas which may have you bound. We will continue to see a distorted image of ourselves and not the image we are capable of being through Christ. As long as those walls continue to build and we meditate on all the negative images which are spoken over us, we will continue to see ourselves based on those images. We will remain bound due to how we see ourselves. You may disagree. You may believe that those bad images spoken over you as a child or young adult have no bearing on your life today. You may say even things spoken over you today do not bother you. You may believe that you do not allow them to affect you. However, if you dwell on it and allow it to fester, you are receiving those images. When we receive those images, many times we will draw away from that which produces life, retreating from those things which are good. We find ourselves literally locked away deep within, not trusting, not socializing, not allowing ourselves to connect. Perhaps, we have found ourselves retreating to areas which felt comfortable as a child. As you answer these questions, look closely at yourself.

1) Do you see yourself as someone who can do all things according to God's Word? _____
2) When something negative is said about you, does it seem to consume your thoughts for days at a time? _____
3) Do you sometimes judge who you are based on how you look on the outside? _____
4) Do you sometimes judge yourself based on how others see you? _____
5) Do you feel you are not capable of doing some things because you are not smart enough or talented enough? _____

When I was told as a little girl, I was not as pretty as my sister or as smart, and when I was told I would never be anything, that is what I believed. This is how I saw myself, but God did not see me as such. Our attitudes have been molded by all those things which have occurred in our lifespan and all those things in which have been spoken over us. We need to go back and look upon all those negative occurrences, and let go of the past in order to move forward. Right now, make a list of all occurrences and everything negative said to you in your past.

152

The areas in my life which caused great pain:

_____
_____
_____
_____

Those things which have been spoken over me which were negative:

_____
_____
_____
_____

When you go before the Father, you need to release all these things to Him. It is healing to get these areas which are on the inside – out. As you release them to God, also forgive each person who was responsible for things done or said to you.

As we work through those negative areas in our lives, we need to look deeper into the life of Moses. We need to ask ourselves this question, *"Why is it that we cannot see ourselves as being used by God as those of old who walked with God?"* We have discussed some of the stories about Moses, and we see that Moses had favor with God.

Exodus 33:12 (NIV) *12 Moses said to the LORD, "You have been telling me, 'Lead these people,' but you have not let me know whom you will send with me. You have said, 'I know you by name and you have found favor with me.'"*

In Exodus, God called out to Moses in the midst of a burning bush in order to give Moses directions to lead His people out of Egypt. Ask yourself, do you believe that God could use you as He did Moses?

Exodus 3:4, 9-10(Amp) *⁴And when the Lord saw that he turned aside to see, God called to him out of the midst of the bush and said, Moses, Moses! And he said, Here am I. ⁹Now behold, the cry of the Israelites has come to Me, and I have also seen how the Egyptians oppress them. ¹⁰Come now therefore, and I will send you to Pharaoh, that you may bring forth My people, the Israelites, out of Egypt.*

As we go on into this story, we see that Moses had doubts he was capable of doing what God was calling him to do. Moses had doubts that any would listen and obey him.

Exodus 4:1(Amp) *¹AND MOSES answered, But behold, they will not believe me or listen to and obey my voice; for they will say, The Lord has not appeared to you.*

God continued to show Moses there would be signs and wonders in order that the people would listen and obey; however, Moses still had no faith in himself. Moses did not feel adequate enough to be that great person whom God desired to use in an awesome way. Do you see yourself in Moses? Do you believe you cannot do what God may be calling you to do?

Exodus 4:10(Amp) *¹⁰And Moses said to the Lord, O Lord, I am not eloquent or a man of words, neither before nor since You have spoken to Your servant; for I am slow of speech and have a heavy and awkward tongue.*

Moses had a stutter when he spoke. He did not feel he was smart enough; he did not feel he was capable; he did not have confidence in himself. However, God chose him. He was God's pick. How many times do we feel the same as Moses did? Do you ever say to yourself, *"I could never do that; I'm not good*

154

enough, smart enough, educated enough, talented enough, gifted enough, pretty enough?" Let's look at God's response to Moses.

Exodus 4:11-12(Amp) [11]*And the Lord said to him, Who has made man's mouth? Or who makes the dumb, or the deaf, or the seeing, or the blind? Is it not I, the Lord?* [12]*Now therefore go, and I will be with your mouth and will teach you what you shall say.*

Moses being of slow speech was not something God did not know. God created each of us uniquely and knows more about us than we know about ourselves. God knows what we are capable of doing. We may not believe in ourselves, but guess what? God believes in us.

Let's look at something else. We know that Moses did not believe in himself. He did not believe he was capable of doing what God called him to do; however, Moses was raised by the daughter of Pharaoh.

Acts 7:21-22 (Amp) [21]*Then when he was exposed [to perish], the daughter of Pharaoh rescued him and took him and reared him as her own son.* [22]*So Moses was educated in all the wisdom and culture of the Egyptians, and he was mighty (powerful) in his speech and deeds.*

We see Moses was educated by the Egyptians, so he was not an uneducated man. Why then did he not feel adequate to do what God called him to do? It even said that he was powerful in his speech and deeds, yet Moses was slow to speak. He had a stutter. I thought about this myself. Growing up, I had an education, yet I never saw myself doing anything great. I spent a lot of time by myself writing and creating. I was very talented when it came to coming up with brilliant ideas and making things with my hands. However, I would not step out of my box because

155

I believed that someone was probably better. Moses believed his brother Aaron was the better choice. Where does this come from? What makes us think this way? We may actually be good at many things, but we do not see ourselves that way. You may be God's choice for something great but be saying, *"No God, send someone else. I cannot do this."* Years later, I found that as I stepped out of the box, I began to excel in things I never thought possible. God began to show me something that I had never thought about. First, if God has called you to do something great, He knows you are capable. He did not choose someone else; He chose you. Second, God had me go back to my roots to think about where I came from, and He had me think about what things I had endured, who had crossed my path, what I had been taught, and what I had learned from the experiences. Just like with Moses, things do not just happen, but they happen because God planned it that way. Does that mean those bad things which happened to us were because God set them into motion? No, but God did know we would go through those things, and years later, we would also be searching for answers and find our truth in Him. Even though, we may never know why we endured some of what we have, we will learn that because of those things, God will turn all of them around and use us mightily.

In thinking back on my own life, as God began to bring to my remembrance my past in detail, I was able to see things I had never seen and never realized. There were those who crossed my path at the right times that I learned from. There were things that happened which taught me valuable lessons. There were impressionable books and sermons which embedded within me for a reason, and when you add it all up, these things are what began to mold me into who God created me to be. The enemy may have had a different plan of action. The enemy deliberately will send those across our path who will hurt us physically, mentally, and emotionally. He will also send those across your path to speak negative images over you. However, if you begin to think back in your life, God will show you that He too was busy sending those across your path to renew your mind to see things according to His way, not that of the world. When we look deep, we will see all of this adds up to a more complete picture of who we are deep within our heart. Yes, we may have been hurt, but our Father has planted good seeds within us in order to heal those pains. Once we receive our healing, others will cross our path suffering from the same afflictions God brought us through, and it will be our time to give back what we received. As God begins to use us to help others, it will all make sense why we went through what we did in order to walk in those things He has called us to do. Looking now at my life, God continually sends those across my path that have so much pain. As I minister to them and spend time staying plugged into their life, things begin to make sense. As I help them walk through their pain, the bigger picture begins to unfold. When I receive text messages or a card expressing how I helped change their life, it was all worth it. As I see the smiles on their faces when it once never showed joy or life, tears come to my eyes. These are the moments when you will say what I have said many times, *"Father, everything you have shown me has been worth it; my life has been worth it; the pain I endured from my losses have been worth it."* I know what it feels like to lose a child, but I can say today, *"Father, everything has been worth it if only one person receives your Words that I go boldly forth to share!"* I understand this concept. We have read that our Father would have sent Jesus to die for us, even if it were only for one sinner. I know the feeling of seeing one come to the Lord, and being set free from their pain. I have seen new Christians begin to love and serve our Father as they come to know Him. Therefore, everything we have endured in our lifetime is worth it when we use our experiences to help others find Jesus.

From my past, I was able to see that things do not just happen by chance, and like with Moses, God intended him to be raised by Pharaoh's daughter. It was intended for him to get an education and did not matter that he was slow to speak. God knew he had what he needed to do what he was called to do. Where he lacked, he had to walk in faith knowing God would make it up. We need to begin to trust God and know that if He is calling us to do something great, then He will walk with us through it. However, most of the time in our walk with God, we cannot rise up to do what He is calling us to do because of the way we see ourselves. We may be capable but the distorted images which we have of ourselves, keep us bound, and of course, we know that the way we portray ourselves has to do with what has been spoken over us. The image we have of God has to do with the image we have of our earthly fathers.

Let's look at both scenarios, first look back upon your own father, and what do you see? Was your father even in the picture? If not, you have no idea of what a father is to be like because there was no example. To you, there is that feeling of rejection of not knowing or having that relationship with a dad. God hates divorce according to the Word, and there is a reason for this.

Malachi 2:16 (NIV) [16] *"I hate divorce," says the LORD God of Israel, "and I hate a man's covering himself with violence as well as with his garment," says the LORD Almighty. So guard yourself in your spirit, and do not break faith.*

God hates divorce because we were created to be one after we get married. When we get married it is with the intention of the man being head over the home. There are many responsibilities that a man has towards his wife and children. What has happened in society is there are far too many homes where there is no father figure. Therefore, the children grow up feeling abandoned by their dads. These children feel rejection, resentment, anger, and much pain. A family was not intended to have just a single mother having to play both roles in order to raise the children and in some cases, just having a single dad. I have seen instances where the dad does have custody of the children for different reasons. This is not one sided; however, the percent of single women raising their children is far greater than of single men. In the single-parent homes, the statistics for those children making it in society is appalling. It was never meant for women to take on the whole burden of raising their children, but what has happened to the extended family? I know that many grandparents have had to step up to the plate to raise their grandchildren, but in many cases, that does not happen. Where are the grandparents, aunts, and uncles? Families were to function as a unit in order to bring balance to the families as a whole. When I say unit, I am not just referring to the immediate family as in mother and father, I mean relatives – everyone! In biblical days, when there was a death in the family and it was a male who still had small children in the home, God commanded the family to tend to the needs of the widow and children.

1 Timothy 5:3-4, 8 (NIV) [3] *Give proper recognition to those widows who are really in need.* [4] *But if a widow has children or grandchildren, these should learn first of all to put their religion into practice by caring for their own family and so repaying their parents and grandparents, for this is pleasing to God.* [8] *If anyone does not provide for his relatives, and especially for his immediate family, he has denied the faith and is worse than an unbeliever.*

In other words, support financially, emotionally, and physically. The family was to step in and provide whatever was needed. We do not see this in our society very much today. In fact, when our parents grow old, it is easier for us to abandon them in a nursing home rather than mold our own lives to be able to care for our relatives. We can make all the excuses we want; however, the bottom line is what is in our heart. I took on the responsibility of promising my earthly dad I would never put him in a nursing home. I did not anticipate the extent of what my commitment meant. Alzheimer's is a disease or rather a curse which had been passed down through my dad's ancestry in the male gene. We watched his dad suffer and die from this sickness. The day came when I had to make good for my promise. It was four long years during the mid to last stages of the disease not to mention the time prior to that. I had never experienced anything like this. I can absolutely tell you that it was very hard. I was also a single mother of three trying to work, manage two households, and take care of my dad. Did it change my life? Absolutely! My children, at a young age, had to help with this hardship. Towards the end, he was unable to get out of bed and had to be tube fed. I had to quit working at one point, and it was around the clock care. Do I regret my choice? No, I do not. There were times that I felt inadequate in caring for him; however, I have also seen the care that goes on inside of nursing homes and know that my father was never neglected or abused in any way. I do not say that to insinuate this is what goes on in nursing homes. However, many times these things do occur due to the help which is hired in, and the management unaware of what may be taking place. The point I am trying to make is to show the decline in the family compared to what we see in biblical days. With the decline, men are not being taught what their responsibilities are. If a man has been raised primarily by his mother and little to no contact with his dad, his image of his dad is very poor. How can this little boy, who grows up without a loving and nurturing father, be able to see that our Heavenly Father is loving, forgiving, bountiful, and will never

160

abandon him? How is the little girl who grows up who has little contact with her dad, if any, be able to see that a father figure is one who loves, nurtures, supports, encourages, and protects in the way that our Heavenly Father does? For those children who have had fathers who were abusive, either physically, mentally, sexually, or emotionally, how are they to grow up to see that our Heavenly Father would never abuse them in any way? Yes, our Heavenly Father does correct His children, but it is not in the way many think. God does not bring bad things in your life when you mess up. This is wrong thinking, and it is not biblical. This will be discussed in depth, in a later series, but the point is that our perception of God has been distorted due to the way we see our earthly fathers. God created man in His image and likeness. The man was to be the head of the home.

1 Corinthians 11:3 (NIV) *³Now I want you to realize that the head of every man is Christ, and the head of the woman is man, and the head of Christ is God.*

Corinthians continues to show that man is the image and glory of God. In other words, what man does should reflect glory to God. If a man is not being a father to those he helped bring into the world, this does not glorify God. We see also that the woman is to be the glory of the man and in the same sense, the way the woman portrays herself should show glory unto her husband.

1 Corinthians 11:7 (NIV) *⁷A man ought not to cover his head, since he is the image and glory of God; but the woman is the glory of man.*

Before we go any further because both of these are touchy subjects, many women feel that their husbands do not show them respect or love. Many men, on the other hand, feel that their wives do not show them respect either and do not handle the

161

affairs of the home as they should. This Scripture says a man is to glorify God the Father. What do your actions say? Are you being a loving dad to your children? Are you being that loving and understanding husband to your wife? If you lack in any areas, it will show in the way your wife and your children show you respect. God intended the man to be head over the whole household. If you are not doing your part, your family will lack and fall apart. On the other hand, if the woman is in rebellion and never satisfied, there may be issues she needs to deal with, especially if the man is being there for the family and doing his part according to God's Word. However, as the man, you have the biggest obligation because it was given to you. God created man in His image; woman was made from you and as your other half to complete you. To add one more aspect because of me being a woman, I do not want any man to think that I am showing favor to women. I have ministered to women whose husbands are not doing what they should be doing, and my response to them is, *"If you line up to the Word of God, God will deal with your husband."* It is not the woman's job to try to change her husband. Your husband will not change by you nagging, continually complaining, giving him the cold shoulder, etc. Your reflection of who God is in your own life will bring a greater change in your husband than anything else. Why on earth would your husband want to serve your God if you portray "God" as someone sitting on the throne dictating to them what they should and should not do? It is not your job to change him, only your job to love him. It is your job as a woman to show respect to your husband and to pray for him. When you do this, you are planting seeds, and God will be the one to cultivate those seeds, not you. However, by no means am I implicating that anyone should remain in a situation where there is abuse in any form. If you feel threatened, then you have every right to leave.

Now, let's look at attitudes. Our bad attitudes and dispositions towards life in general, many times are seeds which were planted by our own fathers maybe even unintentionally. These seeds planted in our life will continue to grow, and eventually, they become huge thorns of deception. We carry these thorns around, and unknowingly, they are planted into our own children as well as others in our lives. I can remember in counseling, when I was younger, being told that the reason my mother did things to hurt me was because an alcoholic always hurts those they love. My mother's pain originated from her own father who was abusive, and she had never received healing. My mother never had a clear perception of God because it was distorted by what was seen in her earthly father. Therefore, those same seeds, which were planted in her when she was a little girl, were also planted in her children. My disposition towards the world when I was in my teens was a very ugly picture. I hated adults; I hated life; I hated authority. I lived a self-destructive life throughout my adolescent years. I would not be where I am today had God not sent those across my path who touched my life and helped me to know Him. My spirit was awakened, and my heart has been healed. Today, the bad has been replaced with good, and I am able to give back what was given to me. Once we are open and receptive, we are able to see how great God's love is for mankind.

Let's look back over those things which have been negatively spoken. When we are raised as small children, what we are being told sticks to us like glue. If you are being told negative things, then you grow up believing that about yourself, but just because someone has spoken something negative over you does not make it true. Years and years of being programmed wrong can make you believe you are not capable of what God has called you to do. This is an area which causes our perception of self to be distorted. If you have not taken the time to write all those negative things down that were said to you, I encourage you right now to stop and take time to do so. When we begin to allow God in to replace those images with godly images, our healing begins, and when something is spoken over us, we do not receive it. Instead of being offended or hurt, we begin to see how those speaking negative words over us deeply need our prayers. Those who have pain in their own lives usually have nothing positive being produced around them. They will continually speak and think on those things which are negative because satan has them bound by lies just as he once had me bound. In order to be healed and set free, take all those negative things which have been spoken and give them to God for healing. You will begin seeing and feeling that healing manifest in your life. God is calling you to greater things, but He wants you healed from your past in every area. We need to step out of our box and cry out to our Almighty Father and say, *"Lord, I am ready to do what You have called me to do. Father, not my will but Yours be done!"* When we come to God with that attitude and mean it, God is going to use us in ways that we cannot imagine.

Ephesians 3:20 (Amp) [20]*Now to Him Who, by (in consequence of) the [action of His] power that is at work within us, is able to [carry out His purpose and] do superabundantly, far over and above all that we [dare] ask or think [infinitely beyond our highest prayers, desires, thoughts, hopes, or dreams]--*

Like it says in Ephesians, infinitely beyond our highest prayers, desires, thoughts, hopes, or dreams, God is able to bring about that purpose in our lives. God does not think as we do, He thinks big. He thinks bigger than we can even imagine and greater than we have ever thought or dreamed. When you let God get a hold of you and decide to believe what the Father of all Fathers says about you, you will begin to see someone that you never knew existed within yourself.

We have years and years of sometimes being programmed with negative images of who we are, and we need to look at this more in depth in order to rise above those images. As we allow God to heal and replace those images, we will begin to see ourselves as capable of walking this abundant life as a Christian. There may be times, in all of our lives, where someone either deliberately or unintentionally spoke certain things over us or compared us to someone else in a negative way. By the time I was considered an adult, I was expected to walk out into the world and exist, but did I know how? Did I know who I was? No, remember I had been told that I was not pretty like my sister. I was told that I would never amount to anything, and I was not smart enough. I was raised in a home where my mother was in denial about her alcohol and drug addiction, and my father wanted to pretend there was nothing wrong. The majority of my memories of my mother are filled with times of drunkenness, anger, and violence. Before I go any further, I would like to say through my walk with God, He did not just heal my past wounds and feelings towards my mother, but the revelation that I have received has helped me to be able to look beyond the addictions and to the heart of a person. If my mother was sober, which was very few times, she was the most giving person you could ever meet. My mother had a heart of gold during the times she was sober. She would give you the shirt off her back. She had compassion for mankind and for those who were less fortunate, but the addictions destroyed her life totally. There are many out there today who are suffering from addictions; however, do not judge a book by its cover. We never know what is on the inside of someone unless we have walked in their shoes. In my mother's drunkenness, her words could be very cold and cruel, but if you knew the person inside, she was very loving and compassionate.

As a little girl growing up in a dysfunctional family, those things I witnessed and those things I was taught were what I considered normal. I did not know any difference. My father was co-dependent, being raised himself by an alcoholic dad. He grew up drawn to those who are dysfunctional because it felt normal. Example: My father detested alcohol; however, he married an alcoholic. I chose men in my life continually who were also from dysfunctional families because it was the norm. I believe there were some things that I did acquire from my father, which were healthy concepts, even though he was very seldom home. I can remember my father would tell me that I could be whatever I set my mind to; however, when my mother tore me down in front of him, he did not stand up for me. Therefore, even though he spoke positive things over me at times, it did not register in my life because I never heard him speak up for me or disagree. Furthermore, my father was quick to point out my shortcomings and criticize my choices after I got older. I then walked out into a cold world after my mother died when I was only 17. I was pregnant having to face being a mother myself, but inside I was still a little girl. My dad had remarried a younger woman within six months of my mother's death, and he basically had a new life that did not include me or my older sister. I found myself trying to fit into a new world, trying to work, support my daughter, make friends, but I was lost inside. I was supposed to be an adult, but I was lost in a world that I had no idea how to survive. It is really easy to see why teenagers today or even young adults make such wrong choices. My life soon became one party after another. Alcohol was a normal part of my everyday life, drugs not too much. I had lived through the drug scene from age 13 to16 and was actually burned out, from that lifestyle, toward my late teens.

166

Having my daughter had also made a huge difference in my life, as I found I did not want her around the partying lifestyle whatsoever. I did not want my daughter to live through the things I had. So my daughter to some extent was a positive influence on my life. We do not always see this in society, but instead, we witness far too often, social services having to step in due to unplanned and unwanted births. However, my first born was also the first grandchild on her daddy's side of the family, and they kept her at least 3 days a week in order for me to work. I began working the nightlife in clubs by the age of 18. This lifestyle came with a price tag. My friends whom I associated with were all focusing on one thing in life, and that was, *"Where is the next party at?"* It is one thing if you are working clubs and bars to help support yourself while in school but if it is all about just being there to party, there is no getting ahead and nothing to look forward to in life. I saw myself as someone who would never amount to anything, someone who was not smart, and someone who would not be anything in life because that was what I thought I was. So, I did not see any need in working towards a goal. What goes on inside of a person when they are living like this? There was a lot of pain and resentment. I hated my dad. I even hated my mother even though she was dead. I blamed them for my life being like it was and would actually go to my mother's grave just so I could tell her how much I hated her. Hate destroys! I was gradually and slowly destroying my self-worth, but God was there. I may not have known Him, but He knew me. Over the next several years, people kept crossing my path with words of light and wisdom. One day, I saw who I was in Christ, and the healing process began.

Rejection is another area that is very real but seldom addressed. Rejection altars the way we feel about ourselves and can go back as far as conception. Research continues to support

167

the belief that babies in the womb can be affected by not only sound around them but also the emotional state of the mother. It is believed that mother's whose babies are wanted and loved, tend to have emotionally healthy children. However, those who may have gone through major emotional disturbances and unresolved stresses, throughout their pregnancy, may give birth to babies who grow to be emotionally troubled children. Extreme maternal distress even poses a risk of hurting a baby physically, and it is also linked to increased risk of prematurity and low-birth weight. So the question is, can what occurred in the womb have greatly affected our emotional state as a child and on into adulthood? Yes, it can and needs to be addressed, if possible. This is an area that you may need to take to the Lord for healing within.

My mother endured many abortions due to my father not wanting children. There came a day when she finally told him, *"No more!"* She gave birth to my sister and then to me; however, she consumed alcohol to extremes the whole time she carried me. No, I do not know what was spoken over me in the womb. I do not know what my mother's emotional state was; however, I do know she spent most of the pregnancy intoxicated which did contribute to my health problems as a child and emotional state. If you have given birth to babies and did not take care of yourself physically, please do not be too hard on yourself at this point. We have all done things wrong. With my first daughter, I for the most part took very good care of myself during the pregnancy; however, my emotional state was a totally different story. My father gave me the choice to either get an abortion or to get married. My first husband had addictions to drugs and alcohol. There was extreme fighting which kept my emotional state elevated to the point that, on one occasion, I took drugs off the street because I could not cope. I remember being really messed up and thinking about what it was doing to my baby. That was the only time during the pregnancy I lost it to that extent; however, my baby could feel the ups and downs of my emotional state. These were all areas which had followed me from birth to adult hood and were not dealt with until I found the Lord. After finding Jesus, I was finally delivered from the pain and rejections of my past. God will forgive you today for any mistakes you may have made with your own children, but we must recognize, admit, and take those things to our Father.

Many Christians today, still walk around with wounds that are not totally healed, and when they continue to do so, those wounds fester in other areas of their lives. We may do well for awhile at serving the Lord; however, there will come a time when we are faced with a situation that requires standing on the rock and not being moved. If you are not fully grounded, meaning that the root has been dealt with, you will fall. Think of it this way, when a tree is first planted, it is weak until it takes root. It takes many years for a tree to become grounded and rooted. Some trees have a much deeper root system than others. Like the Oak, it is very mighty and strong. When faced with a storm, what happens? Those trees that are not grounded will surely fall. If their root system is weak due to not being nurtured, it will not be grounded enough to withstand a storm. In the same sense, when our root system is weak due to neglect and we are faced with a strong test or temptation, we too will fall. We neglect our root system due to not addressing any weaknesses and not being nurtured in the Word of God. During my fall from grace, my root system was damaged. It became very weak, and I began to wither and fall until I could no longer stand. I had taken my eyes off of Jesus and began to find blame in everything. Looking back, I had felt as though the church had given me wrong advice, which made me make choices I should not have made. I felt betrayed personally. Therefore, I retreated to what was comfortable and normal, which was going back into the world.

In order for us to be grounded and strong like the mighty Oak, we must deal with those negative images that have been spoken over us and find the root of the problem. Once we realize where the root lies, we must take it to God. The only way I was able to begin to see myself differently was through Jesus; however, everything negative had to be revealed. The Word is a lamp unto our feet and a light unto our path.

Psalm 119:105 (NIV) [105] *Your word is a lamp to my feet and a light for my path.*

In revealing those things which were spoken negative, we must bring them to the light, and that of course is before the Lord. As we allow God into our lives, He will begin to show us the root cause to our afflictions. Remember, God desires us to be set free. Like I said, there are two sources where we will more than likely find the root, with one being our perception of God, and the other would be the perception of ourselves. Both stem back to our beginning, how we saw our earthly fathers and all those things which have been spoken over us. I had taken everything negative spoken over me and all the occurrences which had caused pain in my life to the Lord and released all to Him. I wrote letters to forgive my mother and father, but there was still pain inside. It became evident that even though I had received healing for past pain in my life, I had not recognized the root. The root is what made me build those walls in the first place, and if they have not been dealt with, those walls which God broke away will only begin to build once again. This is one technique in which satan used to bring me down. Here, I was thinking because I allowed God to begin the healing process and break away those walls which I had

170

built, everything was good, but it was not. I did not look to the root of the problem, and because of this, when I would become wounded again, I also began to build those walls again. It was hard for me to break free, during those 15 years, and come back home because I was dealing with walls surrounding me again. I was not allowing those who God sent across my path to get close enough to see my pain. My root went back to not being able to see God as who He was. I think most Christians today have a hard time seeing God as He really is because their earthly father did not measure up. This by no means is to bring guilt and condemnation on any father out there reading this. On the contrary, like I said many dads today have been living with pain and hurt within their own lives due to their perceptions of their earthly dads. They did not have the role model which was needed in order to heal themselves, so they could be that loving, nurturing father God intended them to be. Even though, my dad to some extent was a positive in my life, he also planted seeds which produced bad fruit. My mother raised me and my sister making sure that we saw no fault in our dad. Mother did not want us to see those things in which he did that were bad; therefore, she did whatever to protect us. My father spent a lot of time away from home in which we were told that he was traveling with business, for the most part. As a little girl, I did not understand why he was not there. I was able to see fault in my mother because I saw her every day. I witnessed her drinking, and there are even memories of her bringing men home which was very disturbing to me as a child. I did not understand but knew there was something wrong with the picture. There were times I would cry to my father because of things my mom would do, and it was though he really was not concerned. This taught me that it did not really matter how I felt, a father was not concerned with your feelings. Years later as a teenager, we would find out that he had another woman. My dad had helped support her all those years. It was like seeing my dad as a "God", who my mother had tried to portray him as for all those years, and then a huge let down to know the truth. I lost all respect for my dad during my teen years. This taught me men were not to be trusted. This was my perception of men. Whatever your perception is of your dad will also be your perception of who God is. There were great trust issues towards men. There were many other things which came to light about my father that I was unaware, which basically painted a much distorted picture of men. If I could not believe that God actually created men in this world to be trustworthy, how could I truly trust God to the point that I would be willing to let go and give Him everything? Even during the 10 years that I walked close to God, there was always that part of me that was unsure and did not trust totally. I believed what God's Word said; however, there were areas of the Word that had not been revealed to me during my walk, not until my coming back home. As a result, I married men who could not be trusted because it was a cycle. There was no trust, and my perception of God was distorted to a sense because the truth in those areas had yet to be revealed.

Even after, you allow God to reveal the root to all your pain and you go through the healing process, the enemy will still try to come in and steal that revelation from you. The devil will send people across your path to criticize and humiliate you; he will make you believe you are not saved or forgiven and that you will never be anybody. It is very important that we pray and spend time with God every single day because when we do not, our spirit is weakened, and there is a door open for satan to come in and plant a seed of condemnation. That seed may begin as these simple words, *"Look at you, you are not a child of God; you are nothing."* That very seed will begin to grow if you dwell on it and listen to it. When you open that door for satan to get in with condemnation and your spirit is not strong, you will listen to what is being said and dwell on it in your heart. Then what happens? It will begin to harden your heart. You will become cold, and God cannot bless you! We need to stand up to who we are in Christ and take our place as a child of God. In order to do this, we must know the Word. We must know what God's Word says about us, and stand up to satan. We should not take anything from the enemy, and we should not let anger or humiliation enter our lives. We should not let those things of darkness come in and bring us down. As we heal from all the negative images spoken over us, we need to replace them with the good images that God speaks over us daily. I remember in my early walk with God, it was nothing to find reminders taped on my bathroom mirror. That was the beginning of my growth, and I needed the reminders. Little things from the Word of God were posted, words of comfort, words of wisdom, whatever I needed at that time. So when I stood in front of the mirror, I could speak out those positive words over myself in order to draw strength and begin to see myself the way God saw me. This was an area of revelation during those 10 years that I had not gotten deep down on the inside of me. Who was I according to what God's Word says? If we cannot believe that we are who God says we are, then how can we say we believe God is who He says He is? If I have restored my trust in men, then my trust in God should be one of believing everything He says about me. As we go through letting go and healing from all we have endured in this life, we will begin seeing God in a different light and seeing ourselves as capable of success. We will begin to see ourselves as somebody, and we will begin to see a different vision of ourselves as the Word speaks over us not as the world speaks. Of course, all of this is only because we are one with Christ and walk with the Holy Spirit. Therefore, we are sons and daughters of the Most High God. We will then begin to believe we can do what God has called us to do. Jesus said all things are possible with God.

Matthew 19:26 (Amp) [26]*But Jesus looked at them and said, With men this is impossible, but all things are possible with God.*

Healing must take place towards your dad or even your mother, and it will not happen overnight. It is something you can do if you spend time with the Lord. Forgiveness has to take place towards your earthly father and mother along with every person who spoke negative images over you or abused you in any way. As you begin your walk with the Lord and through this book, your eyes will be opened to who God is and how men were created to be in His likeness. Even though, we all fall short, Jesus died and shed His blood to redeem us in that area. When you receive all these truths, the next time anything negative is spoken over you, you do not receive it and do not meditate on it.

The Word Versus The World

Do you desire to see mountains move in your life? Do you desire to see God move in your life? As you draw closer to Him, He will begin to walk you through all areas of your life, every situation and circumstance. He will do a complete make-over of your mind, will, and emotions. God will help you to let go and allow Him to be the Father you may never have had. He will begin to show you how an earthly father was created to love his children and nurture them up in the Word and not the world. Your mind will begin to be renewed in the things above and not of this world. You will rise up, just like the great men and women in biblical days, in order that it glorifies the Father. Why do we have a hard time seeing ourselves being used like God used Moses? For the same reason, Moses could not see himself being used in a great way. However, when we overcome all the obstacles in our lives and draw from God, we will be able to see ourselves rise and go forth with whatever it is He is calling us to do.

Our outlook towards the perceptions and beliefs of the world is also an area which has to do with images. When I became saved and began growing in God's Word, I knew that the Word said I could do all things through Christ. I knew God loved me, and I knew I was somebody if God created me. However, there were times those words spoken over me as a child would reflect in my walk with the Lord, and there were times my outlook on life was not always based on what the Word said. I had come to a place where I was walking close to God; however, when trials and tribulation came my way, the way I walked through the test revealed if there were areas that had not been dealt with. When I was faced with a test greater than I felt I could endure, my outlook on life began to, once again, see things according to the world and not the Word. At that point, doubt set in, and I became disappointed in the church. I became judgmental on those who wanted to give me advice, and in general, my attitude became that of the world.

Why do we dwell on things which make us feel unworthy? We know that God sends His people across our path to build us up, and the enemy sends those to tear us down. Why is it that the greater emphasis is on those seeds which are negative than those which are positive? Many times we are consumed with those things which are negative, such as tragedies and horror stories. The movie theaters are packed when a new thriller comes out. When there are horrible tragedies which occur, we rush to watch the updates on the television at night. When we hear about sad stories which happen locally, everyone seems to be talking about it. The media portrays that which is bad over that which is good because it sells! Our minds have been programmed to want entertainment, and if it is not exciting, we are not interested. It is sad to see that those which have tragedies in their lives bring excitement and entertainment to our lives. Those which are

175

famous and face difficult times, with addictions and high profile divorces, draw the attention of the American people. It is no wonder that we dwell on those things which are spoken to us negatively more than those spoken positively. In fact, people in general are more apt to broadcast when everything seems to be going wrong rather than when things are going great. More than likely, we do this because the responses we get from sharing our misfortunes far outweigh the responses from our victories. This is where our minds must be renewed to what the Word of God says and not the world.

The more time you spend on the computer surfing the web or watching ungodly television, the more you are programming your mind to think negatively. It is no wonder Christians today are crying out to God. The majority of Christians do not get it. They want to blame God for their misfortunes because they believe He evidently is not doing His job. After all, if they are never missing a service and their life is still a mess, it must not be their fault, but we have to see that it is never God's fault. We also need to stop blaming the church. If we are not spending time with God, in order to renew our minds to think like Christ, then we are going to think like the world. I do not want to bring condemnation on anyone for spending time on the computer or television. I am not insinuating all programs or websites are bad. What is bad is when it consumes us and our thoughts. A good way to see what your thoughts are consumed with, next time you awaken in the morning or middle of the night, think about what your dreams consisted of. This will also be in another series, but what you are putting in is what will be coming out. Start listening to your conversations with others, if they are solely based on worldly issues, there is not much Word in you. If you would like to see your life as victorious, as God desires for you, then it may be time to make changes. I used to love watching a certain program which came on weekly, but there came a time that I had to realize what I was watching was contrary to what God's Word says. Why then would I want to fill my thoughts with something that is the complete opposite of what the Word of God says? God spoke to me one day and said, *"Fast from that program,"* in other words, *"Do not watch it for awhile!"* I knew if I could not do that, then it became bigger than God to me. Please note, the actual program is not mentioned to avoid conflict with the station; however, I would like to clarify that the program I watched faithfully was not something which would be classified as "R" rated. In fact, the program could actually be watched by all ages. The point I am trying to make is that the majority of programs on television do not fill us with the Word of God but rather with the world.

Another area we need to think about and shed light upon, are areas where we all are guilty of receiving negative images and may not even realize it. Many times we may compare ourselves to someone else. Think back in your life, were you ever compared to someone or to an image of something? Have you ever compared yourself to something or someone else? We all, in one way or another, are guilty of comparing ourselves to some kind of image. Let me give you an example. The world portrays, if you are blond, you will have more fun. The world portrays that women are beautiful when they look like a model. The world portrays that if you are wealthy, then you can acquire anything. How many times do we stand in front of a mirror and judge ourselves based on what the outward appearance speaks? How many times do we look at our bank account and feel as if we are failures? Perhaps, someone close to you has made a comment about your weight or your hair that may have not been meant as a negative remark, but you took it as such. I can remember years ago, my husband saying to me one day, *"You should have your hair bleached blonde like so and so, her hair is really pretty!"* Even

177

though, it was not meant to say my hair color and hair was not pretty, what it spoke to me was that he would love me more if I looked like this particular girl. I never forgot that. I dwelled on it, and even though, I never ran out to have my hair colored, it planted an image in my mind that those who have blond hair are more attractive. How many of us go through life feeling, we will never measure up because our image does not portray what is acceptable to the world's standards. Many times this will keep you defeated; however, God created you and loves you just the way you are. Millions of dollars are spent each year on cosmetics and plastic surgery for women and even men. Many try to stay looking as young as possible, in order to fit into the world's beliefs that you will never be anything or you will never remain where you are today, if your looks on the outside do not measure up. Those who cannot afford this luxury, feel they are limited to what they can do because their outward appearance does not compare to the world's standards. In doing research, statistics show that it is true, those who are more attractive are more likely to achieve greater success. When the decision comes down to one who does not measure up to the world's standards of beauty and one who does, most times someone will be picked because they fit into the world's critique. However, again we are basing everything according to the world's standards and beliefs, not Gods. Statistics do not say that someone who is less attractive cannot succeed, but it does show that the greater percentages that are successful are those who are attractive. This is where we allow the world's perception and beliefs to infiltrate our way of thinking. This is a really good tactic satan uses to keep us defeated. When we take our eyes off of Jesus and begin to look at those in the world or even other Christians and question, *"Why can I not be more like that person, or why is God not using me like that,"* then we open a door for sin. With sin will come destruction, but if you renew your mind to think like God and stop trying to fit into the world, you will be one of the statistics on the lower end which does succeed. When more and more Christians rise up and take their place, we will begin to see those statistics change because God is capable of raising us to levels we never dreamed of. God does not need the perceptions or beliefs of the world in order to bring about His plan for our lives.

Instead of focusing so much attention to our outward self, we should be striving to do everything we can to walk according to the Word of God. In order to do this, there are areas that keep us from achieving. One such area may be our associations. Perhaps, you are in a place where you are struggling to do according to what the Word says. Maybe, you are trying to pray, read the Word, or spend time with God. When you first get saved and go back into the world, chances are those you were associating with prior to getting saved may not be in your best interest. There may be family and friends that you love and do not want to let go of. You do not necessarily have to rid them completely out of your life; however, you do have to be aware of your time invested with them and how it is affecting you. We have all heard the phrase, *"Birds of a feather flock together."* This is so true, if you spend a great deal of time associating with those who think like the world, it will have an effect on your way of thinking. When you are beginning the walk to renew your mind, it is extremely important to spend your time wisely. If you continue to put more of the world in you, that is what will come out. There is also the saying, *"What goes in must come out."* The world is full of negative perception; in other words, everywhere you look you see what the world proclaims things to be. The world looks at those without an education, as being unable to succeed. The world looks at those who commit a crime, as being a hindrance to society. The world looks at those who may not have a slim figure and beautiful face, as being unattractive. This is just a few perceptions according to the standards of the world, but who sets the standards? We live in a world which has from the beginning of time began setting standards of the way man perceives things, not the way God perceives things. The world continually strives to fit into certain categories and certain perceptions in order to be accepted. The world strives to be successful according to the standards which have been set down by man and not by God. They believe in order to achieve success, you must be taught through man's philosophies. Man may say that their methods are godly methods, but if God is not in the equation, it is not God! God does not look upon each of us and judge us according to the standards of man. God created each one of us uniquely. It does not matter if you fit into the standards set by man, what matters is if your heart is pure enough to be acceptable to a God who loves and desires for you to be all He created you to be. This has nothing to do with all the things in which the world has handed down to you. It has nothing to do with your bad hand of cards, which was dealt to you in order to keep you from rising to that level which God sees you capable of doing. It does not matter if you did not get your education. It does not matter if you grew up in a dysfunctional family. It does not matter if you have been in prison. It does not matter if you have committed adultery. It does not matter if you are addicted to drugs, and it does not matter if you have committed murder. The world may say that because of your past, you will never be anything. To paraphrase, God says in His Word, *"Seek Me My child; seek My love, and let Me renew your way of thinking; let Me heal your heart."* There may be much pain, which has happened to you in your past or even present, but God will take everything that satan has used to try to destroy you, and turn them around. He will turn all the bad around in order to bring glory to Him. God desires that glory, and it cannot happen unless He raises you to a place for others to see.

Isaiah 26:15 (Amp) [15]*You have increased the nation, O Lord; You have increased the nation. You are glorified; You have enlarged all the borders of the land.*

God increases nations, and He increases His children in order that it glorifies Him. In Genesis, God spoke these words to Abraham…

Genesis 12:2 (Amp) [2]*And I will make of you a great nation, and I will bless you [with abundant increase of favors] and make your name famous and distinguished, and you will be a blessing [dispensing good to others].*

God desires to increase us in order that it gives glory to Him. God has given His children favor with all of mankind. He desires that we are set apart and distinguished among those of the world. In Luke, everything God promised to Abraham was not just for him but also for all of his descendants. If you are a child of God, you are a descendant of Abraham.

Luke 1:55 (Amp) [55]*Even as He promised to our forefathers, to Abraham and to his descendants forever.*

Your family, who may not be saved, has favor with God once you have received the gift of salvation. However, it is important for you to continue your walk and be that positive influence in their life. You cannot allow your family to pull you back down. If you desire your family to walk this walk with you, it will take you standing firm. You may have to make decisions which may eliminate or limit the amount of time spent at certain family gatherings in which you once attended. What I mean by that, if there are family gatherings for certain occasions which include heavy drinking, drugs, or fights, which break out regularly every time the family comes together, it may be time to avoid those particular get-togethers. This by no means is implying that you totally avoid your family. On the contrary, you will be walking with the light, and it will take the light to shine out the darkness. God has really been doing miracles in my own family. There was a time when I just stayed away; however, God spoke to me to begin ministering to them. I love my family dearly, and I know what their pain is because I also dealt with many of those same areas. By bringing them Words of truth, as God instructed me, He has begun to move in several of their lives. God will change your family, but remember, it is not in ourselves this happens. We simply plant the seeds, and God cultivates. We cannot put a time frame on when anyone will be awakened to the truth. It will be in God's timing.

Finding Purpose

Throughout history, every man and woman of God had a purpose. When they rose up to do the calling which God set on their lives, they increased in stature, favor, and wisdom. As they increased in all things, this gave glory to God. Everyone that followed the path God had set before them were increased in some way. If you are a child of God, you have a purpose. Even Jesus had a purpose which was to redeem mankind and provide eternal life for those who believed on Him. John the Baptist also had a purpose, to prepare the way for our Lord and Savior, but what happened after Jesus rose up and began walking that course the Father had set before Him?

John 3:29-30 (ESV) [29]*The one who has the bride is the bridegroom. The friend of the bridegroom, who stands and hears him, rejoices greatly at the bridegroom's voice. Therefore this joy of mine is now complete.* [30] *He must increase, but I must decrease."*

This Scripture shows us that John the Baptist's time was complete. He had completed his purpose of what God had called him to do. He had done the works set before him by preparing the way for Jesus. It was time for John to decrease in order for the increase to go rightfully to the Son of God. We all have a purpose just like John, winning souls for the Kingdom of Heaven and preparing those for the end times. God will increase us, just as He did John the Baptist. John was increased prior to Jesus, and we shall be increased prior to Jesus' return. We are to bear witness for our Lord and prepare for his coming. After Christ returns for the church, prophecy will be fulfilled, and there will be no need for increase. We will be glorified in our heavenly bodies and dwell with God forever and ever.

*1 Corinthians 13:8 (Amp) *[8]*Love never fails [never fades out or becomes obsolete or comes to an end]. As for prophecy (the gift of interpreting the divine will and purpose), it will be fulfilled and pass away; as for tongues, they will be destroyed and cease; as for knowledge, it will pass away [it will lose its value and be superseded by truth].*

We all have one purpose as sons and daughters of our Father. Our purpose is to go forth and win souls. How we each go about fulfilling our purpose will be according to our own particular calling on our lives. God has a specific calling on each of our lives, and those He calls, He justifies and glorifies.

*Romans 8:30 (Amp) *[30]*And those whom He thus foreordained, He also called; and those whom He called, He also justified (acquitted, made righteous, putting them into right standing with Himself). And those whom He justified, He also glorified [raising them to a heavenly dignity and condition or state of being].*

In 2 Thessalonians, on the day of the coming of Christ, He will be glorified through the saints.

2 Thessalonians 1:10-12 (Amp) [10]When He comes to be glorified in His saints [on that day He will be made more glorious in His consecrated people], and [He will] be marveled at and admired [in His glory reflected] in all who have believed [who have adhered to, trusted in, and relied on Him], because our witnessing among you was confidently accepted and believed [and confirmed in your lives]. [11]With this in view we constantly pray for you, that our God may deem and count you worthy of [your] calling and [His] every gracious purpose of goodness, and with power may complete in [your] every particular work of faith (faith which is that leaning of the whole human personality on God in absolute trust and confidence in His power, wisdom, and goodness). [12]Thus may the name of our Lord Jesus Christ be glorified and become more glorious through and in you, and may you [also be glorified] in Him according to the grace (favor and blessing) of our God and the Lord Jesus Christ (the Messiah, the Anointed One).

As we read on in Thessalonians, we are constantly being perfected in the calling God has set before us. We are to bring glory to Jesus in all we do, and we are glorified through Him because of the grace of God. In other words, remember we discussed that the man is to bring glory to God, and the only way he can glorify God is by living according to what is commanded. God desires that glory. When others can see that what we do is not in ourselves, but only because of who sent us, it gives the glory to God the Father, Son, and Holy Ghost. The glory does not come to us but through us to glorify our Father. A good example is when we are witnessing about how our lives have changed. We do not want to give the impression that our lives have changed because of something we were able to do in ourselves. No, my

184

life today is an example of the work in which God has done in me. My life today is only because Jesus died on the cross for me, and I have been redeemed. My life illuminates that change today because the Holy Spirit walks with me on a daily basis. In myself, I can do nothing, but with the Holy Spirit and in the name of Jesus, I can do all things.

We all may have our insecurities, but if God has called us to do something, He knows what we are capable of doing. If we step out of our box and allow God to use us, God gives us everything we need to accomplish that which He sent us to do.

Ephesians 3:20 (Amp) [20]*Now to Him Who, by (in consequence of) the [action of His] power that is at work within us, is able to [carry out His purpose and] do superabundantly, far over and above all that we [dare] ask or think [infinitely beyond our highest prayers, desires, thoughts, hopes, or dreams]--*

In Ephesians, it shows that God gave us a purpose. God's power is at work within our lives to accomplish that which He gives us. God does not just send us out into the world to fulfill what He has called us to do without what we need to accomplish it, no matter what our calling.

Some of us may still say, *"All this may be true, but the great men of old lived purer lives than we do today."* Yes, they did practice living according to the Ten Commandments, but they still had to sacrifice animals, which was innocent bloodshed, in order to be in right standing with God. Today, we need to practice living according to the commandments as well, but we also need to realize that our day can begin every single morning with a prayer of pleading Jesus' blood over us. Jesus' blood sanctifies us daily so that we are in right standing with God. We may not be living in the Old Testament times; however, by faith, we still have to recognize the importance of pleading the precious blood of Jesus over our lives daily. Remember, when we plead the blood over us, we are actually making a statement that we believe by faith Jesus' blood is flowing over our lives. We believe by faith that this is in order to sanctify us so we can come before the throne of grace, before our Father. When we asked Jesus to come into our heart, did we see anything different? No, but by faith, we believed that our sins were forgiven because the Word of God says when we repent, we are forgiven. By faith, we believed that we received salvation and eternal life when we called out to God. Today, we also believe that Jesus abides with us and it is by faith we will come to know there is power in Jesus' blood.

Galatians 2:20 (Amp) [20]I have been crucified with Christ [in Him I have shared His crucifixion]; it is no longer I who live, but Christ (the Messiah) lives in me; and the life I now live in the body I live by faith in (by adherence to and reliance on and complete trust in) the Son of God, Who loved me and gave Himself up for me.

However, we also know as long as we live in these fleshly bodies, we will miss it and sin. Remember, that is why we should plead the blood over our bodies daily. When we get saved, we do not just assume that it ends there. In Old Testament times, as God was giving Moses all the instructions on building the tabernacle, which would hold the Arc of the Covenant, instructions were also given on preparations for the sacrifice of innocent animals. God spoke to Moses and instructed him that the sacrifice of animals was to be done on a daily basis, in order to make atonement for the children of Israel. Atonement is the payment of damages done for an offense to cover our sins on a daily basis.

Exodus 29:36 (ESV) *^{36}and every day you shall offer a bull as a sin offering for atonement. Also you shall purify the altar, when you make atonement for it, and shall anoint it to consecrate it.*

According to Scripture, Jesus came and made that payment for our sins with the blood of One who is not only innocent but pure.

1 Corinthians 6:11 (Amp) *^{11}And such some of you were [once]. But you were washed clean (purified by a complete atonement for sin and made free from the guilt of sin), and you were consecrated (set apart, hallowed), and you were justified [pronounced righteous, by trusting] in the name of the Lord Jesus Christ and in the [Holy] Spirit of our God.*

Remember, Moses was no different than we are. He did not see himself being used in the great way God had called him. We all have a purpose, and where we go with God depends totally on how much we are willing to give of ourselves. If Moses could have seen himself the way God saw him, he would never have questioned the Father when his calling was set before him. Do we question God because we are not convinced that God can lead us in such a mighty way? Moses questioned God because he did not see himself the same as God did. There are many great men and women in the bible who went on to do extraordinary things for the Kingdom of Heaven; however, they were no different from you and me. God created them, and He knew their faults but chose them to do great things because it is through Him, we are capable, not through ourselves. God knows our faults and has already designed a path specifically for each of us, one which is far greater than we could ever imagine. However, many will never walk that path because they struggle with seeing what God sees! In Corinthians, it says we are set apart. God sets us apart as being different from the world. We are His children, and He declares us righteous because we trust in the name of Jesus and in the Holy Spirit. When we acknowledge that Jesus is the Son of God, this glorifies God, and He is very pleased. Just like when we learned that all heaven rejoices over one sinner who is saved, God is pleased because we acknowledge who Jesus is, and we acknowledge the Holy Spirit. We may not understand everything yet, but He does not expect us to. The Holy Spirit will teach us all we need to know in God's timing and as we put forth effort to grow.

John 14:26 (NIV) *26But the Counselor, the Holy Spirit, whom the Father will send in my name, will teach you all things and will remind you of everything I have said to you.*

Remember, God wants the glory, and the glory cannot come to God if His people are not increased. To be increased can only be accomplished because of the blood of Jesus today, and it will not be accomplished through our own efforts.

Isaiah 9:6-7 (Amp) *6For to us a Child is born, to us a Son is given; and the government shall be upon His shoulder, and His name shall be called Wonderful Counselor, Mighty God, Everlasting Father [of Eternity], Prince of Peace. 7Of the increase of His government and of peace there shall be no end, upon the throne of David and over his kingdom, to establish it and to uphold it with justice and with righteousness from the [latter] time forth, even forevermore. The zeal of the Lord of hosts will perform this.*

In Isaiah, this was referring to the Son of God. This Scripture prophesied about Christ even before He was born. The increase we receive with Jesus and His peace, there shall be no end. We are joint heirs to the Kingdom of Heaven. Increases should follow us where ever we go. As long as we are saved, live according to the commandments, and as long as we set our sights on those things above and not beneath, we should have increases daily. Peace should dwell among everything which we do, this is the way our Father sees us. Just like an earthly father who loves his children, they love us no matter what we have done and desire for us to have those things which are good. Of course, we look at this pertaining to those earthly dads that are there for their children, but a father's love never ceases to exist. Along with the love, a father has for his children, is everything else which the father has worked for. When we make wills, who do we leave our inheritance? I know there are some instances this may not be the case, but in the normal sense, our inheritance is left with our children! By being saved and coming into the kingdom, under the blood of Jesus, everything which the Father owns becomes our inheritance. Our Father desires to increase us in every manner while here on earth and eternally, when we go to live with Him in heaven. In Revelation 21, John writes, in the end, man will be God's people and dwell with Him. God desires for His children to rise and know He is our God. He desires for us to increase and looks to the day that we will once and for all dwell among Him.

Revelation 21:3 (NIV) ³And I heard a loud voice from the throne saying, "Now the dwelling of God is with men, and he will live with them. They will be his people, and God himself will be with them and be their God."

In order to increase, we must acknowledge our purpose and set our sights on accomplishing those things which we are called to do. Our sights should be set to run the race which is set before us.

Hebrews 12:1(ESV) ¹Therefore, since we are surrounded by so great a cloud of witnesses, let us also lay aside every weight, and sin which clings so closely, and let us run with endurance the race that is set before us,

In other words, we are to lay aside every weight and sin, in order to endure that course God has specifically designed for each of us. We are to run it enduring to the end. What are the weights in our lives, which try to keep us from running the race set before us? A weight is anything which weighs us down, in order to keep us from accomplishing the purpose God has set before us. When you begin to know what your calling is, where God is leading you, and your purpose, satan will try to put obstacles in your path that will weigh you down. He will try to keep you from being able to succeed. satan may use a person to distract you from your purpose. He may use material things, or he may attack you in other ways without using objects. When you begin walking in your calling, you will begin to be more aware of the tests and trials as they come. As these tests come, we must stand firm on our beliefs because the enemy is going to try to put so much weight on us that the thought of giving up will come. However, one thing which will help, to keep you grounded, is to look back at where you have already come. When we do this, it helps us realize that we really do not want to go backwards. We already know what is back there, and we came this far because we made the decision to continue forward. Once we have taken so much ground, why would we walk away knowing if we do, one day we may be right back trying to regain the ground we lost. The last thing we should want to do is start over again to regain that which we once had with Christ. I did this and regret having to start again, when I never had to leave in the first place. Think about if you have set out on a course to hike across a certain terrain, and you have already come so far, but yet, you still have quite a way to go. What do you do when you are faced with a storm? Are you going to retreat and try to make it back to your original destination, or are you going to weather the storm in order to continue the path you set out to take? If we have made up our minds that we are going to endure, no matter what, then we weather each storm as they come knowing we will walk through them. Of course, any storm we endure, we do not do this alone. The Holy Spirit walks with us as we welcome Him into our lives daily.

In my walk, many times, it has been evident when it is the work of satan. There have been times that I was faced with a great obstacle in my life which would try to keep me from going forth to minister the gospel. Many times, I have planted seeds into someone else's life, and all of a sudden, a problem would arise. I have found myself at times ministering where my voice would start going. As soon as I would leave the place I was at, it would become worse, and I knew there were other homes on my calendar I was expected to share and minster the Word. The enemy wanted me to quit and give up. The enemy wanted me to call and cancel. However, I stood strong on the Word and rebuked the infirmity satan was trying to put on me. There were times that I did have to cancel, and I would become that much more determined to go and serve God's people in order to show the enemy he had not won. The enemy only wins when we give up; otherwise, he never wins our battles. Of course, when you get to the place that you are on fire for the Lord, God will also begin to show you balance, which is an area that will be discussed in a later series.

5 The Journey through Adolescence...

The Search for Maturity...

Life Choices

Our focus in this chapter will be on our own free will and that of the Fathers. We face life choices every day. Some choices may be good, and others will lead us down paths we soon will regret. As a Christian, how are we to make those choices in order to reap the blessings of God and not the curses of mankind?

James 1:18 (Amp) [18]And it was of His own [free] will that He gave us birth [as sons] by [His] Word of Truth, so that we should be a kind of firstfruits of His creatures [a sample of what He created to be consecrated to Himself].

We must first look at the meaning of free will. In James, it shows us that it was God's own free will that brought us in as His sons and daughters. In the Scripture below, it shows that Jesus was the Word. Jesus is the Truth because God's Word is Truth. *(John 17:17)* He was made flesh in order that, through His blood, we become children of God. This was God's free will and His choice because He wanted to redeem His children back from the deceptions of this world.

John 1:12-14 (Amp) [12]But to as many as did receive and welcome Him, He gave the authority (power, privilege, right) to become the children of God, that is, to those who believe in (adhere to, trust in, and rely on) His name-- [13]Who owe their birth neither to bloods nor to the will of the flesh [that of physical impulse] nor to the will of man [that of a natural father], but to God. [They are born of God!] [14]And the Word

(Christ) became flesh (human, incarnate) and tabernacled (fixed His tent of flesh, lived awhile) among us; and we [actually] saw His glory (His honor, His majesty), such glory as an only begotten son receives from his father, full of grace (favor, loving-kindness) and truth.

It is with our free will that we accept Jesus because God desires those who willingly want to serve and walk with Him. We need to realize that we owe our birth to God, not to the will of our flesh. This is not the physical birth but our new birth of being born again. We might have made the choice to seek God, and in seeking, we found the truth; however, it was God's will in the first place that we became sons and daughters of His.

We may not realize it, but daily after becoming a Christian, we battle with our will and the will of our Father. Every day, from the time we climb out of bed, we make choices of what we are going to do and when we are going to do it. God did not have to make the choice to send a Savior to redeem us, but He did so with His own free will. Being created in the likeness of God, we have that same free will. However, how many times do we make mistakes in our lives by exercising our own free will? You may be in a place where you never miss church, and you still struggle in life not understanding why. We may, for the most part, be doing everything right; however, we are leading and not being led. This is because we are trying to do things in ourselves and not allowing God to be in charge. Our choices often reflect decisions made based on selfish desires, other than what is in our best interest. The result, far too often, cost us in more ways than we may have expected. Poor decisions rob our finances, our health, our joy, our peace, and our happiness. Our decisions also affect not only ourselves but those who are close to us. We need to be able to see that, even though we may have been given a free will, God desires that we look to Him for all things. In James, it goes on to say that we need to listen.

James 1:19 (Amp) [19]Understand [this], my beloved brethren. Let every man be quick to hear [a ready listener], slow to speak, slow to take offense and to get angry.

We need to think back to adolescence, during our teen years. During that time frame, teenagers do not always want to listen to their parents. We thought we knew what was best, but later in life, we realized that our parents were much wiser than we thought. I think most of us would admit, in our younger days, we made many mistakes because we did not listen to our parents. My parents were not even Christians, yet there were still wise things they tried to impart upon me. I know I did not want to listen to their advice, and the results were many poor decisions. We pay for our mistakes and in more ways than one. I believe we all understand this, after the fact. We cannot go back and change anything we have done wrong; however, hopefully, we learned from those mistakes. Although, sometimes we do not learn from our mistakes, and there is one area that we continue to walk in even after we are all grown up with children of our own. Perhaps, you have children today, or perhaps, you are a teenager reading this. Whatever the case, this is something we need to be able to see in order to grow. We will all go through the adolescent years at some time in our lives, and we will all realize at some point that the teen years are growing years. During these years, we do not know as much as we think we do. Adolescence is a very hard time in our lives where we feel like an adult, yet our minds are not fully developed. Then, we grow up, or do we? After becoming an adult, God may be saying the same thing about us that we say about our young people. Many times teenagers are saying things such as:

•Why won't they just let me do what I want? I am not stupid!
•I am capable; I can take care of myself.
•They treat me like a baby; why can't I make my own decisions?

On the other hand, adults may not be speaking this, but their actions towards God are saying things such as:

•I pay my own bills, and I do not need someone else showing me what I need to do.
•I am responsible, and I do not need your advice.
•I know how to do this, and I do not need someone else telling me how.
•I have done this before, and I think I can handle it.
•You may mean well, but I did not ask.

I am sure there are more things I could add to this; however, the point being, when we receive salvation there is a totally different world to explore. It is not this world; it is a world that focuses on those things above which have greater value and greater wisdom. God desires from the moment we make the decision to be saved, to surrender to Him. He desires that we allow Him to begin to transform us to where we think and act, walk and talk just like Jesus. In doing so, we produce good fruit and not bad, and the decisions that we make, will produce good choices and not bad. Our good choices will not cost us in our finances, our health, our happiness, etc. We have to realize that, even though, our definition of the word adult may mean we have come to a place of being mature, real maturity only comes with the wisdom from above and not that of the world. So, the next time you get frustrated with your own children, you need to realize that God may be speaking the same language to you, and you are not listening. He wants us to wake up and see that our frustration comes from trying to change something that is blinded from the truth. Just as, our children may not be able to see our point of view because of immaturity, we are also blinded from the truth instead of surrendering all to our Father. The most rewarding thing we can do as parents is to raise our children to know the wisdom of God, not that of the world. No, God does not want robots, just like we do not want our children to be robots. God wants obedience, the same as we want obedience with our children. Ask yourself, why do we desire our children to do what we say? Your answer is the same answer of why God wants us to listen and obey!

1 Corinthians 8:9 (Amp) ⁹Only be careful that this power of choice (this permission and liberty to do as you please) which is yours, does not [somehow] become a hindrance (cause of stumbling) to the weak or overscrupulous [giving them an impulse to sin].

Our bad choices will affect those around us. In 1 Corinthians, it says to be careful, why? As parents, we know that those choices we make are setting an example to our children. Children do not hear, *"Do as I say, not as I do."* Children believe if you can do it, they can do it also, and any choices you make are affecting those who are close to you whether it is what happens behind closed doors or in public. Everything we do affects those who look up to us either in a good way or a bad way. Ask yourself, what kinds of seeds are you planting? Good or bad? There are many instances in the Word where men and women made choices they soon regretted. Here, is an example in Hebrews where it speaks of Esau, from the Old Testament times, who sold his birthright for a single meal.

Hebrews 12:16-17 (Amp) ¹⁶That no one may become guilty of sexual vice, or become a profane (godless and sacrilegious) person as Esau did, who sold his own birthright for a single meal. ¹⁷For you understand that later on, when he wanted [to regain title to] his inheritance of the blessing, he was rejected (disqualified and set aside), for he could find no opportunity to repair by repentance [what he had done, no chance to recall the choice he had made], although he sought for it carefully with [bitter] tears.

You can read this story beginning in Genesis 25 of the Old Testament; however, the point here is to show you that many times, we make a split-second decision based on our feelings at that moment. Esau was very hungry after being in the field all day. His brother Jacob, who loved to cook, offered him food only if he would give up his birthright. In those days, the first born son received the birthrights of his father, which were all rights to that of his father's inheritance. However, it shows that when the time came, and his father Isaac was dying, he called for Esau in order to bless him. Esau was also cheated out of his blessings. The point in the book of Hebrews was to show that due to his bad choice, it affected Esau for many years. Our choices can affect us for the rest of our lives. Now later on, Esau was blessed by God; however, there were hardships he endured by following his will and not that of God. You may think, I would never give up something so great for a single meal, but perhaps, you have given something up for a single night of pleasure. Maybe, you desired that one night of passion that you gave up your virginity to someone who deceived you. Perhaps, you lied to your spouse to keep them from knowing about a mistake you made in hopes of not hurting them. You may have cheated on someone you loved. You may have stolen something from someone which affected them immensely. You may have done something in which you have never told anyone due to fear of the consequences. All these things were split-second decisions not thinking about the consequences upon your life, upon the life of those you love, and the life of those whom you may not even know. Just like the split-second decision to get behind the wheel of an automobile, after having just a few drinks, you never thought about that choice

198

causing an accident which resulted in the death of someone else. The result of our split-second decisions can affect lives forever. There have been many children brought into this world by split-second decisions and many men who do not even know those children, which they helped bring into the world. Even worse, are the abortions that are the result of split-second decisions, and then, there are the over-whelming number of children in our society who are abused or neglected because many were never wanted. You may say that you would never give up your inheritance for a single meal, but when you make these bad choices, in reality you did give up your inheritance for a single meal. The curse of this world is upon you, and rather you realize it or not, you lost your inheritance with God until you repent and make things right. God will show you how to restore those relationships. He will show you how to mend those broken hearts, which may have been the result of your choices in life. God will also show you how to release the guilt and pain you may be feeling as the result of your actions.

Come as You Are

Many today, struggle with taking that step forward and surrendering all to God. There are many in church today that keep this to themselves and do not express it to others. For many, being in church has nothing to do with that desire to change. Many in church today are not seeking God or trying to find Him, and they know deep down inside that they do not feel the presence of God in their lives. However, they find themselves in a place spiritually where people expect them to be at church every time the doors are open. In fact, some may even be leaders within their churches, but if the truth were known, many do not understand that one on one intimate relationship with the Father. Many have not found that excitement and passion with every day being a new day with the Lord. Many feel disappointed in the churches today and seldom attend for various reasons. There are those who contemplate in their minds that God is real, but they are not where they need to be just yet to make that commitment. Many today feel the churches are full of hypocrites who believe they are better than everyone else. This outlook on the church leads many to fall away rather than associate and try to fit into the cliques often seen within the walls where the believers come together. There would be those who would say, they do not have appropriate clothes to feel acceptable in the churches today. You may say that you do not have transportation to attend church or that you work on the days of church services. However, many of these individuals who have reasons for not attending services would say they do believe in God. We will look at the reasons we should lay down our lives today and just come to the Lord. We will examine why too many today are trying to live with one foot in the door and one foot out, and we will explore the various reasons or excuses which people use in order to keep from making that commitment to the Lord. If we want to know God and see Him work in our lives, we have to come to the place where we make a one on one commitment. We have to come to the place where we will lay down our lives and come just as we are. It does not matter about our attire. It does not matter what the reasons, if our heart is right and we desire to meet Jesus, He will open that door.

John 10:9 (Amp) [9] I am the Door; anyone who enters in through Me will be saved (will live). He will come in and he will go out [freely], and will find pasture.

Jesus said that He is the door in which we enter. In John, He said anyone. It does not implicate that you must have certain attire in order to come to Jesus. In finding Jesus, we enter, and then, we go out freely and find our pasture. There are many

Christians today who may be saved but are dead inside, and they are not growing because they are not giving God 100%. We need to look at this in depth because in order to begin to reap the benefits of being a Christian, we must be willing to surrender everything to God. We see that we need to "come as we are". Jesus did not say you need to get rid of all the sin in your life first and then come. No, He just said to come. I have ministered to those who have no problem letting you know that they know they need God in their life, and they know their life is messed up. They know they are living in sin; however, when it comes to taking that step forward, why do they stop? Before we go any further, answer these questions honestly.

1) Are you willing to surrender all to God? _____
2) Are you willing to go where God wants you, to whatever church He leads you, knowing that if you are obedient, God will meet you half way? _____
3) Are you willing to step out of your box and open up to a leader in the church where God sends you, in order to reveal your sin, so that God can begin to deliver you from whatever addictions you struggle with? _____
4) Are you willing to go forward, despite your past experiences, with whatever church or denomination which influenced you to give up and have a bad outlook on the churches as a whole? _____
5) Are you willing to be open-minded enough to explore the possibility of perhaps another denomination other than what you have been taught from childhood? _____
6) Make a list of every area of your life which needs deliverance *(this will be any addictions to drugs, alcohol, sexual addictions, or any sin which has you bound and controls your life in a bad way)*.

_____
_____
_____
_____
_____

Many of us spend too much time comparing ourselves to others when all we need to do is allow Jesus in, and let Him begin a complete makeover of our whole being. God made you unique. He does not want you to be like someone else. God just wants us to be ourselves, and allow Him to transform us into what He created us to be. We need to stop looking at the world as our examples, such as:

• The way we should dress in order to come to church
• What kind of job we should strive for
• Who we should marry
• How we should act
• What we should say

Every day, we make a mess of our lives. By the time we come to our Creator, He has a lot of work to do. God has to begin by bringing us back to the beginning. From there, He begins the transformation within us.

How much time and money have we spent, trying to make ourselves be something that we are not? After going through the process of trying to transform ourselves to be more like the world, we later come to realize, this is not who we are. I know in my past, I spent a lot of money trying to look like I had money that I did not have. I did this in order to impress people that I thought were important. I spent a lot of money trying to be in the right places in order to be somebody that I was not. I lied in order to make others think something about me that was not even true, and I know that I am not alone here because my girlfriends were all doing the same thing. Today, millions of dollars are spent on trying to look like someone else, be like someone else, and to portray to be something that we are not. Instead of living a lie, we just need to go before our Father and say, *"God, show me how to love me."* That is it! When we allow the Father to come in and show us who we can be because He is the One who created us in the first place, we may actually love ourselves! In fact, I know you will love yourself. When we stop spending foolish money on trying to accomplish things that we were never meant to accomplish and allow God to lead us, we will find our way. Then, we will see that His way was better than all those other paths we tried in our past, and God's way will not cost you the time, money, and energy that you have spent on trying to do something that was not you. You see, when we follow God's path, He also will provide everything we need to accomplish the task. God will provide the finances, time, and energy. You will blossom and have that inner peace and tranquility that you would never have known doing it your way. Here is an example, in Matthew, of all we need to do. Jesus gave a parable about a wedding banquet.

Matthew 22:1-10 (Amp) ¹*AND AGAIN Jesus spoke to them in parables (comparisons, stories used to illustrate and explain), saying,* ²*The kingdom of heaven is like a king who gave a wedding banquet for his son* ³*And sent his servants to summon those who had been invited to the wedding banquet, but they refused to come.* ⁴*Again he sent other servants, saying, Tell those who are invited, Behold, I have prepared my banquet; my bullocks and my fat calves are killed, and everything is prepared; come to the wedding feast.* ⁵*But they were not concerned and paid no attention [they ignored and made light of the summons, treating it with contempt] and they went away--one to his farm, another to his business,* ⁶*While the others seized his servants, treated them shamefully, and put them to death.* ⁷*[Hearing this] the king was infuriated; and he sent his soldiers and put those murderers to death and burned their city.* ⁸*Then he said to his servants, The wedding [feast] is prepared, but those invited were not worthy.* ⁹*So go to the thoroughfares where they leave the city [where the main roads and those from the country end] and invite to the wedding feast as many as* *you find.* *¹⁰And those servants went out on the crossroads and got together as many as they found, both bad and good, so [the room in which] the wedding feast [was held] was filled with guests.*

What does this tell us? This parable shows us who exactly is invited to the feast. This is a comparison of what heaven is like and how God sees things. Those who thought they were too good were not interested in this banquet. Maybe, they were too busy, or perhaps, there was a movie they were planning on watching. Perhaps, there was another party they wanted to attend with their friends, or maybe, they wanted to go shopping. Maybe, they were planning a trip somewhere, but for whatever reason, they were not interested in this so-called "banquet". They were already in a clique with the right kind of people and did not know this guy very well. Besides, this banquet just did not interest them. The king told his servants to go into the streets and find any who wanted to come. Who showed up? Those who were good and bad, according to the story, came to the banquet. The guests included those who may not have had much, the insecure, sinners, and those who the world looked at as nobodies, but it did not matter who they were because the king invited them to come. Here is the deal, Jesus died for those who know they need Him. He died for those who would come – just come. Jesus did not say you have to have money. He did not say that you have to be that person with a great personality. He did not say that you have to be full of life. He did not say to clean up your life first. Jesus just said come, and that is it! There is a banquet, and we are the guests of honor. Today, Jesus just wants you to put down your pride, cast down those thoughts which make you feel defeated, and allow Him to dress you in the finest for the feast at the banquet of your Father in Heaven. Allow Jesus to come in and remake you on the inside to be who you were created to be today!

Straddling the Fence

Why should we give up our life and come to the Lord? We have a free will. We can continue to gratify our flesh and do whatever it is that we enjoy doing. Why would we want to die to self? I believe if you are reading this today and engaged in trying to live in both worlds, you are not completely content. If you really loved your sinful nature and those things which gratify your flesh, you would not be trying to keep one foot on the side of the fence which leads to heaven. However, I believe when you are straddling the fence, and you know if that is you, you really desire that stronger commitment and stronger relationship with the Father. Although, many times, we do not know how to step over completely to the side which will bring us into a world full of blessings and excitement. Today, I will lead you to the place where, once and for all, you can make that choice to climb over to the light and away from darkness.

John 12:47 (Amp) ⁴⁷*If anyone hears My teachings and fails to observe them [does not keep them, but disregards them], it is not I who judges him. For I have not come to judge and to condemn and to pass sentence and to inflict penalty on the world, but to save the world.*

Jesus said in John that He came not to judge the world but to save it. When we continue to live according to our own free will, doing all those things our flesh enjoys, we bring condemnation upon ourselves. Condemnation is what makes us feel unworthy. It makes us feel that we are not good enough to come to the Father. Many times, this condemnation is what keeps us from pulling away from the world, but Jesus did not come to condemn you. However, the enemy wants to condemn you because he can keep you in a state of feeling unworthy. When we feel unworthy, we will run from the Father deeper into the world where the enemy can keep us defeated. If we run to the Father, we will receive forgiveness and love.

Romans 8:1(NIV) **¹***Therefore, there is now no condemnation for those who are in Christ Jesus,*

There is so much revelation in *John 10:10* below. Through this Scripture, we need to realize that the thief/satan wants to destroy our existence. He is a liar, and he will keep you defeated. satan will keep you bound until you make that decision with your own free will that you are tired of your life like it is. He will keep you bound until you decide that you are ready to give God a 100%!

John 10:10 (Amp) **¹⁰***The thief comes only in order to steal and kill and destroy. I came that they may have and enjoy life, and have it in abundance (to the full, till it overflows).*

Here is what I want to show you. Those who are trying to live with one foot in the church and one foot in the world, though, they have a free will to chose to do whatever it is they desire, their choice to remain in sin actually keeps them in bondage. We are only free when we live in the Truth and not in a lie. We know that the Word of God is the Truth, and in John, it says that knowing the Truth is what sets us free.

John 8:32 (NIV) **³²***"Then you will know the truth, and the truth will set you free."*

When we make those decisions to try to live in both worlds, we are listening to a lie from the enemy. satan does not want us free; he wants to keep us in bondage.

Romans 1:25 (Amp) ²⁵*Because they exchanged the truth of God for a lie and worshiped and served the creature rather than the Creator, Who is blessed forever! Amen (so be it).*

According to Romans, when we make choices knowing that it is not what God wants us to do, we have exchanged the Truth of God for a lie from satan. We make these choices when we go to church pretending that we are Christians and then go back into the world to act like the world. We cannot serve God and satan both. In Galatians, Paul warns us, as children of God, we are called to be free not bound. When we indulge in sinful nature knowingly, eventually it will catch up with us.

Galatians 5:13-15 (NIV) ¹³*You, my brothers, were called to be free. But do not use your freedom to indulge the sinful nature; rather, serve one another in love.* ¹⁴*The entire law is summed up in a single command: "Love your neighbor as yourself."* ¹⁵*If you keep on biting and devouring each other, watch out or you will be destroyed by each other.*

Therefore, we are not free when we are living in sin. We are only free when we are walking with God. When we are in sin, we will be judged by the law. If we use that freedom in Christ to indulge in sinful nature, rather than to serve and to love, we will be destroyed. There are many who indulge in sin on a daily basis and believe as long as they pray each day or maybe pray weekly to be forgiven, they can continue to indulge in what gratifies their flesh. This is not so. If you fall in this category, you are using that freedom to live to satisfy self and not to serve. The Scripture says we are to serve one another. We must learn to serve before we can lead. To serve one another, we must die to self. How can a servant be to his master all his master desires if the servant's main focus is towards himself? The Word says that we cannot serve two masters, for we will either hate the one and love the other.

Matthew 6:24 (NIV)[24] "No one can serve two masters. Either he will hate the one and love the other, or he will be devoted to the one and despise the other. You cannot serve both God and Money."

Why then should we put away that sinful nature once and for all? Why should we climb completely over that fence to serve only the one master? In John, it says for those who make that choice to believe totally in Jesus, totally trusting the Father, will not face judgment. The enemy will not be able to condemn those who are sold out for Jesus.

John 3:18 (Amp) [18] He who believes in Him [who clings to, trusts in, relies on Him] is not judged [he who trusts in Him never comes up for judgment; for him there is no rejection, no condemnation--he incurs no damnation]; but he who does not believe (cleave to, rely on, trust in Him) is judged already [he has already been convicted and has already received his sentence] because he has not believed in and trusted in the name of the only begotten Son of God. [He is condemned for refusing to let his trust rest in Christ's name.]

We know that there is no condemnation for those who believe. If you are straddling the fence, you continually face condemnation. You continually will feel, as though, you are not good enough. When things go wrong in your life, you contemplate if it happened because of what you did last night or at another time. However, if you climb that fence to serve only the one Master, the condemnation is going to go. You will rise up to know that you are in right standing with the Father, and there is no condemnation because you believe!

John 3:18 (NIV) ¹⁸Whoever believes in him is not condemned, but whoever does not believe stands condemned already because he has not believed in the name of God's one and only Son.

We have to come to the place where we are honest with ourselves in answering this question, *"What keeps you from climbing over that fence and serving the one true Master of all Masters?"* I'm sure there would be many answers to this question, and only you can answer it about yourself. However, if you are a believer trying to serve our Father and still have one foot in the world, I believe that there has to be something there that will not let you walk away from God. I believe God is working on you and desires that you wake up before it is too late. In this world we live in, we all recognize that there is light and darkness. Those who continually practice doing those things which are good are operating in the light; however, those who continually practice doing evil are living in darkness. Many times, we do not see ourselves as operating in darkness because we feel that our sin does not fall on the level of being evil. However, the question to ask would be does your sin condemn you? Do we feel that guilt associated with sin?

John 3:19-21 (Amp) ¹⁹The [basis of the] judgment (indictment, the test by which men are judged, the ground for the sentence) lies in this: the Light has come into the world, and people have loved the darkness rather than and more than the Light, for their works (deeds) were evil. ²⁰For every wrongdoer hates (loathes, detests) the Light, and will not come out into the Light but shrinks from it, lest his works (his deeds, his activities, his conduct) be exposed and reproved. ²¹But he who practices truth [who does what is right] comes out into the Light; so that his works may be plainly shown to be what they are--wrought with God [divinely prompted, done with God's help, in dependence upon Him].

satan will try to deceive us in believing that whatever little sin we may be continually walking in, is not enough to be concerned. However, to God all sin is sin, and there is no gray area but only black and white. If it is contrary to His Word, it is sin. Like I said, we will only be completely free when we no longer feel that guilt of condemnation in our lives. There may be times we try and miss it; we try again and miss it. I was ministering to someone who said that it did not matter how hard they tried to be like Jesus, they could not do it. My response to them was to stop trying! God never expected us to walk this walk alone. When we try to do something and find ourselves struggling, our problem is that we are trying to do it in ourselves. The reason we came to the Lord in the first place is because we realized that we needed a Savoir, and we realized that we needed someone to help us walk this walk. We need a savior to show us how to walk it, talk it, and conquer this world. If you are struggling, go to our Father and say, *"Lord, I cannot do this; I need you to show me how!"* That is all God wants us to do anyway, trust in Him with our whole might! Remember, Jesus said that it was better for Him to go because the comforter would come. The comforter is the Holy Spirit who will walk this walk with us. He will remind us of all truths and teach us all things. The Holy Spirit is the one who will show us how to climb that fence and make that decision to serve the one Master.

Galatians 5:16-18(NIV) *[16]So I say, live by the Spirit, and you will not gratify the desires of the sinful nature. [17]For the sinful nature desires what is contrary to the Spirit, and the Spirit what is contrary to the sinful nature. They are in conflict with each other, so that you do not do what you want. [18]But if you are led by the Spirit, you are not under law.*

When we walk with the Father, we know the Holy Spirit is with us, and it is no longer a struggle. We will live by the Spirit and not gratify the desires of the sinful nature. If you are living by what you desire, then you are not being led by the Spirit, and your life will be a struggle. I remember getting back in church and beginning my life again after being backslidden. There was one area where I was in sin, and I justified this because to me, it was not in the Word of God. Literally, I could justify that it was not in the Word; however, in a sense it was. The point I want to make is that when I began to focus my life on Jesus and not those things of the world, which may at some time have gratified my flesh, all of a sudden that desire just left me. It was that simple. I do share further back on this subject to a greater degree; however, my point is if you are weak in an area of your life and continually struggle trying to have control in that area, do not be surprised if after you begin to draw close to God, the desire leaves you. Take smoking for instance, you begin walking close to God, and one day, you notice that the desire is gone. Would that be a bad thing? If it is something you struggle with, it does not matter to God. God did not say for you to struggle with anything, just give it to Him. All of a sudden, you will realize that the desire just left, just like that. If you are ready for some peace and you desire to let go of your past, or those things which bring you condemnation, then ask yourself where does God fit in? Do we continually do what we want and not what God wants? Are we being led by the Holy Spirit, or do we just make our own rules as we go?

Galatians 5:19-21(NIV)[19]The acts of the sinful nature are obvious: sexual immorality, impurity and debauchery; [20]idolatry and witchcraft; hatred, discord, jealousy, fits of rage, selfish ambition, dissensions, factions [21]and envy; drunkenness, orgies, and the like. I warn you, as I did before, that those who live like this will not inherit the kingdom of God.

We can see what sinful nature is. You may say, *"I am married, and there is no sexual immorality in my life; I do not have any idols; there is no hatred in my life or jealousy, and there are no fits of rage or selfish ambitions of any kind."* You may believe that you do not fall into any of these categories, but anything you put before God is your idol. If you spend time doing anything and do not give time to God, then you have idols in your life. If you live according to the world, always wanting what someone else has, then you covet what your neighbor has. This will be discussed in another series to a greater degree, but for now, we need to look at where God fits into our lives? If you are not living according to God's commandments, then you are living according to the flesh which is sin, and the result of sin is death.

Romans 6:23 (NIV) [23]*For the wages of sin is death, but the gift of God is eternal life in Christ Jesus our Lord.*

We have to make a decision that we are sold out for God 100%. We are not going to live trying to be a Christian sometimes and not other times. I believe that it is crucial to see what the world will miss out on, and for those who diligently seek God, what benefits will be received. In Matthew, this is a conversation between Jesus and Peter.

Matthew 16:16-17 (Amp) [16]*Simon Peter replied, You are the Christ, the Son of the living God.* [17]*Then Jesus answered him, Blessed (happy, fortunate, and to be envied) are you, Simon Bar-Jonah. For flesh and blood [men] have not revealed this to you, but My Father Who is in heaven.*

Jesus asked His disciples who they say that He is. Peter replied that He was the Son of God. Then Jesus replied back, and He told Peter that he was blessed because he knew this only

212

because His Father had revealed it to him. We need to ask ourselves, how do we know that Jesus is the Son of God? If we believe this because of something a man or flesh and blood has revealed to us, then we do not really know nor do we understand. When we pray for salvation and go before the Father to repent of our sins, we then ask Jesus to come into our heart. However, is it heartfelt? Do we believe this deep within? Your words are meaningless to God because He is a God of action. The only way we can believe that Jesus is the Son of God is if the Father revealed this to us. This is the only way. Jesus knew Peter's heart. He knew that Peter had that heartfelt relationship deep within. Jesus knew Peter's heart was right because he had an encounter with God, and God revealed to Peter who Jesus was. When we are ready to be saved, we first come to the place where we realize that we cannot do this in ourselves. We realize that we can no longer walk in this life without a greater power. We begin searching, *"God, are you real?"* We begin seeking for that revelation to know the Father. It is during this place in our lives when our salvation will be heartfelt! It is at that point in our lives that we know this is real. We seek, and we find. We continue seeking until we find. *(Luke 11:9)* We need to go back to the day when we prayed for salvation and repented of our sins. We need to ask ourselves, *"Was there a change within on that day? Did we feel different? Did we feel God's presence?"* All of this matters because we do not need to go through life unsure of our relationship with God.

I remember in my own walk I married into a family who were all church goers and most went regularly. They did not all walk the walk outside of church, but they regularly went to church. I remember feeling the pressure to go forward and say the prayer to be saved. I remember the pressure of the pastor coming to the house to witness to me, and finally, I did go forward to recite the sinner's prayer. I felt no different; however, I consistently went to church believing that was what I was supposed to do. I believed that I was saved because I was told that I was. No one told me that I should feel something different. Not long after that, tragedy happened in my life. I was faced with my second miscarriage. The first miscarriage was prior to going forward to say the sinner's prayer; however, this second time, I believed that I was saved because I was told that I was. I remember being by myself and crying out to God, *"This is not fair; how could You take my child?"* I was saved now, how could He do this? It was at that time, when I cried out to God, I finally felt His presence in my life. It was not by the words which came out of my mouth the day that I walked forward, but it was the words which cried out to God in my time of trouble that acknowledged I knew He existed. In my hour of need and pain, I believed there was a God and believed Jesus died for me. From that day forward, I never doubted that My God was real. From that day forward, God revealed Himself to me in greater degrees many times, and my walk with Him continued to grow. You may have experienced something similar, where you cried out to the Father and then knew that He answered you. God is who revealed to you that He was real, and through His Word that Jesus was real. I have heard many testimonies of those who were at a place in their lives where they questioned if God was real. In a time when they needed him, they would cry out, and His presence would become real. If you desire to feel this and really know that God is who He says He is, cry out to Him in your hour of need. If you want to feel His presence bad enough, He will meet you half way, but do not go through life having a mediocre Christian walk. We should expect a dynamic and exciting Christian walk, it is our choice. The Word says that we do not receive what we ask for because it is for the wrong motives.

James 4:3 (NIV) ³When you ask, you do not receive, because you ask with wrong motives, that you may spend what you get on your pleasures.

If you desire to feel God's presence and want more of Him in your life, He will meet you half way. This is not a selfish or self motivated prayer when we ask for something which will glorify God. If your motives are right, you will receive it. In reading John, you need to ask yourself, *"Who do you desire to receive praise from?"* Are our motives to receive praise from an employer or perhaps our spouse? Are our motives to receive praise from our friends and family? When you line up your way of thinking to what the Word of God says, the way the world sees you will no longer matter. Our desires will be to know God is looking down upon us, and He is smiling because He sees that our hearts, motivations, and desires are right.

John 5:44 (Amp) ⁴⁴How is it possible for you to believe [how can you learn to believe], you who [are content to seek and] receive praise and honor and glory from one another, and yet do not seek the praise and honor and glory which come from Him Who alone is God?

Have you met Jesus at the cross and surrendered everything to Him? Does your life show the world that you are a believer in the Most High God?

Making Excuses

Excuses are something that we have become very good at in life. If we do not feel like doing something because our flesh does not want to participate, we have every excuse in the book memorized in order to get out of doing what we would rather not do. We make up excuses when a friend or family may need us to help them with a project. We make up excuses when we really are not interested in doing something with someone else. We make up excuses to get out of doing something that would help someone or help a good cause. Why do so many of us feel that we have to make up excuses? Why are we not honest with ourselves and others by admitting that we just do not want to do something? When we are asked to do something we would rather not do, we make excuses in order to justify why we did not do what was asked. I believe that many times it is not a matter of not being honest with others but not being honest with ourselves. Many times, we refrain from doing those things which would be good for us. Many times, we avoid getting involved or giving too much of our time because we are afraid of facing the truth. Our reasons for not going through with something has to do with many times, just not having the motivation. Some of us would not admit it, but we are actually too lazy to conquer that which we should strive for. There are thousands of excuses, and if our flesh decides it just does not want to participate, it will pull an excuse out of the book – that simple! Let's do away with the excuses. This is a bad habit which will get us nowhere. We need to make a stand today that we will not allow excuses to rule our lives. Think about it this way, if there is something that you really want to do, you will find a way to do it. We know this to be true. Nothing stands in our way if there is something that we have a desire to do. So with the excuses thrown out the window, let us begin looking at this walk with God differently. What do we desire? Think about this and answer the questions below.

1) What is it that you do not like about your life currently?
   _____

2) If you could change any one thing in your life, what would it be? _____

3) What do you believe keeps you from striving to reach that one goal in your life? _____

4) Deep down inside, do you really desire that one on one walk with God? _____

satan would love to keep you bound with all those excuses, and sometimes, our excuses may be legitimate. However, most of the time they are just excuses. Today, we are going to touch base on some of the most frequently used excuses which keep us right where satan wants us, away from the blessings of God. Many would say that they feel disappointed in the churches today. You may have walked into a church needing to feel the presence of God. You may have reached out really wanting that relationship, growth, and connection. However, when you walked into the church, you felt nothing different by the time you left. Perhaps, the church felt cold, or perhaps, it seemed to be no different from the world. In Revelation, it speaks of the churches today. Just like with anything, there are those who may be on fire for the Lord and those who have fallen, forgetting their first love. Let's look at the seven churches which are spoken about in Revelation. Every church in this world today, falls into one of these categories. When God is calling you to be connected, it does matter where you are connected. We should not just assume, as long as we walk through the doors of a church today, this is the place God has put us.

Revelation 2:2-4 (NIV) ^{2}I know your deeds, your hard work and your perseverance. I know that you cannot tolerate wicked men, that you have tested those who claim to be apostles but are not, and have found them false. ^{3}You have persevered and have endured hardships for my name, and have not grown weary. ^{4}Yet I hold this against you: You have forsaken your first love.

Here, we see a church which seems to be doing everything right. This is a very active church going about doing the Lord's work. This is all good, but what does God hold against them? This church has forgotten their first love. What is our first love? That is Jesus. Jesus is the reason we can have eternal life, the reason we are able to go before the Father, and the reason that we have the ability to live an abundant life. What happened to this church? Sometimes, we get so busy doing works, we forget our purpose. God does not want us to be too busy that we do not take time out to worship, give praise, and honor the One who created us and the One who sent us. We must remember that God gave each of us gifts to do the works in the first place, but those gifts are to benefit His Kingdom. There have been times in my walk that I became so excited with where God was leading me, I just took off and ran and ran and ran. Eventually, we will all be faced with a test and may fall. The reason is that when we get so carried away with our calling and a test comes, we are not strong enough to fight and weather that storm. Our strength comes from the Lord, and if we are not drawing on that strength daily, we will fall. When we go about putting everything into our works, we stop spending those intimate times with our Father, and we stop seeking and learning of Jesus in order to walk imitating the One who sent us. We must remember that Christ sent all of us into the world to continue doing what He began. If we do not spend time where the anointing is, we will only operate in the flesh. When I get too busy doing works that I no longer feel the presence as strong, I get still before the Lord because I realize that I missed it somewhere. It is during these times in which God has been waiting for me to slow down, come to Him, and just listen – not talk but listen. Many times, it is not that we are doing anything wrong but that God is trying to teach us something.

Revelation 2:9 (NIV) *⁹I know your afflictions and your poverty—yet you are rich! I know the slander of those who say they are Jews and are not, but are a synagogue of Satan. ¹⁰Do not be afraid of what you are about to suffer. I tell you, the devil will put some of you in prison to test you, and you will suffer persecution for ten days. Be faithful, even to the point of death, and I will give you the crown of life.*

This church suffers from afflictions and poverty, yet they are rich. This church is doing everything right. They may not have a huge building that shows great wealth; however, inside they are rich. This is to show us that it is not about what a church has on the outside; however, this is not to say that God will not bless a church to rise to be great in order to glorify Him. We should never judge by the outward appearance because we can be deceived. Many today want to go to the biggest churches and those which seem to be covered by wealth according to appearances. What is on the outside is not what makes the church, just as what is on the outside of a person is not what makes the person. We have all heard not to judge a book by its cover, and I believe that is a great comparison when we are seeking God for direction. It goes on to say that this church is encouraged to continue being faithful, but they are warned they will face persecution and tests. However, by their faithfulness, they will endure to the end. Do not judge a church by its cover. Until we walk in a church and experience what is on the inside, we do not know that church at all.

Revelation 2:13-14 (NIV) [13]I know where you live—where Satan has his throne. Yet you remain true to my name. You did not renounce your faith in me, even in the days of Antipas, my faithful witness, who was put to death in your city—where Satan lives. [14]Nevertheless, I have a few things against you: You have people there who hold to the teaching of Balaam, who taught Balak to entice the Israelites to sin by eating food sacrificed to idols and by committing sexual immorality.

This church is faithful. They stand firm on claiming what they believe; however, there are those members that are wicked and influencing those on the inside to sin. This is probably seen more in the churches than we may know. Yes, there are those who attend church regularly and engage in sin outside of church. When these become planted firmly within the churches, they are leading astray those on the inside. What fault is this of the church? Many times, it is because the church is not teaching the full gospel. If a church is teaching messages of truth, sin will not be able to remain. If churches today teach the Truth, regardless if it offends, convicts, or condemns those hearing the message, those who are willfully living in sin will make a choice to repent and come clean, or they will look for another church that does not make them feel guilty. If someone feels condemnation because of truth coming from the Word of God, then they are allowing satan to condemn them. On the other hand, if they are convicted and repent, that Truth spoken may have saved them from eternal fire. Let me say this again, we have gotten too comfortable with our sins today. It is the churches responsibility to bring the whole truth of the Word of God not just part of it. People do not want to hear that they are in sin if they engage in sex outside of marriage. People do not want to hear that they are in sin if they are not tithing. However, if the church is not preaching the whole gospel, then that church is in sin and will be held responsible. I can tell you that when a pastor preaches a sermon that people do not want to hear, the following week attendance will drop. Those who felt uncomfortable are living that sin and do not want to change their lives. Those who are willfully living in their sins would rather find a church that makes them feel good about themselves, but why bother going to church if you are not being taught the whole truth? Why would we want to pretend that we are doing what God has called us to do when, in fact, our sin will find us out eventually? If we are not living under the blood of Jesus, we will be judged according to the law? We will never receive the blessings that God intended for us if we keep running from Him and run to a false sense of worship. If it is not all God, than it is not God at all.

Revelation 2:19-20 (NIV) [19]*I know your deeds, your love and faith, your service and perseverance, and that you are now doing more than you did at first.* [20]*Nevertheless, I have this against you: You tolerate that woman Jezebel, who calls herself a prophetess. By her teaching she misleads my servants into sexual immorality and the eating of food sacrificed to idols.*

This again is much of what we discussed with the previous church. This church does many deeds and services; they love the Lord and are faithful. They are evidently growing because it says that they are doing more than in the beginning. However, they put up with sin and immorality in their congregation. Also, we see that they tolerate idols. What are idols in our lives today? Idols are anything which take up our time to the extent that we are not doing what God called us to do. When we engage in doing those things to that extent, we are feeding our inner man with things which produce bad fruit and not that which is good. This should be evident in the churches today. What type of fruit are the churches producing today? As Christians, we should be producing fruit which is good. Good to God is anything which edifies and lifts Him up, such as obeying all the commandments, taking care of those who cannot take care of themselves, helping the church grow to reach the community, and to share Jesus in every avenue which is available through the church, community, and nations.

Revelation 3:1-2 (NIV) ... I know your deeds; you have a reputation of being alive, but you are dead. [2]*Wake up! Strengthen what remains and is about to die, for I have not found your deeds complete in the sight of my God.*

221

This is very evident in a church today. There may be a church which puts on a show with great advertisement, many members who have been there for many years, and a lot of attention in the community. However, when you walk into this church, there is no life. There is no presence of the Holy Spirit; there is no presence of being active in deeds in the community, and there is no evidence of bringing Jesus to the world within this church. This church is cold, and it is dead. There is no fruit which edifies God.

Revelation 3:8 (NIV) [8]I know your deeds. See, I have placed before you an open door that no one can shut. I know that you have little strength, yet you have kept my word and have not denied my name.

This church is doing everything right and doing it with little strength. We gain strength with numbers. This could be a small church which is doing amazing things with what little they have to operate with. We see that God is pleased and will bless this church greatly.

Revelation 3:15-17 (NIV) [15]I know your deeds, that you are neither cold nor hot. I wish you were either one or the other! [16]So, because you are lukewarm—neither hot nor cold—I am about to spit you out of my mouth. [17]You say, 'I am rich; I have acquired wealth and do not need a thing.' But you do not realize that you are wretched, pitiful, poor, blind and naked.

To God, He would rather you be either cold or hot but not lukewarm. What does this tell us about this church? We see that this church has become wealthy according to the world's standards, but to God, they are poor and blinded. What is the difference in a church being cold and one being lukewarm? A church, that is cold, does not have truth within them at all because they have never received the truth in areas where needed; therefore, they do not have that fire within them to grow in the Lord. Yes, they may believe in God and believe in Jesus, but they do not have that one on one relationship with the Father which brings that dynamic fire inside of them that cannot be contained. However, if a church is lukewarm, this means they have had a touch of knowing enough truth and chose not to walk in it. They chose to walk according to their ways and not God. Many times, we learn something new and then decide to incorporate it into our way of thinking by changing it. Man likes to be in charge. It is our nature, and this is what we see with a church that is lukewarm. Everything within the church is conducted according to man and not God. This is not God's church; it belongs to man. These churches may have faithful members that are all about helping to grow the church but for what reasons? They continue to expand and continue to have different programs popping up everywhere; however, what are their motives? This is where we must look at the fruit which is being produced. The church should be on fire for the Lord, and the fruits should be evident by the seeds they are planting. Is the church planting into the Kingdom of Heaven, or is the church planting seeds into the growth of that ministry? This is a tough question. If they are planting seeds into the Kingdom of Heaven, what must we see? We will see the church going forth to bring Jesus to the world, but it will not be about growing their church. If the church is doing what God called them to do, they will sustain and be blessed, and God will be the One who grows their ministry. You can always tell the fruit by those who are leading. What do their lives speak outside of church? Is it all about the church or about Jesus? Do their lives proclaim victory and peace? How do they walk through their storms?

I believe we should all agree that we are able to see a clearer vision of churches today. With this new acquired knowledge, we also need to put away our excuses of not attending church based on our opinions of those churches we have attended. There are many churches out there today and many denominations. My suggestion would be to find a church which teaches the full gospel, meaning that they study in depth all of the Word of God not just part of it. If you want to grow and want to be fed properly, then you need to explore the options out there. According to Revelation, all churches are not the same. We should not assume because of a bad experience this is the case. We should test the spirits.

1 John 4:1 (NIV) *[1]Dear friends, do not believe every spirit, but test the spirits to see whether they are from God, because many false prophets have gone out into the world.*

Another excuse used many times for not making that step forward with God are those who say, *"I am just not ready to make that commitment; one day I will take that step but not today!"* Sadly, many have said this, and that day never came. Life many times ends tragically with no time to make things right with our Creator. As long as you feel this way, satan will make sure that your day to get things right will never come. He will continually put obstacles in your path to keep you from making that decision. When I was out in the world for 15 years there were times I made up the same excuse, waiting for the right day to come. However, that day was not going to just happen. I can tell you that satan continually put things in my path to keep me in a place where I felt defeated and felt there was no way out, but there was a way out. My mind was being programmed to believe all those lies the world tells. Remember, the creator of those lies has every person in bondage, one way or another, just like he had me. Are you ever concerned with a thought such as, *"What if I do not make that choice?"*

Psalm 55:19 (Amp) [19]*God will hear and humble them, even He Who abides of old--Selah [pause, and calmly think of that]!--because in them there has been no change [of heart], and they do not fear, revere, and worship God.*

We need to think on this because the day will come that many will regret not having that change of heart. We know there is no straddling the fence. We either worship God, or we worship this world.

There are other excuses, which are used many times such as − no transportation to church and working on the days of church services. To address these excuses, I would like to say that God knows your heart. If it is a real excuse and you are sincere about stepping out to make that commitment, God will open a door. Here, are some solutions − if it is transportation, many times if another church member is aware of this they would be more than happy to pick you up. Many times, I have gone out of my way to pick up those who needed a ride, and I have done so gladly knowing that I was serving which is what it is all about. If it is your job keeping you from being able to connect to a church, I too had a job in which I worked every Sunday. Finally, I made the decision to cut back my hours because I had the authority to do this. However, a few weeks down the road, the owner respectively told me that he had to have someone there that day. I resigned because this was not a permanent position. Within a few weeks, I was called and rehired with an agreement on how much time I could give. God does not always just open doors, sometimes He closes doors, and when this happens, another door will open. If you pray and believe for a way, God will provide that way.

We must make the decision to come now and not allow anything to stop us. No excuses, no circumstances, or situations can keep you from serving God if you are determined. Jesus said that whoever trusts and relies on Him will never be hungry or thirst. We will not hunger for anything; our needs will be met. Ask yourself, are you trusting in the Lord today, or do you invest your trust in the world? The world will leave you empty; Jesus will fill you up.

John 6:35 (Amp) [35]Jesus replied, I am the Bread of Life. He who comes to Me will never be hungry, and he who believes in and cleaves to and trusts in and relies on Me will never thirst any more (at any time).

Do you sometimes feel rejection from the world? Jesus said He would never reject anyone who comes to Him.

John 6:37 (Amp) [37]All whom My Father gives (entrusts) to Me will come to Me; and the one who comes to Me I will most certainly not cast out [I will never, no never, reject one of them who comes to Me].

Remember, Paul said that Jesus died for all, not for some. Jesus died so that we would live for Him and not for ourselves!

2 Corinthians 5:15 (Amp) [15]And He died for all, so that all those who live might live no longer to and for themselves, but to and for Him Who died and was raised again for their sake.

God was not being selfish wanting us to live like Jesus and not like ourselves. On the contrary, in the beginning, God created a perfect world that man messed up. Even though, we messed it up, God loved us so much that He is still fighting today to redeem His children. However, as long as we live in our sin, it will produce bad fruit in our lives. Look around at your life right now. We need to stop for a moment and write down everything that is wrong in our lives currently.

_____

_____

_____

_____

_____

_____

_____

Now ask yourself, if you knew making that choice to live without sin would fix all these things you just listed, would you desire to walk with God in order to learn how to do this? It is that simple. People try to make it hard, but where is our motivation? Our motivation has the power to be able to change those things on our list. Our motivation should be in the assurance that those things which are currently causing stress, affliction, depression, and infirmities to bombard our lives will completely turn around when we submit to our Father. Jesus just said to come and rest; He will give us rest. Are you ready to allow Jesus into your life completely?

Matthew 11:28 (NIV) [28] *"Come to me, all you who are weary and burdened, and I will give you rest."*

Jesus died for all, and if you know you have sin in your life and you are not living right, come as you are. You may be hurting emotionally, physically, or even spiritually, but Jesus died for those who recognize they are not righteous. He died for those who know they are sinners and need Him in their life. Jesus said in Luke that He did not come to call the righteous but to call those who are not free from sin. If you have emotional scars or physical scars, Jesus is your answer. If you are not where you need to be spiritually, Jesus is your answer.

Luke 5:32 (Amp) [32]I have not come to arouse and invite and call the righteous, but the erring ones (those not free from sin) to repentance [to change their minds for the better and heartily to amend their ways, with abhorrence of their past sins].

Do not wait for something drastic to change before you make the decision to seek God. If that is what you are waiting for, satan will see to it that it never happens. Come as you are. It does not matter if you have an alcohol or drug problem. It does not matter if you are living in sexual sin or what your current circumstances are. If you are saying that you need peace in your life, blessings, or a change in your life, Jesus is the answer! Give God a chance! I have heard many people say, *"You do not know what you are asking me to do; I cannot do what you are asking."* When in reality, I have never asked anyone to do anything. If someone reaches out to me and begins to share their problems, and they want my prayers, I give them the answer. The answer is Jesus. I am not telling anyone what they have to do, but I am sharing Jesus because He is the solution. It is not my place to tell someone to stop drinking or using drugs, and it is not my place to tell someone to stop living in their current sin. It is not my place to tell someone to leave their spouse or to get out of the relationship they are in, but if they open up to me for prayer, I will let them know Jesus is the answer. It is not my place to make the choice for their current situation, but if they ask for answers, I can lead them to the truth; I can lead them to Jesus. Jesus only expects us to meet Him half way. He cannot begin to work in our life when we will not step forward and come. The answer is to stop looking at your circumstances and begin to look at God. I have had people call me on Sunday morning hung over from a bad night, and I would ask them to come to church. Now notice – they called me! People in the world do not call me unless they want to hear the truth, and then when I give them the truth, they reject it. The response I got one Sunday morning was, *"You do not want me coming looking like I do!"* I did not ask how they looked, and Jesus never said when you come to Him, make sure that you have had a good night's sleep, you are properly groomed, and above all, make sure it is not a night that you missed it. He did not say to make sure that it is not a night that you got drunk or committed a sin before you come to church. Jesus just said to come; that is all He said! It does not matter what the church says. If there is anyone that looks at you with judgment because you walk in a mess, then that is something that God will deal with on their part because they missed it. You get out of bed and meet Jesus half way. Jesus did not say for you to change things in your life first. He knows that you will not be able to make those changes by yourself. If you could, then you would not need Him. It does not matter if you are hanging out with sinful people, drug dealers, prostitutes, etc. Jesus never asked you to give up your friends, but what happens when we meet Jesus half way? We just come and show up at church. We begin to listen, and maybe, we go back to the way we were living. The next Sunday, we do it again. We come as we are; we leave and go back to our life. This begins to become a habit of meeting Jesus and going home, but what happens next? As God begins to minister to your spirit, things begin to click inside. Then you begin to notice that you think differently. You begin to look at things differently, and gradually, some of your desires for those things which were sin begin to leave. We find that as those bad desires leave, God begins to fill us with His desires. At some point, if you are not saved, you will take that step for salvation and mean it in your heart, or you may be at a place where you need to rededicate your life. However, you will find that you want to seek more and more of God. Whatever the desires you now have which are causing destruction in your life, God will gradually take those desires away and fill it with good. Then all of a sudden, you realize that you actually have good days and happy days. You begin seeing God change things around you, and blessings start to come your way. Then all of a sudden, some of those friends, you did not want to give up, begin seeing your life change. They begin to desire some of what you have, and they wind up walking this walk with you. However, this time you are not sitting around crying about how bad your life is. In fact, you are talking about how great things are now and how you only wish you had found the answers sooner.

What Is Your Motivation

We need to look a little deeper into motivation. Many today are always saying they are going to do this and going to do that; however, that day never comes. We even see during the beginning of a new year, many people will make resolutions. These resolutions sometimes are carried out, but far too often, the goal is left undone with the person feeling defeated. We must ask ourselves, what are our motivations? What will make us get up and do what we have set out to do? We need to answer the questions below.

1) Are you bad about procrastination, putting something off until tomorrow what can be done today? _____
2) Are there areas of your life that you do not procrastinate? _____
3) What is that motivator which makes you carry out some things and not others?
_____

I believe there are probably areas in all of our lives, which we put off and other areas where we do not. This is what we need to look at in order to set goals and priorities in our lives. Those things we give a greater priority to are the areas we are less likely to procrastinate. I thought about this in my own life, what are my priorities besides doing those things which God has called me to do. My 3 year old grandbaby, which lives with me, is a huge priority in my life. It is imperative that my focus is on her well-being. Being three, she can do very little for herself. I have to make sure she has healthy things to eat. I have to make sure she gets bathed and is in bed at certain times. These are areas that I do not procrastinate in. Other areas of my life would be my work. I do not procrastinate in doing those things which bring in finances in order to support myself and my grandbaby. Right now, take time out and make a list of areas in your life that you do not procrastinate.

_____
_____
_____
_____
_____

Now your reasons; write down why those things listed above, you do not procrastinate.

_____
_____
_____
_____

Usually, we will see two things. We do not procrastinate on those things which bring in finances, in order to pay our bills and survive, and we do not procrastinate on those things which have to do with taking care of those we love. What does this tell us? This shows us where we place our greatest value. We do not procrastinate when it has to do with people we love and money. Now we know according to the Word, that it is not money that is the root to all evil but the love of money.

1 Timothy 6:10 (NIV) [10]For the love of money is a root of all kinds of evil. Some people, eager for money, have wandered from the faith and pierced themselves with many griefs.

I do not believe for those of us who are just trying to make money, to pay their bills and survive, would necessarily have a love for money that has become an idol to them. Let's look at this picture a little more clearly. We say that we want to have that one on one relationship with the Lord. We desire to know God to a greater degree; however, we see by this picture that what motivates us to do those things, which are of high priority, are love and necessity. However, God desires for us to love Him deeply, just like He loves us deeply. How can we do that if we have just begun this walk with Him? Just like with any relationship, it has to be nurtured, for the love, to grow deep; otherwise, it is only on the surface. God knows that overnight, you are not going to understand the depth of the kind of love He is all about, but we have to have that desire to love Him deep within. What will it take to motivate us to step out and strive for that deeper relationship with the Father? Ask yourself if you are confident in the outcome of where you will be in the next 5 to 10 years doing it your way. Are you confident in the outcome of where those you love will be in the next 5 to 10 years, relying on chance? If your answer is no, I can tell you that your motivation needs to be in trusting the Father. Without Him, your life and those you love will be by chance. Trusting and relying on the Father, will produce a different outcome, and I can promise you that. The apostle Paul writes and shares some really good points, for us to contemplate, in 2 Timothy below.

2Timothy2:3-7(NIV) ³Endure hardship with us like a good soldier of Christ Jesus. ⁴No one serving as a soldier gets involved in civilian affairs—he wants to please his commanding officer. ⁵Similarly, if anyone competes as an athlete, he does not receive the victor's crown unless he competes according to the rules. ⁶The hardworking farmer should be the first to receive a share of the crops. ⁷Reflect on what I am saying, for the Lord will give you insight into all this.

Who is our commanding officer? Do we want to be in the army of the Lord, or do we want to be the one on the sidelines who does not get involved? Do we want to share in the rewards which are promised for those who work hard like the farmer? A farmer produces good crops, but only because he is diligent in his work. The farmer perseveres until the end of the harvest, at which time he can finally step back to enjoy the fruits of his labor. Why put off tomorrow what we can accomplish today? Why would we not want to be all we can be in order to reap the fruits of our labor? We have the ability to be greater than we are; however, our ability rests in the Lord.

2Timothy2:11-13(NIV) ¹¹Here is a trustworthy saying: If we died with him, we will also live with him; ¹²if we endure, we will also reign with him. If we disown him, he will also disown us; ¹³if we are faithless, he will remain faithful, for he cannot disown himself.

Dying with the Lord is dying to self. We put all our trusts and efforts in Him. We make the decision to walk His way and not our way. If we do this, we will reign with Him, and if we disown Him, He will also disown us. It continues in 2 Timothy showing us a glance at the world where we live. People everywhere today are quarreling. You may have days that everything goes great; however, disagreement will come and arguing many times follows.

233

The things that people would love more than anything is for peace to reign in their lives; however, we know that this is something that is few and far between. When God begins doing a work in us, our lives will begin to be transformed differently than those of the world. Never think that peace is something you cannot obtain, but it will never be acquired without Jesus.

2Timothy2:14-15(NIV) ¹⁴*Keep reminding them of these things. Warn them before God against quarreling about words; it is of no value, and only ruins those who listen.* ¹⁵*Do your best to present yourself to God as one approved, a workman who does not need to be ashamed and who correctly handles the word of truth.*

At some point, we all must grow up and let go of our youthful ways. Many today strive at staying young. They strive to continue living doing the same things they did in their youth, for fear of letting go of those years and realizing that those days are gone. This kind of thinking is foolishness, and in order for our lives to change, regardless of our age, we must desire the wisdom from above and not the world.

2Timothy2:22-23(NIV) ²²*Flee the evil desires of youth, and pursue righteousness, faith, love and peace, along with those who call on the Lord out of a pure heart.* ²³*Don't have anything to do with foolish and stupid arguments, because you know they produce quarrels.*

I have met and ministered to people who seemed to love the Lord, and yet, their life seemed to be one struggle after another. After spending quite a bit of time with these individuals and sharing the Word, as it pertained to their lives, I could see why they could never rise above their circumstances. Many out there today know what the Word says and claim to love the Lord; however, when it comes to putting any effort forth, they have no motivation. Many today fall into this category and continually look to other resources to be able to get by. In other words, they may be getting public assistance to housing, food stamps, child-care, etc. They also may have family and friends who constantly help them out and even their church. Do not take this in a negative sense; if you are currently getting public assistance, these programs were set up for those who need them in order to get on their feet. In fact, in my younger days, I too had help from some of these agencies. However, what I am getting at is sometimes we get so used to these programs and others bailing us out, that it becomes our crutch. We come to expect the assistance and consider it a blessing, perhaps even from God. Then we see no reason to try and rise above these circumstances. We continue day after day, week after week, month after month, and year after year expecting the assistance, and we have no desire to be able to stand on our own two feet. These programs are designed to help people get on their feet, not to cripple them to where they have no desire to be anything, do anything, or achieve anything. There are also programs to assist those to go back to school. Perhaps today, if you can see yourself in this situation, instead of being offended, it may be time to reach out to one of those programs and take advantage of the opportunities offered by our government. It may be time to get your education, so you can rise above your circumstances. Remember, our God is a God of action, and many times, we do not see blessings because we are waiting on Him to act. However, God desires to see us step out and do what we can do with what we have. God will meet us half way but not if we do not show any effort on our part.

Back in my early 20's, I lived in California with my first born. I was a single mother and had to have assistance. I had no income coming in other than what I made with my job, which was not enough to support me and my daughter. At this time, I did not have a college education; however, I did not abuse the system. I used it to my advantage. I went back to school, while the state helped support me, in order to get on my feet where I did not have to depend on any assistance from anyone again. The Word talks very bluntly about those who have no motivation. If it takes them putting out more effort than they are currently doing, it will not happen.

Proverbs 10:4 (NIV) [4] *Lazy hands make a man poor, but diligent hands bring wealth.*

Your life will remain exactly as it is unless you are determined to put the effort forth needed in order to succeed. God is not going to bless those who continually lay around waiting for others to provide for them. Unless you are handicapped, disabled, or in some other way incapable of making a living for yourself, God will not open doors in your life to bless you. You can pray all you want, but it is not biblical and will not happen. God is a God of His Word, and His Word clearly states that if you are lazy, if you have no motivation, you will be poor. Think about this, being poor does not just mean that you will have no wealth, but being poor means in every area of your life. Those that God has brought across my path who have no motivation because they desire to get by with public assistance, it was sad for me to see how these people walk around day after day being beat down by the world. Those living in this place do not understand why they cannot find peace, happiness, and why their life is so hard. If you do not have peace in your life and you struggle, God is trying to wake you up to the fact that there needs to be a change. That change has to come within ourselves, many times, before God can begin doing work in our lives. If we have no motivation, we need to wake up and realize, even though, life seems easy by not having to put forth much effort to survive, due to support from other sources, what is this worth? Is it worth our happiness? Is it worth our life? There is much more to life than living off the government. There is much more to life than living with no inner peace and that feeling of shame. Sometimes, we just have to put our pride aside and make that decision that we are going to do something with our life.

Hebrews 6:11-12 (NIV) [11]*We want each of you to show this same diligence to the very end, in order to make your hope sure.* [12]*We do not want you to become lazy, but to imitate those who through faith and patience inherit what has been promised.*

We are encouraged in Hebrews, to be diligent in our lives and put forth as much effort as possible in order to have that hope for a better life. What we choose to do every day is what we are teaching those who look up to us such as our children, our younger siblings, and anyone else that may be in our lives. What is your life speaking to those who love you? Our lives need to imitate those who are diligently walking with the Lord, and the fruit in which they produce is the result of their hard labor.

Discipline

We have discussed those things which motivate us to accomplish tasks, while other areas of our life we fall short. With this, I believe it is important to look further into how to obtain that discipline in our lives to accomplish those things which have been thus far unobtainable. For instance, our desires should be to seek the Father in order to gain that wisdom and knowledge through the Word. Our desires should be to come to that place where we see things through Jesus and not through the eyes of the world. In obtaining this goal, our minds will be renewed. We will find inner-peace, and blessings will begin to transform around us. To reach any goal in life takes discipline. I believe it is important to

237

take a look at statistics for goals set each year during the New Year.

Basically, a New Year's Resolution is merely a goal set. As Christians, we each should set goals in our lives; however, there are lessons to learn about achieving goals. Here are some statistics among the American people.

40 to 45% of American adults make one or more resolutions each year. Among the top New Year's resolutions are resolutions about weight loss, exercise, and to stop smoking. Also popular are resolutions dealing with better money management/ debt reduction.

The following shows how many of these resolutions are maintained as time goes on:

- *Past the first week: 75%*
- *Past 2 weeks: 71%*
- *After one month: 64%*
- *After 6 months: 46%*

While a lot of people who make New Year's resolutions do break them, research shows that making resolutions are useful. People who explicitly make resolutions are 10 times more likely to attain their goals than people who do not explicitly make resolutions. [1]

Statistics say that almost half of all American adults make a resolution to begin the New Year, but the resolutions are all basically things to make them healthier, more attractive, and have more money and less debt. While none of these things may be bad, they fail to strive for the one thing that can accomplish all of the things in which they desire. Notice what the Word says about the wisdom of the world:

1 Corinthians 3:18-20 (NASB) [18]Let no man deceive himself If any man among you thinks that he is wise in this age, he must become foolish, so that he may become wise. [19]For the wisdom of this world is foolishness before God For it is written, "He is THE ONE WHO CATCHES THE WISE IN THEIR CRAFTINESS"; [20]and again, "THE LORD KNOWS THE REASONINGS of the wise, THAT THEY ARE USELESS."

Our goal as a Christian should be to strive for those things above not those things of the world.

Matthew 6:33-34 (NIV)[33]But seek first his kingdom and his righteousness, and all these things will be given to you as well. [34]Therefore do not worry about tomorrow, for tomorrow will worry about itself. Each day has enough trouble of its own.

Should we set goals? Absolutely! The statistics show, people who do make resolutions or do set goals are more likely to achieve that which they set out to accomplish than those who do not. God expects us to strive for those things which are above not of this world.

Colossians 3:2 (NIV)[2]Set your minds on things above, not on earthly things.

God expects us to prepare ourselves for action.

1 Peter 1:13 (NIV) [13]Therefore, prepare your minds for action; be self-controlled; set your hope fully on the grace to be given you when Jesus Christ is revealed.

If we simply do nothing, then we are not preparing. The word "prepare" is an action verb; it shows action. People who have no goals, which simply do nothing but get up each morning and do whatever when ever and nothing is planned out, accomplish nothing! To prepare ourselves for the kingdom to come, we must set goals because goals are the driving force which is a plan of action that we desire deep within our being to accomplish!

What should our goals be? The statistics for resolutions say that after 6 months only about 46% of all who made resolutions have stuck to them. Much of this has to do with the personality of a person, the motivation, and the mindset; however, this all comes down to discipline! If we are not disciplined, we will never succeed.

Deuteronomy 8:5 (NIV)[5] Know then in your heart that as a man disciplines his son, so the LORD your God disciplines you.

In order for children to grow up in a manner that is considered worthy of mankind and be an asset to society, takes discipline. Parents who have the wisdom of God go a step farther to discipline them in the ways of the Lord. For each of us to be where we are today, a lot had to do with a strong hand from our earthly parents trying to keep us on a path that was good and not bad. If we were not fortunate to have that upbringing, then perhaps, we are where we are today because of the grace of God and much correction and discipline on the Lord's part. Whatever the case may be, we cannot ever achieve those things we desire unless we have had discipline in our lives. Even if there are areas that we do have discipline, we may still lack in certain areas. Just like the statistics for those who fall after 6 months from their commitment to their New Year's Resolution, we also will fall at some point if we do not willingly receive the corrections and discipline from the Lord.

Job 5:17 (NIV) [17] *"Blessed is the man whom God corrects; so do not despise the discipline of the Almighty."*

In Job, it says blessed are those whom God corrects, and we should not despise that discipline. With discipline, character is built. When we begin to discipline ourselves, we will then begin to see those things we desire to manifest in our lives. It says in Proverbs, fools despise wisdom and discipline.

Proverbs 1:7 (NIV) [7] *The fear of the LORD is the beginning of knowledge, but fools despise wisdom and discipline.*

We need to come to a place in our lives that we welcome discipline. Whether the discipline comes from reading God's Word or another source such as a spiritual book, a minister, teacher, evangelist, or even a Christian friend, we must accept that correction for our own good. Many times, we are able to see ourselves in what we read, even though, it might be an ugly picture. Whatever the case, God speaks to us in various ways. We need to recognize when something in our spirit is touched by a Word from God, even though, it may wound our flesh. We need not to be foolish but wise in knowing that God is trying to teach us. He desires us to rise to a place in this life and receive those things which He desires for us, and this cannot be accomplished without discipline.

Psalm 94:12-13 (NIV) [12] *Blessed is the man you discipline, O LORD, the man you teach from your law;* [13] *you grant him relief from days of trouble, till a pit is dug for the wicked.*

Blessed are those who are disciplined and taught of God's laws. In being disciplined, we are kept from days of trouble. To me, not enduring days of trouble would mean that everything works out for the good. If I desire to achieve a goal in my life to lose weight, not to just feel better about the way I look but to be healthier, then I believe that I need to listen to the Word of God. He will give me the discipline and wisdom, not to be troubled by the way I feel or look, knowing my successes will come through Him. In His wisdom will be enlightenment on how to achieve that which I desire, but it will only be accomplished if I welcome discipline.

Let's look at what kind of goals we should set? Remember, Jesus is our example, and we should do according to all that He did. The temple is our body, and we should keep it holy. We should take good care of our physical bodies.

1 Corinthians 6:19 (NIV)[19]Do you not know that your body is a temple of the Holy Spirit, who is in you, whom you have received from God? You are not your own;

If Jesus is our example, then we should look to Him. God does expect us to take care of our bodies. He does expect us to have balance in our lives. Recently, God taught me a valuable lesson on balance in my life. Daily, I spent as much time as possible sharing Jesus with those God sent across my path that were not in church, as well as a group in my home. Every day, after working all day, I would head to someone's home. During this time, I was also taking care of my grandbaby and getting home in enough time to get ready for bed and start this same process over again on a daily basis. I was not getting the sleep I needed and seldom home except for sleeping. I began to get sick and tried to breeze through without stopping. I got better and then sick the second time. This time, I was down. I could not understand why this was happening because what I was doing was the Lord's work. It is funny how when we get sick, all of a sudden, we have to get still in order to hear God's voice. Prior to going to bed one night, I cried out to God for answers to know why I was getting sick. Yes, I knew that I was not getting adequate sleep. However, in my mind, I thought that as long as what I was doing was the Lord's work, He would see to it all my needs were met including my health. It does not work that way. In going to bed, I pulled out a spiritual book that I had been reading and began to read where I had left off the night prior. It was unbelievable, but what I was reading were my exact words that I had just spoken to the Lord. *"Why God, why; I am going every day doing your work, why would You allow me to get sick?"* My answer was very simple. Balance! If we do not balance out our life, it does not matter if you are living for the Lord, you will get sick. Your physical body requires balance, and the health of your family life also requires balance. We cannot be super heroes in these earthly bodies. Therefore, I had to slow down and do what God called me to do not over and above. It is balance, and in God's timing. Yes, He does expect us to take care of our earthly bodies as long as we are on this earth.

God desires to use us in mighty ways, but we have to be wise with our time. We have to balance our lives between family, ministry, and work. If you desire to meet goals in your life, make a list of a normal work day and a list of those days off from work. Look at your time and determine those things which are wasted times and those which bear good fruit. Good fruit is not just doing things for God. Good fruit can be things which you do with those you love as well, even friends. God expects us not to neglect our family as well as other relationships. Memories of good times are important to leave that legacy when you are gone. If you only give to God and the ministry and lack in areas with those you love, you basically are leaving behind nothing for those who were perhaps closest to you. When you balance everything out, below are memories of what you are leaving behind to those lives you have touched:

1) How you not only gave to those you did not even know, like that stranger you crossed paths with, but also of how you gave to those you loved in the form of knowing how to **love** like Jesus did.
2) Always having **joy** in your heart, which was made complete through Christ.
3) That **peace** which passes all understanding seemed to flow all around you at all times.
4) **Patience** rose up in you when you were tested and walked through trials.
5) **Kindness** towards others even those who were not kind back.
6) Within your heart showed **goodness** towards all of mankind even those you did not know.
7) Your balance between God, family, work, and play spoke miles of **faithfulness** to the Lord God Almighty knowing that the answers to life are only through Him, where your trust rested.
8) Compassion and **gentleness** were exhibited towards strangers, animals, as well as all of those you loved.
9) And, in times of great tribulation and trials, **self-control** rose up above all circumstances and situations knowing that God would walk you through as He always had.

These are the Fruits of the Spirit, which will be taught to a greater degree. However, when we are dead and gone, how do we want to be remembered? What examples do you desire to leave for your children and grandchildren? These are things that we need to think about, but none of this is accomplished without that discipline in our lives.

244

What goals should we seek? We should be striving for more of what is above and not here on this earth. We should be striving for more wisdom, knowledge, revelation, faith, and anointing. What happens when we gain all these things? We will not lack in any area of our lives. Does God not know if we need to lose that added weight? Does God not know if we need to have more discipline with our finances and perhaps a better job? Does God not know if we need a miracle? Like the Word says, if we seek those things above, what will happen? All other things will be added. God spoke to me several months ago about my health. I listened and agreed, but I did not take a step towards changing any of it, why? Because, I was too busy – too busy doing God's work and thought that God would just miraculously keep me healthy. Even though, I was not eating right and getting enough rest that He had spoken to me about, I believed all was good. God intends us to be balanced, and He gave us a day of rest each week. The purpose for that day is because as long as we are in these earthly bodies, they require good nutrition and enough rest. If we allow God to take control of those things which concern us, those goals which we desire to accomplish will happen! All things are possible for those who believe.

Mark 9:23 (Amp)[23]And Jesus said, [You say to Me], If You can do anything? [Why,] all things can be (are possible) to him who believes!

Let's look at guidelines on how we should set our goals. I believe many people set goals that are hard to reach. Many people set long-term goals, and they become discouraged because there is nothing short term to be able to reach in order to feel successful. Let's look at this differently. We desire for certain things to change in our lives like that greater walk with the Father. Therefore, the first thing we need to do is make a list of what we need to accomplish. How do we achieve these things? We first seek God. We begin by surrendering all to God, surrendering the way we think, the way we feel, the way we act. Let's start with goals that are obtainable and have a progressive goal by setting small goals. We work on those small goals for a few months and then add to them after we become grounded for a couple of months.

1) Set a goal or commitment to God that begins small, such as: *"Lord, I commit to daily reading one chapter of the bible."* This is not one book of the bible but one chapter. Commit to read it and think on it until you receive something. When we set a goal to read more than that daily, we wind up not understanding what we read and really receiving nothing. Begin with small and grow from there.

2) If you have access to a computer, search for "bible" and go into one of the sites where you can search for particular words in the bible. Then commit 2 or 3 times a week to study one word in the bible such as: love, forgiveness, peace, obedience, commandments, wisdom, etc. Search for that word and then read down the list. Any Scripture that relates to something you desire to know, read them thoroughly. Go to several and study those things which will begin to enlighten your understanding of God's Word.

3) Set a goal to daily pray to God even if it is for 10 minutes. Spend that time just talking to God like He is your dad because He is, and tell Him how much you love Him. Ask God to put the desire within you to want to serve Him. Ask Him to put the desire within you to want to know Him.

4) Daily set a goal to lift up others to God, even if it is just a few minutes. Spend this time asking for God's favor for those you lift up to Him. Ask God to forgive them, bless them, and let this time be not just for those you love but for those that may be your enemies also.

5) Daily, when you rise in the morning, speak the prayer below. Tape it on your mirror in your bathroom, but have it somewhere that you can see it and repeat it.

Father, I thank you for the blood that Jesus shed on the cross for me. I plead that blood over my life this day that it flows over me continually, and it not only sanctifies me but protects me. I thank you Father that I am your son/daughter and that Your wisdom, knowledge, and understanding flow into my spirit. I thank You that the fruits of the spirit are evident in my everyday walk with You... love, joy, peace, patience, kindness, goodness, faithfulness, gentleness, and self-control. I thank You that You are continually perfecting every gift and talent that has been given unto me. I thank You Father that my desires continue to line up with Your desires and that as Jesus is my example, I desire to go where He went, say what He said, do what He did, and pray what He prayed. I thank you Lord God that as I die to self and look to those things above and not those things which are carnal, that You Father are continually at work in those things that concern me.

Luke 16:10 (NIV) [10]*"Whoever can be trusted with very little can also be trusted with much, and whoever is dishonest with very little will also be dishonest with much."*

As we show God that we are disciplined in the little things, He will continue to give us more. Those who have walked through this understand this concept. Those with huge ministries or who have prospered much can tell you that they began with little. As they used what they had and diligently on a daily basis showed God that they desired all that He entrusted them with, He began to give them more. If you desire to lose weight, it can be accomplished through wisdom from the Father. If you desire to make more money and live better, not having to struggle, it can be accomplished by looking to those things above and not the world. If you desire to grow more spiritually, it can be accomplished by

247

asking the Father for more insight. If you desire to quit a bad habit and have been unsuccessful in the past, it can be accomplished through the strength of the Lord. If you desire that a loved one change from the life-style they may be living, or for them to be saved, it can only happen with prayer and by you first getting your life right to lead the way. Whatever you desire, do not look to the world for your answers because the answers that will be lasting and rewarding can only come with the wisdom from above.

Correction versus Criticism

One last thing, which needs to be touched on briefly, is the difference between correction and criticism. Many times, the Lord sends people across our path to correct us and our defenses go up immediately because we take it as criticism instead. We have to come to that place of maturity, in order for God to be able to correct us, listening instead of taking everything negatively. How can we grow to be all God desires us to be if we already think we know everything? When correction comes, instead of looking at it like criticism, why not look at it like constructive criticism or just correction? However, there may be those in our life which have always been critical about everything and everyone, but as a child of God, we have to overlook those things which are spoken even if they are intended as criticism. If, on the other hand, the criticism comes from someone we work around or a close friend or even family, it may be time to choose how often we are around them on a personal level, especially if their words do not line up with the Word of God. We may be at a place where it is time to refrain from those things in the world which bring us down, as our family and friends may not be trying to walk this life with us. Therefore, we need to be sensitive to the fact that even though their words are hurtful, they actually need our prayers in order for God to begin doing the same work in them, He is doing in us. Many times, we are in places where daily we are around people who are not Christians or people who live like the world and sometimes, they may even be in positions of authority. I know I have ministered to some who find themselves in situations beyond their choice, such as at work or school. If that is the case, we do not have to get involved in idle conversations while at work, school, or any other place. We can choose our conversations and can choose to either walk away or engage in idle talk. Rather at work or school, our focus should be on the task we are there for. Although, we can still show the world Jesus instead of allowing the world to bring us down. This is our choice, as we grow and become stronger, we should strive to share Jesus. Once those you are around daily know your value system and your commitment to the Lord, they will not be as apt to discuss just anything with you as they may have in the past. We have to ask ourselves why we would want to associate with people who constantly are trying to make us look bad, feel bad, or bring us down. This does not make sense!

I know even in my younger years, it became evident to me those who knew how to point out my mistakes in a constructive manner by not making me feel beneath them, and there were those who did not have that gift but were critical. As soon as anything was taken negatively, my defenses automatically went up. Yes, we learn at a very early age, we do not like to be spoken at harshly. Our defenses usually come up, and our outlook is that feeling of criticism. *"Why is that person always trying to make me feel as though I am nothing?"* This, of course, is a tactic of our enemy which will be discussed in a later series. However, there are those who know how to lead and those who do not. I believe it is a gift to be a great leader, and with that gift, it comes natural. For those who know how to do this constructively, they gain a totally different response, and they attain far better workers.

There are probably, by far, fewer leaders who know how to lead, where you do not mind following, than those who do not. Many times, there are those who are very critical and controlling. This type of leader, many times, will make us want to give up before we even begin. This shows that many out there today, do not have the concept of how to lead in order for those to follow. However, being a Christian, we are not to act as the world even towards negativity. Being a Christian, if we are in a place of leadership, we need to allow the Holy Spirit to be our guide. Even though, we may not be a gifted leader, the one we should be following knows how to lead better than any man. We forget, where we are weak, He is strong. We can be good at anything when we are doing it through Christ. Of course, we know that there are probably far fewer Christian leaders than worldly leaders. As we get older and more mature, we learn to walk through any difficult situation without taking things personal. We quickly learn, there are many personality types out there, and some are easier to work with while others are not. Where we need to go with this, is to the place where we look at everything as a possible statement which could bring us wisdom in one way or another. We should not take everything said to us on a personal level and allow our youthful ways to have precedence. Let me clarify this, in my younger years, I was always on edge waiting for someone to criticize me because it was what I was used to. However, I was fortunate enough that during those first years in the workforce and school, most of those who led me were great at building me up and encouraging me to make me see myself as being able to succeed. I can remember a few leaders during this time who were very critical. I took this personally as an assault. It made me want to give up believing in myself and to give up on my performance. After all, if we are constantly criticized, what would be our motivation to try harder? There is no motivation when we find ourselves under a leader who tears us down continually. My point is this, if we are to be Christ like then we do not act as the world. Instead, we act above what the world would do. Our performance at our job or school should not slack down because of words. We should be above those words knowing that the approval we seek is not from man but from God. God will be the one to reward us of our efforts not man. God knows if we are not performing in a way which brings glory to Him. We are expected as Christians to glorify God in all our works, not just some of our works.

Now as time went on, there were those I worked for who were trying to promote me because they believed I could do better. They would build me up in all those areas that I was good at, and then, they would tell me things that I needed to work harder on in order to be promoted. The way they did this, I took as constructive criticism because they cared about my future and wanted to see me be successful. Now, in your lifetime, if you encounter many career changes, there may come a time that you will have someone who is harder to work for in which nothing seems to please them. We do not need to take this kind of criticism as destructive, but rather, we should look upon it in a constructive way. That person may not be gifted in leadership abilities, and they may be unaware of the way their words are being received. It is up to us how we choose to receive the words which are coming at us. The norm would be for our guard to go up automatically, our defenses go up, and we become ready to fight for what we believe. The norm would be that we do not allow someone to make us feel that we are nothing, and we are stupid. Here is the thing, even as a child, we never liked to be told by others when we did something wrong or that we needed to do it another way because our way was not good enough. We have become a society that wants to go out into the world and be accepted just as we are. We want others to think that we are not the ones with the problem because it is always someone else's fault. We feel that if someone does not like something about us, then they should stay away because it is not our problem.

We need to think about this deeply when we become Christians. God wants to do a work in us, and if our defenses are constantly going up, how can He get through to us? God speaks to us in many ways. For those of you who do not know what someone is referring to when they say, *"I got a Word from God"* or *"God spoke to me"*, this does not necessarily mean that God came down and spoke to them in an audible voice like you and me. When God speaks to us, He tries to speak in that still quiet voice, which is within us. However, many times we have tuned Him out just like we tune out our children, our spouse, our parents, our employer, etc. When God cannot get our attention, by speaking to us, then He has to take other measures. This is where God either sends an obedient servant, a pastor giving a sermon, that TV Evangelist, perhaps a spiritual book across our path in order to get a message or Word which is needed for growth. However, many times, we are offended when someone gives a sermon or message on a particular subject that we take personally. If you become upset because of a sermon a pastor or Evangelist gave, then you are not in a place to receive from God. If you become offended because another Christian friend shared something with you that God had showed them pertaining to your life, then you are not at the place you need to be in order for God to do His perfect work in you. If you become offended, you probably need to work on those areas which feel uncomfortable to discuss. If you become offended, it is evident that your flesh does not want to listen because your flesh does not want to change in that area. It's funny how someone who does not even know us can say something which upsets us. We become offended and cannot wait to be around someone else in order to vent about what that preacher said or what that Evangelist on TV said. If we are

252

offended, that message was meant for us, and more than likely, God has been trying to get our attention to hear what was said. Now, here is the problem - us! We are the problem. God goes to a lot of trouble getting our attention to give us a Word that is going to better our life; however, we cannot handle constructive criticism. How are we going to be where God desires us to be if we continue wanting to do everything our own way? How can God use a people who are so insistent on having their own way?

Now let's look at this in a different perspective. Many times, it may be someone we know very well who will come and share something with us. Even when I was walking with the Lord for those 10 years, there were areas of my life that I was sensitive in because I did not have the revelation in which I have today. If someone came along and spoke one little thing over me which sounded like criticism, I took it as such. God may have actually sent someone across my path to correct me in love, but I did not take it that way. It would wound me, and when I became wounded, I retreated! There may have been areas that I was in sin and did not want to look at myself. I wanted to believe that everything was okay, and it was not me. If there are areas which are sensitive, it is more than likely due to what has been spoken over us as a child, and we have not completely given it all to God. We are so accustomed to doing many of the same things we did as a child in order to comfort ourselves. Most of us probably do not even realize our actions are showing, *"Do not go there and do not get too close!"* Red flags begin to go up everywhere. We begin to back away from that person who may not even be aware that they said something which wounded us. Maybe, they were not even aware that they said it in a way where we took it as criticism. As a Christian who desires to grow strong, we have to rise above words which may or may not be spoken wrong. Whether it is done purposely or done out of love, as a Christian, we have to come to the place where words do not affect us. We need to come to a place where words do not move us unless it is God's Word, and that move should be one of action and getting involved! Jesus is the same yesterday, today, and tomorrow. Jesus is our example! We need to strive to be more like our Creator. When a word is spoken which takes us back a few steps, we need to get by ourselves as soon as possible and give it to God. You may be surprised that sometimes, God is actually trying to teach you something and the more teachable you are the greater God can use you. Do not fall into the category, *"You cannot teach 'an old dog' new tricks."* If you do, you will be limiting yourself to how far you can go, how much you can do, and to be all God created you to be.

We need to do an attitude check. Take a positive approach to every situation and know that it is an uphill road from this point. Yes, we are climbing a hill, and it may not be as easy as walking down the hill. As we climb to greater depths, we achieve greater victory and freedom. It is our choice to wake up each morning and make the decision that we are going to look at life in a positive way and not a negative way.

6 The Journey through Defeat...

The Search for Victory...

The Lord Is Our Strength

Psalm 18:2 (Amp) ²*The Lord is my Rock, my Fortress, and my Deliverer; my God, my keen and firm Strength in Whom I will trust and take refuge, my Shield, and the Horn of my salvation, my High Tower.*

When we first get saved and begin our walk with the Lord, we have no idea the extent to what this Scripture means. God is our rock. He is our Fortress and will deliver us from all. This is where we take refuge in knowing that the Creator of the entire Universe desires to be everything to us. He desires to shelter us from all which the enemy or the world throws at us. However, in order to reap this benefit as a child of God, we must first understand it in its entirety and know what part we play in this role.

I believe, we can all agree, when we first begin our walk with the Lord, our life is not exactly like that of our Savior. We fall short on being able to achieve portraying our lives to be like Jesus. After living in the flesh for many years, each of our lives probably paints a picture that is far from perfect, but that is okay. Jesus said to come as we are, and that is what we did. None of us are capable of cleaning up our lives and then coming. Our lives can only be cleaned up once we have the Holy Spirit walking with us. God knows that our lives need drastic changes to take place in order to be new creatures in Christ. Remember, the old man is no longer there *(2 Corinthians 5:17)*; however, we probably do not even have a clue of what our new man is supposed to be.

Psalm 18:32 (Amp) *³²The God who girds me with strength and makes my way perfect?*

According to Psalm, God will be our strength and make our way perfect. We will not and cannot ever do this in ourselves. This is where we need much help in order to achieve what God desires for us in its entirety. We know we are transformed in our spirit because Jesus came to live in our heart, and He is part of our inner man.

Philippians 3:10 (Amp) *¹⁰[For my determined purpose is] that I may know Him [that I may progressively become more deeply and intimately acquainted with Him, perceiving and recognizing and understanding the wonders of His Person more strongly and more clearly], and that I may in that same way come to know the power outflowing from His resurrection [which it exerts over believers], and that I may so share His sufferings as to be continually transformed [in spirit into His likeness even] to His death, [in the hope]*

Our inner man still lives in that fleshly body which has been used to doing whatever it feels like doing, living how it feels like living, and carrying out those plans which gratify our flesh. So now the transformation needs to begin, and Jesus said to come as you are because He knows once you accept Him into your heart, you will become a new creation. The Lord was not implying that we come as we are and remain as we are; however, it is okay that we are a mess right now. Our God wants us to see a different world. He wants us to see a world that is far better than we could ever imagine. Old things are going to pass away, and you will gradually start seeing that you find no enjoyment in doing some of the things you used to do which produced bad fruit. The Holy Spirit will walk with you daily, and you will begin to recognize that little voice which will make you feel uneasy when you are doing things that are not godly. You will start to see that you do not like who you were, and you will gradually start trying to do things differently to become that new person. Old desires will begin to leave you. You will even begin to receive revelation on why you did things in ways which were unhealthy. This is revealed in order to be able to see who you were prior to Jesus. After being enlightened into the ways of Christ, we begin to see how selfish we were in so many areas, and many times, we never even noticed. I know after 15 years when I walked back into God's arms, I had struggled to keep that relationship with Him while not going to church. I had felt that I could go to heaven just staying close to Him and did not need the church. This was just one piece of revelation I received, and this revelation painted a picture of what I had become during those 15 years. The picture painted was much like the world which generally operates in a self-centered state of mind. I thought I could make the correct decision based on what I believed, and I did not take into consideration that maybe it was not God's way of doing things. Of course, I learned that I could not stay close to living a holy life, according to His commandments, when all I was associating with were people of the world. We do not realize how much we are like the world, which is essentially the opposite of Jesus, when that is what has been absorbing our whole being from the time of birth. In order for God to begin the transformation process, it does take a lot of effort on our part in listening and obeying. One thing we must do is spend our time with those who believe likewise. The world will swallow us up if we allow it.

We may say that we do love God and desire that closer walk with Him. However, if all our time is spent in association with those of this world, we will never reach that goal. We will become too much like the world which is all about self, consumed with

257

fulfillment of the flesh. When you are doing fleshly things and not spiritual things, it is impossible to draw close to God. When I drew close to God after coming home, I found that my desires began to change drastically. At that time, I was divorced and found myself in the dating world to some extent. However, I knew what I needed to do in order to get my life right with God and go home. When God began to fill me totally with His presence, I no longer had the desire to feel like I had to have someone in my life to love me because I had Him! I was loved totally. It is the most awesome feeling to know God's love because you totally feel complete. I did not need those things of the world that I once thought I had to have. I spent most of my life feeling like I had to be married in order to be complete. I spent most of my life thinking that I had to have someone to grow old with so I would not be alone. I do not feel that anymore. I feel totally complete wrapped in my Savior's arms, loved and blessed! The desires to be married left! I had to come to a place where God showed me that I had been doing everything my whole life my way. He had to show me what a mess I had made of my life with three marriages! It was an ugly picture, but this is not to say my marriages did not work as the result of my fault totally. However, the point is that I had to do it my way instead of looking to God to bring the right person across my path. When we are unequally yoked, God will allow us to make that mistake; however, it is not to say it is going to work. Therefore, I have to look at those three marriages as my fault, especially the last two because I knew the truth and still chose to do it my way. I was saved on the last two, but I did not allow God to lead me. I did not look to God for the right decisions. It was my way, and I made a total mess of the relationships. So today, it is no longer my way. This is great revelation I received from God which revealed the mistakes I had made. This revelation began cleaning up and transforming my way of thinking into that of my Savoir. I look to Jesus as my example today in

258

order to follow and not lead. It is quite evident that we do not know what is best for us because if we did, our lives would not be such a mess. I make it a point every day to pray, *"Father, Your will be done not mine!"* I know now that if marriage is ever in the picture again, it will be for a reason, and it will be God that makes that decision. The person who He sends will be His choice and it will work.

Today, my life is quite different. When you begin to be obedient to God and stop fighting Him, He then begins to reveal much of His perfect plan for your life. My strength rests in my Lord today. In 2 Corinthians, it says that His grace is sufficient; it is all that we need. I do not have to rely on my own strengths. I do not have to rely on my own power because where I lack, He makes up.

2 Corinthians 12:9 (Amp) ⁹*But He said to me, My grace (My favor and loving-kindness and mercy) is enough for you [sufficient against any danger and enables you to bear the trouble manfully]; for My strength and power are made perfect (fulfilled and completed) and show themselves most effective in [your] weakness. Therefore, I will all the more gladly glory in my weaknesses and infirmities, that the strength and power of Christ (the Messiah) may rest (yes, may pitch a tent over and dwell) upon me!*

We should glory in our weaknesses and infirmities because when we are weak, all we have to do is call on the Lord during these times. We know that God is there, and He will see us through to the finish. My God has never forsaken me when I needed Him. Yes, there will be tests, but we will also count it all joy knowing that as we walk through these tests, we will gain much insight into the mind of Christ. Growing up, I did not have enough confidence in myself. I did not believe that I could do anything or be anything; therefore, I did not step out of my box. Today, I challenge myself to do those things I would never have attempted in my past. Today, when I am walking the path God laid before me, I see that I never fail because He is right there to see me through to the finish. It is not with my strength but His strength.

Philippians 2:13 (Amp) [13]*[Not in your own strength] for it is God Who is all the while effectually at work in you [energizing and creating in you the power and desire], both to will and to work for His good pleasure and satisfaction and delight.*

God has begun to reveal to me many things in store for my life; however, in Acts, Peter tells us that God is no respecter of persons. If you listen and obey, He will bless you just as much as He has blessed anyone else.

Acts 10:34 (Amp) [34]*And Peter opened his mouth and said: Most certainly and thoroughly I now perceive and understand that God shows no partiality and is no respecter of persons,*

God desires for all of His children to know, when we begin seeking, we are going to find. With obedience, we are going to be blessed. It does not make any difference your nationality or in what culture you were raised. It does not matter what background you came from or what education you may or may not have. It does not matter what sex you are or your age because God is going to cause a storm to come into your life that you will not be able to contain. With this storm, excitement and anticipation will come knowing that you are heading down a path designed by the God of the Universe. As you carry out His purpose totally for your life, your course will continue to increase and be blessed. Notice in 2 Chronicles, it says that the eyes of the Lord run to and fro throughout the whole earth to show His strength for those who are in right standing towards Him.

2 Chronicles 16:9 (Amp) ⁹For the eyes of the Lord run to and fro throughout the whole earth to show Himself strong in behalf of those whose hearts are blameless toward Him...

If we are born again, redeemed by the blood of Jesus, we are in right standing with our Father. He is continually looking for those who love Him. He looks for those who are faithful and obedient. God is looking for you today. He desires for you to rise and submit yourself to Him, and He will begin that perfect work within you. We have to realize that walking the course He designed will be a perfect plan for our lives with no imperfections. It amazes me today why anyone would not want to walk in God's plan. Why would we choose to walk our way and in 10 years or more regret our decisions? My only regret today is that I did not die to self totally 15 years ago; however, it is never too late. It does not matter your circumstances or what you may be feeling inside. Wherever God is taking me today, I am confident in His direction for my life because as long as I know I am doing what He called me to do, it will be a much better plan than doing it my way. Remember, we have all tried it our way and many times unsuccessfully. When you answer these questions, think about your reasons behind your answer.

1) Has your life up to now been victorious or defeated?
   _____

2) Are you tired of doing things your way and failing?
   _____

3) Are you willing to let go of your selfish ways in order to begin to learn from a higher wisdom that even the world does not understand? _____

Today, my desires are to walk ever so close to Him that I do not stumble and fall into the world. God will show each of us how to obtain this if we truly desire that wisdom. You may not realize this yet, but after you become saved, God is already doing a work in you. Eventually you will begin to see this, but this is also a continual process. I have shared with many, God knows us better than we know ourselves, and when we come to Him after being in the world, He looks at the whole picture. God sees everything that needs to be transformed. We may have thousands of things that need to be fixed; however, God patiently begins working on one area at a time. God sees the importance of what needs to be fixed first and so forth. As He begins working on these different areas, we will begin resisting in some places because it feels unnatural to us to let go of certain things. However, once we quit fighting God, the transformation goes much smoother, and we actually begin to like the new person within.

Today, my desires are still being transformed deep inside. This is a process that continues no matter where you are with the Lord; God is continually at work in you in order to perfect you.

Philippians 1:6 (Amp) *[6]And I am convinced and sure of this very thing, that He Who began a good work in you will continue until the day of Jesus Christ [right up to the time of His return], developing [that good work] and perfecting and bringing it to full completion in you.*

After God begins working on one of those areas in you which need transformation and He brings it into completion, He begins on another area. We must pass our tests in whatever area we are

262

facing in order to go to another level. When we begin to realize that most of the circumstances we are faced with are merely tests that we go through to complete us, we will begin to look at it differently. Instead of becoming agitated that we are again facing a trial or temptation, just submit and say, *"Okay Lord, I am ready for the next test."* With a positive outlook, it gets much easier.

About a year ago, God began showing me how to be sensible with my finances. I have been blessed for many years on how to make money; however, I have also tended to spend it without giving much thought to what I was spending it on. As long as my money went towards those things which were of importance and there was money put back, it did not matter to me if I wasted money on things which were not a necessity. However, He had begun to show me that if I spent my money more wisely, I would have much more. The most important concept that He has shown me with this revelation is that in order for Him to complete His perfect plan for my life, He totally has to transform me in all areas. The test which I faced was not necessarily about how I was spending my money, it was an area of discipline which I needed to grasp. When God has a plan for your life which is greater than you could ever imagine, He must begin to prepare you for that plan. Any time America has gone to war, prior to sending men into battle, they have to spend countless days in boot camp in order to be ready for the task at hand. God cannot just open a door that is absolutely fascinating without preparing us for that task. Therefore, He begins to discipline us in all areas of our lives. The purpose of me spending less had nothing to do with God not wanting me ever to purchase anything which was not a necessity, but it did had everything to do with my ability of being disciplined with my finances. God was trying to bring me to the place where my life was disciplined. If it is a matter of buying something I need versus something I just want, could I walk away from that temptation? God spoke to me some time ago and many times since, and He has said, *"Jolene, where I am taking you, you must be strong."* That was all I knew; however, it was enough to know that one of the things I must learn is the key to know how and when to spend my money. By doing this, I know it is God and that I am being sensitive to His voice. Through my obedience, my money would go where He desired it to go. God will lead all of us through obedience whether it is with our spending, our tithing, our giving, our choices, etc. We become obedient when we draw from Him and only Him, knowing that our strength through our weaknesses is obtained through the Father.

We all have areas where we are weak; however, God will give us revelation in those areas in order that we gain strength. Once we become strong in those areas and it is no longer a stronghold that satan can use against us, we have conquered one aspect which used to keep us defeated. That weak area becomes a strength which we have obtained. We all have areas where we are strong, and we need to look at this in order to be able to see how it can be possible for our weaknesses to become strengths. A strength in our life is merely something we have conquered deep within. We know if we act a certain way or we say certain things what will take place. We also know if we do or do not do certain things, what the end result will be. In other words, it can be those areas we conquer based on our knowledge or skills, and the end result produces victory. In looking at this, we need to stay focused to gain this perspective in simple terms. The truth to gain strength in any area becomes a matter of getting the formula down on the inside of us. Meaning – what we need to do or not do, what we need to say or not say, and how we need to act in order to know the end result will always be in our favor. We realize those things which we are good at as our strengths; however, there are many areas which are also strengths that we take for granted. These areas have become so natural to us that we do not see them as strengths. These are the areas we need to look at. Many of these areas we have been taught from as far back as our childhood, and we never even think about them. Strengths can be looked at as talents or gifts, and they can also be acquired or learned knowledge. For instance, from the time we came into this world, we began to get revelation that if I do this, this is the result. If I touch something that is hot, I am going to get burned. If I walk in front of a car, I am going to get hit. We do not do these things because we know the end result produces destruction. In a sense, God gives revelation in this same way to where eventually it can become natural to us just like any other area where we are successful. In other words, if we say certain things, it is going to initiate an argument; therefore, we naturally learn how to think like Jesus to where those thoughts are no longer in us which would trigger an argument. It becomes natural or learned! What may not seem natural to our flesh will seem natural to our spirit man within. Once we have the revelation we need in order to do something or not do something because this will be the end result, it also becomes our motivation. Our spirit man must become greater than our fleshly man in order to be all God desires for our lives. If we want the end result to be what God desires, the formula must be to listen and obey. In other words, we are obedient to listen and learn, and then we acquire the results we desire. If we learn this formula, we can never go wrong, and the end result will be very rewarding.

I walked away from the church and fell from grace because I believed something someone said and because someone hurt my feelings. What was the end result? Fifteen years of struggling, no longer having the power of the Holy Spirit, and no longer having guidance or revelation to keep me on the course God planned for me. Everything I did was in me which resulted in sin, and sin brought destruction. What did I learn? I learned that I cannot do this walk in myself. I learned that I cannot remain strong without being fed, and I must follow God allowing Him to lead me.

We draw our strength from the Lord. We can do all things according to Philippians through Christ who strengthens us. How do we claim this strength in our lives? What do we have to do as Christians? We may desire to have all our weaknesses become strengths; however, how do we begin the process where God will begin to give us that revelation in order to conquer defeat in our lives? What is our part that we play?

Philippians 4:13 (ESV) *13I can do all things through him who strengthens me.*

In Luke, it talks about building our house on the rock, a solid foundation, which is Jesus. For those who do not have a solid foundation and a storm comes, the ruin will be great. When trials come our way, we will not be able to stand!

Luke 6:48-49 (ESV) 48he is like a man building a house, who dug deep and laid the foundation on the rock. And when a flood arose, the stream broke against that house and could not shake it, because it had been well built. 49 But the one who hears and does not do them is like a man who built a house on the ground without a foundation. When the stream broke against it, immediately it fell, and the ruin of that house was great."

We can be doing all the right things; however, if we are not grounded and a storm comes, we will fall. I was building my foundation as I walked with the Lord, but our house does not become strong until we are grounded on that rock. We must be deeply planted. Tests and trials will show if your foundation is strong enough to weather through the storms of life. As you begin to face tests, will you grow weary and give up? If you give up in the midst of a test, you will never grow in strength. How much can you endure to gain greater things? The tests will come, and you will fall if you are not grounded. Those first years of my walk with the Lord were full of knowledge and wisdom; however, there still remained much to know in order to withstand the enemy. Besides being healed from all our past pain and knowing we are sons and daughters of the Most High God, daily we must seek God's wisdom, guidance, and knowledge in His Word in order that we remain strong. In Luke, when a storm came, Jesus' disciples immediately began to fear and immediately cried out to the Lord.

Luke 8:23-24 (NASB) [23]*But as they were sailing along He fell asleep; and a fierce gale of wind descended on the lake, and they began to be swamped and to be in danger.* [24]*They came to Jesus and woke Him up, saying, "Master, Master, we are perishing!" And He got up and rebuked the wind and the surging waves, and they stopped, and it became calm.*

In our life, we cannot actually see Jesus, and we definitely have a hard time believing He is in the midst of our storms. If we are going to conquer our fears and have victory in our lives, we have to hold fast to God's Word which states, He is always there with us.

Joshua 1:5 (NIV) [5] *No one will be able to stand up against you all the days of your life. As I was with Moses, so I will be with you; I will never leave you nor forsake you.*

In order to become strong, we must take our eyes off of the storms of life and look to Jesus. We must be grounded in the revelation that our Father is always with us. He will never forsake us, and we must build our foundation on the rock of Jesus. We must know that because of God's love for His children, Jesus died in order that we live and that we do so abundantly.

John 10:10 (Amp)[10]The thief comes only in order to steal and kill and destroy. I came that they may have and enjoy life, and have it in abundance (to the full, till it overflows).

In the midst of a storm, it is hard to keep our eyes on Jesus. Most of our storms in life have titles such as: financial problems, marriage problems, depression, addictions, etc. However, when we look at our circumstances and the current situations we are facing, we miss it. When those tests come, far too often we run away from our source. Far too often, we run into the world for comfort, and this opens a door which allows satan to enter. satan, seeking whom he may devour, comes in to steal, kill, and destroy. satan will destroy our marriages and our families. He will steal our peace, joy, our finances and our children. satan will continue until we have lost everything or until we wake up and get back on the right path. satan will put before you temptations, and most will be areas that you were once weak in prior to being saved and set free. When we open that door, and we lose what we had, we then become weak again. We wake up each morning and go about our lives in our own strength, not that of the Father. In my life, I became weak and fell. I had been healed. I had let go of my past pains and rejections of being emotionally and mentally abused as a child. I had let go of the past pains of being physically abused as an adult. However, I fell because I was not solidly grounded in every area where there were once weaknesses. My way to handle failure or what I would perceive as such was to create a place of hiding. Building those walls gave me a place of refuge. It was a place where on the outside I could pretend all was good, but on the inside, those insecurities and feelings of not being good enough would begin to resurface. I would stop seeing myself as a child of the Most High God. I would stop believing that God desired to use me in great ways. I would stop dreaming that it was possible to be all that He called me to be. After once believing, how can we stop believing? We can see how this happened to the children of Israel. They saw all God was capable of doing, yet they quit believing. This is because satan attacks us in those same areas, and once again, we are blinded. I once again quit believing that I was good enough. I once again began to see myself as nothing because I stopped following and began to lead myself back into the path of destruction. I stopped drawing my strength through Him and trusted the strength within myself. We need to run to God daily for that revelation we need in order to stay focused. We need to draw strength in those areas which we are weak. Understanding our weaknesses will help us to stay strong and trust in God so that we look to Him and not fall back into the world. Here is the point – revelation from the Father is more or less like the blue print into our lives and into our way of thinking. In order to change our way of thinking, we have to have a new set of blue prints.

Let's think about it like this, if you have ever had to study to understand how something worked, then you did what it took to achieve that goal. Like when we first start using a computer, there were times that we may have thought we would never get this. However, once you spent time on the computer and began to get it deep inside of you, it is just like riding a bicycle. Not that we are all "computer geeks" but most of us that spend any amount of time on a computer have learned to grasp how to make it do what we need it to do. Just the same, when we ask for revelation to understand why we do what we do and God begins to show us, it is like turning on that light bulb. We begin to see why we do this and why we do that. When we understand this concept, we begin to have control over that area. At that point, we rise up and refuse to allow satan to continue using those same strategies He has used on us for many years. After satan realizes that it will not work, there will not be any reason for him to attack us in that area again. What I am trying to have you grasp here is this, in order to grow strong with God, we have to get the revelation within us that will make us strong. We need strength in two major areas, in the area of being committed and dedicated to our Lord Jesus Christ and our commitment to the church. We need commitment and dedication in these two areas to be successful Christians in order to begin to grow stronger and begin to mature in the wisdom and knowledge of God. Once we grow in these areas, we can walk in His strength and not ours.

We also need to realize, the strength we draw from God is there for us to walk in daily regardless if our day is going good or if we have a storm arise in our life. It is much better to learn to be obedient while being faced with the small tests, before we are hit with a big test. If we learn to conquer those small tests, we should be able to withstand the bigger ones much easier. If we are walking obediently, God will not send us through any trial or temptation without being there to give us strength. That strength will arise in us when we need it.

Psalm 18:39 (Amp) [39]*For You have girded me with strength for the battle; You have subdued under me and caused to bow down those who rose up against me.*

God desires for us to be strong which is another benefit of being a child of God.

1 Corinthians 1:8 (NIV) *⁸He will keep you strong to the end, so that you will be blameless on the day of our Lord Jesus Christ.*

At some time, we are all faced with trials that may be overwhelming; however, in 1 Corinthians, it says that God is faithful and will not allow us to be tempted beyond what we can bear.

1 Corinthians 10:13 (NIV) *¹³No temptation has seized you except what is common to man. And God is faithful; he will not let you be tempted beyond what you can bear. But when you are tempted, he will also provide a way out so that you can stand up under it.*

I remember this Scripture coming to mind after my daughter died in 2000. I can remember crying out to God saying, *"Lord, I do not know why you think I can bear this because I am literally dying inside."* To lose a child is the greatest loss there is and not understanding why is so hard for parents to bear. I can remember, prior to her death, going to many funerals of her friends and a few of my other daughter's friends, as well. It was so sad, and I can remember leaving after giving my condolences to the parents, and saying to myself, *"I could never endure losing a child."* Then I was faced with just that. I can remember friends who stayed by my side for several weeks saying, *"How are you doing this; you seem to be holding up so well; I could never do this?"* My reply was, *"I am not doing this; I am just going through the motions."* I was numb and in shock. I was in disbelief and could not imagine why God thought I could walk through this. My strength was the book of Job at that time. I read it and meditated on it. How could one man have lost everything, so much more than me, and not given up? God was faithful to give me my revelation in order that I drew strength and received my answers. Today, I can see that I was capable of going through my

271

daughter's death and in the same way that Job did. I never wavered from my belief, and I knew that my God would bring me through my pain. This was not to say that it was an easy road; however, it was a road that I did not walk alone. So yes, our God is faithful and will be there when we need that strength to see us through any situation. He is there by our side and will firmly plant us on the foundation of our Savior, Jesus Christ.

2 Thessalonians 3:3 (Amp) ³Yet the Lord is faithful, and He will strengthen [you] and set you on a firm foundation and guard you from the evil [one].

What is God's will? His will is to perfect us! He is there continually to do a perfect work in us, in order to strengthen us, so that we are equipped with everything we need to be able to walk the path He intended us to walk.

Hebrews 13:21 (Amp) ²¹Strengthen (complete, perfect) and make you what you ought to be and equip you with everything good that you may carry out His will; [while He Himself] works in you and accomplishes that which is pleasing in His sight, through Jesus Christ (the Messiah); to Whom be the glory forever and ever (to the ages of the ages). Amen (so be it).

How do we faithfully walk in this strength? We should look away from anything that would distract us from keeping our eyes set on Jesus. We should keep our eyes on those things which are above and not of the world. Jesus is our example. He is our leader and the source of our faith. If we look to Him, we will be able to endure and increase. However, if we do not stay focused on those things above, we will grow weary, and our minds will begin to wander and faint. Therefore, if we are struggling with sin and struggling trying to live according to the way God sees us, our minds are wandering, and we will lose heart. This is not what God desires for us, and He has given us the answer in order to live according to His promises. As in 2 Corinthians, it was for our sake that God made Christ to be sin for us, so we can become the righteousness of the God who created us.

2 Corinthians 5:21 (Amp) ²¹For our sake He made Christ [virtually] to be sin Who knew no sin, so that in and through Him we might become [endued with, viewed as being in, and examples of] the righteousness of God [what we ought to be, approved and acceptable and in right relationship with Him, by His goodness].

Christian or Disciple

Where was the word "Christian" first used? We see in Acts, the word Christian was used to refer to the disciples, and this is where the word originated.

Acts 11:26 (Amp) ²⁶And when he had found him, he brought him back to Antioch. For a whole year they assembled together with and were guests of the church and instructed a large number of people; and in Antioch the disciples were first called Christians.

What is a disciple? A disciple, in biblical days, went from town to town sharing the gospel of Jesus, helping to spread the good news or the doctrine of Christ. In other words, a disciple is one who walks as Jesus did and brings the gospel to the nations as was commanded. Therefore, we should acknowledge that if we consider ourselves Christians, then we are Disciples of Christ.

In my ministry, I have seen that most people consider themselves Christians, but they are real quick about clarifying that God has not called them to go and share Jesus. Many today believe that all a Christian has to do is attend church and try to live a good life. We could still go a bit deeper, and many would add to this and say, a Christian does not necessarily even have to go to church. Many assume all a Christian has to do is just believe in Jesus. However, now is the time to bring clarity into what a Christian really is and how a Christian is to live. If we want that closer walk with God and want to see victory in our lives, we must begin to grasp one revelation at a time in order to renew our minds to that of Jesus.

According to the Word of God, we see that a Christian in the bible was in reality a Disciple of Christ. A disciple's primary focus is to share the doctrine of Christ to all that God sends across their path. If we consider ourselves to be Christians then we are Disciples of Christ; therefore, it is our responsibility as such to share Jesus. We will go even deeper into the Word of God and see just what disciples are required to do according to the bible. In Matthew, it shows where Jesus went out and said to come after Him and follow Him, and as a disciple, He would make you fishers of men. Being a fisher of men would be to turn from gaining those things in the world and allow your motivations instead to be that of saving souls.

Matthew 4:19 (Amp) **¹⁹***And He said to them, Come after Me [as disciples--letting Me be your Guide], follow Me, and I will make you fishers of men!*

This was not just meant for the first 12 men that Jesus called to walk with Him. In Matthew 16, we see that Jesus said if anyone desires to be "My disciple", not just certain ones but anyone, he must deny himself and take up his cross and follow Him.

Matthew 16:24 (Amp) [24]*Then Jesus said to His disciples, If anyone desires to be My disciple, let him deny himself [disregard, lose sight of, and forget himself and his own interests] and take up his cross and follow Me [cleave steadfastly to Me, conform wholly to My example in living and, if need be, in dying, also].*

Jesus said, if anyone desires to be "My disciple" and disciple being another word for a Christian, then in reality, He said, if you desire to be a Christian, you will deny yourself. This means that we will disregard what we want because it is no longer our decisions any longer, not if we desire to be a Christian. We should lose interest in those things which we desire and our flesh desires. Our focus should be to share the gospel. We see in Matthew 28, Jesus told the 12 they were to go into all the nations and make disciples of all. This is for all who believe on Jesus and desire to be baptized in the name of the Father, Son, and Holy Spirit.

Matthew 28:19 (Amp) [19]*Go then and make disciples of all the nations, baptizing them* [a]*into the name of the Father and of the Son and of the Holy Spirit,*

As we read in Romans below, Paul said for all those who are disciples, they need to be going and making more disciples. Therefore, we see that we are called not just to share Jesus to all those God sends across our path, but we are to minister and make them Disciples of Christ. The church was never meant to stop functioning in reaching out and making more disciples. The church is to continue this same process today. Too many believe that we are just all happy Christians coming together once a week to learn of Christ, and we leave the church keeping what we learned to ourselves instead of helping to grow the Kingdom of Heaven. If you are a Christian, you are a disciple, and Jesus has called you to go and make more disciples. In fact, Jesus said if you claim to be His, you will do this. We were never given a choice in this matter. Jesus did not say, after you become a believer in Him that you can go save souls and make disciples if you feel like it. He did not say, you can just stay at home doing what your flesh desires to do, and hopefully, people will be able to see Jesus in you enough to make it to heaven. Perhaps, you may even get lucky enough to win a few souls for the Kingdom of Heaven if someone by chance can get a glimpse of Christ in you. Jesus also never said, if you believe in Him, you can wear the name "Christian", and you do not have to do anything to claim this name. No, we are commanded to go and make disciples. If we want the full benefit of being a Christian, we have to own up to the fact that every one of us has this calling. It is not a gift to share Jesus. It is not a gift to make disciples but a requirement if you want to be a Christian.

Romans 1:5 (Amp) [5]It is through Him that we have received grace (God's unmerited favor) and [our] apostleship to promote obedience to the faith and make disciples for His name's sake among all the nations,

We need to bring clarity to the famous Scripture, John 3:16. This Scripture would have us believe that all someone has to do is just believe Jesus is the Son of God, and they will receive eternal life.

John 3:16 (ESV) [16]"For God so loved the world, that he gave his only Son, that whoever believes in him should not perish but have eternal life."

276

We cannot take one Scripture in the bible and just assume it to be the only Scripture which talks about eternal life. Yes, it says that as long as we believe in Jesus, we will have eternal life; however, for us to say we believe are just words. I have spoken about words, and to God, words are just words unless followed by action. Words are meaningless if there is not action to go with those words. Just as your spouse or someone special tells you they love you, if they do not treat you like they love you, you are not going to believe it based on just words. Same with God, if there is not some kind of action behind our words, they are meaningless. To know if you really believe in Jesus, look at this Scripture and see if your actions show you believe. Jesus said...

John 14:12 (ESV) [12] *"Truly, truly, I say to you, whoever believes in me will also do the works that I do; and greater works than these will he do, because I am going to the Father."*

You see, Jesus went to the Father and left His disciples with a great and awesome gift. The Comforter, which is the Holy Spirit, lives among those who are His disciples. These are the ones who daily, by their actions, are demonstrating to the Father that they believe. These actions are done by doing those same things Jesus did when He walked on this earth.

You may be saying this is too hard or that you do not know how to do this. You may be saying that you are too shy or that you do not know enough about the bible to share. Maybe you feel that you are not confident enough to be His disciple. That is okay, remember, Moses too felt insecure and lacked confidence, but with God, all things are possible. God does not expect us to jump right in there not knowing how to win souls. As previously discussed, our government does not send our men and women off to war without proper training. How much greater is our God than our government? God will prepare you, and Jesus will prepare the way. All God desires to hear from you at this point is a willingness to obey. God desires for His children to recognize they do have this calling on their lives. He only wants us to be willing to do what we are called to do and be honest with our insecurities. Whatever reservations we may have, we need to bring those fears to the Father. Allow God to begin bringing you to the place you need to be in order that He can use you. As you are obedient, God will begin to bless you wherever you go.

Let me share a story. In my church, our pastor recognizes that all of us, not some but all, have this calling. We began a program where we were all required to go out into the community and minister Jesus in homes of those who do not attend a church. When this was first brought to the church, my first thought in my mind was, *"God, this cannot be you because you know my life; it is too busy."* My life at that time consisted of raising my grandbaby, a full-time job and a part-time job on top of that, managing my rental property in two other states, attending church every time the door was open, working on this book, and ministering to a few inmates in prison. I no more spoke those words in my mind when that voice came and said to me, *"Jolene, are you going to deny me?"* If, it was God of course, I was not going to deny Him. However, in the natural sense, I did not see where there was time to do this. I replied, *"God if this is you, I will try to do one home a week."* The next voice I heard was, *"Are you going to limit me?"* I laughed at that point because it sure sounded like God to me. I could not believe my words were such that I had declared what I would and would not do for God. My reply was, *"God, if you bring them, I will go."* Now let me tell you how this worked, first, we were to make a list of those we knew who did not go to church and invite ourselves in to pray for peace in their home, sharing a brief lesson. I made my list and did not

278

call one person on that list because within the next 3 weeks, I had 8 homes to go into weekly. Remember, I had said to God, *"You send them, and I will go,"* well He sent them, and I went. How was I doing this? Was my life a mess? No! In fact, about 3 months went by, and I began to look back wondering how in the world I was doing this. Then I realized that my life was full of peace. Everything in my life just fell into place, and there was just a presence of the Lord like I had never seen. I knew what our pastor did was provide an avenue for those who would never step out and begin to be that disciple. It was an open door to show those who have never ministered to anyone that they can do this. My advice to anyone reading this would be to find a church which has programs set up in order for those to be encouraged to go out and be that disciple they were called to be, or you may need to be that person who begins a program in your church to open avenues for people to minister. Too many times, we see the churches today having a certain amount in leadership positions within our church body which consists of leaders and members. We see that the job of the member is just to attend, give their tithe, and go home. This was not seen in the churches during the days after Christ died and was resurrected. The disciples were instructed to go and make disciples. The churches began to sprout up, and with that, the members were taught to be disciples. They were taught to go and make more disciples, and the process just continued to grow and grow. We were never meant just to sit in a church for the entirety of our lives and do nothing until time to go home to be with Jesus. We are to get involved and be active. Did you know that God is a God of action? Everything you will read in the Old or New Testament shows God as action. His love is an action; it is not just words. Faith is an action; it is not just words. If we do not get involved, we grow stagnant and do not produce fruit. We grow up; we grow old, and we die. That is it! There is nothing left behind to show how we contributed to winning souls for the Kingdom of Heaven. We have no legacy.

Now for boot camp, in order to go forth as a disciple, we must learn how. The 12 disciples with Jesus, as they went into the various cities and places, remained there as long as it took to train others to be disciples. Then, the next group would rise up and do it again and again. This was how the gospel was spread in those days, and the way it should also be spread today. We cannot assume there are enough evangelists reaching all parts of the world or enough pastors. Think about all those who do not attend church, if you and I do not go forward to share Jesus, they will not be reached. Therefore, your boot camp is merely getting plugged into the right church which believes we all need to be trained and led. We cannot lead until we have been led. God does not expect us to be in a place of leadership until we have paid our dues, so to speak. We must first learn to serve and allow for that training needed. However, God does expect us to be obedient and submit to the training we need in order to share Jesus and make disciples. The shepherd leads the sheep to springs of water. In our case, that is springs of living water. Jesus is our Shepherd. He is the living water which is available if you seek to find Him.

Sin Is A Choice

We have to realize there are no gray areas with God; it is only black and white. Sin is sin. There is no greater sin and no less sin. Sin is not necessarily doing something wrong, but it is also not doing something we are commanded to do. There are doctrines today which teach to come to church and ask for forgiveness for your sins, and you are still saved. These doctrines go on to say if you continue to do the same sin week after week, it is okay as long as you just keep asking for forgiveness, everything is good. However, if we are using this to justify our sin and we have no intention of not doing the sin, then our heart is not right. We have already discussed that our words mean nothing to God. Let's clarify what sin is. Sin is knowingly doing something we know we are not supposed to do according to God's laws, the commandments. It is willfully doing that sin anyway or not doing something which we are commanded to do. Many today believe that when Jesus came the commandments were abolished; however, we can see according to Matthew below, Jesus said…

Matthew 5:17-20 (NIV) [17] *"Do not think that I have come to abolish the Law or the Prophets; I have not come to abolish them but to fulfill them.* [18] *I tell you the truth, until heaven and earth disappear, not the smallest letter, not the least stroke of a pen, will by any means disappear from the Law until everything is accomplished.* [19] *Anyone who breaks one of the least of these commandments and teaches others to do the same will be called least in the kingdom of heaven, but whoever practices and teaches these commands will be called great in the kingdom of heaven.* [20] *For I tell you that unless your righteousness surpasses that of the Pharisees and the teachers of the law, you will certainly not enter the kingdom of heaven."*

Of course, there are none who live a pure and righteous life which would surpass the commandments in Old Testament times. Therefore, it is accurate to state that we are held accountable for our sins according to the Ten Commandments.

1 John 3:9 (Amp) [9]*No one born (begotten) of God [deliberately, knowingly, and habitually] practices sin, for God's nature abides in him [His principle of life, the divine sperm, remains permanently within him]; and he cannot practice sinning because he is born (begotten) of God.*

In 1 John, we see if someone willfully chooses to practice sin, they are not born of God. If they are in sin based on their own free-will, they do not know the Father and do not have that deep, heartfelt relationship of knowing Him. Most of us really know our parents, and when we are raised in a good nurturing home, with awesome parents who also brought us up in the ways of the Lord, we do not deliberately want to do anything to disappoint them. Many of us, even if we were not raised in the best of families, still did not want to disappoint our parents. In the same sense, if we really know the Father, we desire to make Him pleased with our conduct and with every step we take. We should continually strive to make our Father proud of us. I know over the years many of my friends or acquaintances when they would do something wrong, even mentioning you were going to tell their parents, the conversation went to, *"No – don't you dare tell my parents!"* I believe many of us can relate to this through our teen years and into our 20's, but why were we so concerned with our parents knowing our sin? Many times because of consequences; however, many of us even though we may not have wanted to admit it, did not want to disappoint our parents. We are supposed to look at God as our Father because if you are born again, He is your Father. Why then do we not take into consideration what He thinks? Why do we not take into consideration the disappointment He feels? Why do we not think about the consequences to our sins? God sees all and hears all. We cannot do anything in which He is not aware of, yet we act as though we could care less what He is thinking during our disobedience. When we grow up to the age of accountability and knowingly commit sin day after day, week after week, and we run to church to ask for forgiveness, we then feel justified that we did what was needed. Therefore, we can run back into the world and do it all over again. Do we think that God is just okay with us knowingly committing the same sin day after day? Do we think God understands because after all, we live in these fleshly bodies, and they are going to sin? We show more respect to our earthly parents than we do to our Creator, the One who gave His only Son to die for us and pay the price for our sins. There have been instances in our lives where we may have done something which cost someone we cared about a debt rather it was in money or consequences. We felt horrible for the pain we caused and did everything to make it up. Yet, God gave His Son to die on the Cross to pay the price for me and you deliberately sinning day after day, not even caring the pain that He endured to give us a better life. Our family and our friends gain greater respect than we give to our Creator. God desires a people who are sensitive to His will. He desires those who want to strive daily to walk free from sin. You may say it cannot be done, but ask yourself, that sin you knowingly commit every day, does it have control over you? Are we not able to make the choice to either sin or not to sin? If, we were to admit the truth, we choose to commit that sin every day in order to satisfy our fleshly desires, and we do not want to give it up. Ask yourself this, *"If, it was a matter of life or death would you give it up?"* Let's look at some specifics here in order to clarify sin of the flesh in which we choose to engage. Perhaps, you are involved in premarital sex outside of marriage; perhaps, you are involved in making money in a way that is not legal; perhaps, you are involved with someone who is married or you are married; perhaps, you are taking money from your employer or a friend without them knowing; perhaps, you are cheating the government. Whatever your sin is, think about it right now. I am not referring to those who have addictions at this time because these areas are strong holds, which will be addressed in a later series. What I am referring to are those sins that we willingly commit because we do not want to stop them. I am referring to those sins which satisfy our flesh. Now, let's look at some consequences. These are consequences which could happen or will happen if you continue, but in any sense, there will be a consequence, and that will depend on what tactic satan decides to use on you. If you continue long enough, eventually you will pay for that sin. Even if, you do quit and do not make things right, you will still pay for that sin, not only you but your children.

Premarital sex has many consequences, which you may not have considered, such as unwanted pregnancy, STD's or AIDS. Do not think just because you use protection that you are okay. When we willingly commit sin, we open the door for destruction into our lives. In Isaiah, it says those whose feet rush into sin are willingly committing that sin. If your feet are carrying you and you are allowing it, you have voluntarily made that choice to walk away from God and into darkness.

Isaiah 59:7 (NIV) [7] *Their feet rush into sin; they are swift to shed innocent blood. Their thoughts are evil thoughts; ruin and destruction mark their ways.*

What is innocent blood? We know men are not innocent; therefore, what is innocent? Animals are innocent and our children are also innocent up until they reach a certain age of accountability. Many times, we see that abortion is so rampant in our society in which innocent blood is shed because of one night's pleasure. Perhaps, you are saying that you would not be part of an abortion, but ask yourself if you are willing to give up your life to raise a child that was not wanted. When a child is brought into this world which was never really wanted, they bear this burden upon their lives. Many times, children are born into this world where the mom may love them, but the dads are not even in the picture or vice versa. In many of these families, that child bears the mark of rejection. Many times, that child suffers because of being an unplanned pregnancy. These children suffer from lack in areas of attention, nutrition, structure, discipline, guidance, education, and I could go on and on with afflictions suffered by those who are innocent. This is not fair to our children, and we have to be responsible for our actions.

Let's go a bit deeper. Suppose you are involved with someone steady and are engaged in premarital sex. According to Isaiah, you are still in sin, and sin brings destruction to your life. I can remember years ago being taught that as long as you are walking with the Lord, you have that umbrella of protection over your life. However, when you willingly sin, you step out from under that umbrella. Suppose you are living in this sin and one day, satan decides He wants to put tragedy on your life. Was this tragedy caused by your sin? Our actions play a big part in what happens in our lives. God desires for us to obey in order that He can protect what is His. When we willingly commit sin, we open that door for evil to come. When we willingly commit sin, we are obeying the evil desires of our flesh.

Romans 6:12 (NIV) [12]Therefore do not let sin reign in your mortal body so that you obey its evil desires.

Maybe, you are involved in making money in a way that is not legal or you are stealing from your company or a friend. Either way, you are taking that which is not legally yours; therefore, what could the consequences be? There are many bad things which could happen if you were to get caught. We need to think about the consequences because if we continue, we will get caught. You could wind up in jail, lose your job, lose your friend, or become a statistic of a violent crime by someone you never meant to hurt. Do we think about the consequences to our sin? No, we do not because if we did, we might do things differently. Think about this, if you have children or people who depend on you, what would the consequences do to them if you were caught? How would it affect or hurt those who love you? Would getting caught be enough to make you wake up? Remember, satan loves it when we are in sin because he knows we have turned our back on God, and our lives fall under his mercy. When in sin, we are not under that umbrella of protection. Hopefully, you have someone who loves you and has that deep relationship with God because you may have favor due to their prayers. Let's look at one more, suppose you are involved with someone who is married or you are married. There can be many consequences, but the end result is never a good one. When you get caught, there are many people who are hurt. When your sin is exposed, you will pay a big price. I do not believe I have to go on about the consequences on any of these; however, there is one more consequence that has not been mentioned. What we do today, will come back on our children and their children to the fourth generation.

Numbers 14:18 (NIV) [18] *'The LORD is slow to anger, abounding in love and forgiving sin and rebellion. Yet he does not leave the guilty unpunished; he punishes the children for the sin of the fathers to the third and fourth generation.'*

These are generational curses. You may say this is unfair; however, there is nothing which hurts us more than to see our own children go through hard situations. These curses can be broken off of a generation, but you have to be walking with God in order for this to happen and then it takes prayer. Here is the thing, even if you do not have children at this time in your life, think about your own father and the sins he committed. We pay for the sins of our fathers. When I first gained this revelation many years ago, it totally made sense. I thought back about my own father's sins. He cheated on my mother through their whole marriage. My life was full of men who cheated on me. At one time, I felt there were no men out there that did not cheat. I did have a bad outlook on men; however, there are good men out there today. For a dad to see his daughter suffer from one relationship to another because the men always cheat on her, it is very painful. That dad is paying for his mistakes, and his dad paid for his. It is nothing more than paying for our father's sins. Yes, it is a cycle which is what the world calls it, but God called it first. The world says we choose to marry into what we perceive is normal based on our childhood experiences. However, this is the same thing as generational curses which have been handed down to us. The world says we can go through counseling in order to heal from the past, and God says we can renew our mind and our way of thinking when we learn of Him. It is our choice to walk with the world's beliefs or choose God's way. I believe to go with that which has been founded the longest and has the best success rate. God's wisdom has been around from the beginning of time, and the success rate beats that of the world by far. So, if you are a man today and you are engaged in any kind of sin, your children will reap the bad seeds which you have planted. If you are alive to see it, you will witness your daughters and your sons paying a horrible price for what you have committed. It is not to put the blame on anyone out there because if you have committed these sins, it is because you too are paying that price of what your dad has done. This does not leave women out. There are many women today which are the head of the household. You are responsible for your children's spiritual upbringing, and everything which you do will either produce good or bad seeds in your own children. As for the fathers to these children being raised in a single parent-home with their mothers, even though you are absent, you hold the greatest responsibility towards your children. When divorce happens, you cannot divorce your children. God hates divorce for many reasons, but our children bear the worst pain of all by growing up in homes which are fatherless. Hopefully, these teachings will wake up this generation and generations to come, to be able to see there is nothing good which comes from our sins. Generational curses are very prevalent in our society today due to our forefathers before us. The good news is these curses on our families can be broken, and our children can be set free once and for all. In order for this to happen, we need to make changes in our lives today for generations to come. You need to ask yourself today, if that sin in your life is worth your children having to pay the price. Perhaps you think what I am saying bears no merit; however, I challenge you to study this in the Scriptures, and if I am right, why would you want to put this sin upon your own children?

In order to follow Jesus, we have to be obedient to obeying all the commandments, and in doing this, we have to be sensitive to recognizing those things which are sin in our lives. Once we recognize our sin, we must be obedient to making the right decision and walk away from those things which keep us in bondage. We need to be ready to come clean and be set free from those fleshly desires in order that we begin planting good seeds for generations to come.

We all understand what sin is, but we must also look at what sin is not. Sin is not doing something the Word commands us to do. Perhaps, we did not know it was sin. There may be things which have become habits since we have become accustomed to doing them for so long. However, God may be trying to help us break those habits because they are contrary to His Word. These sins are usually done without even realizing that what we are currently doing is sin, but the Holy Spirit is there to lead and guide us away from those sins. He is there to teach us and remind us of all truths. When we hear that small, quiet voice saying, *"You know* you should not do this" or "You need to do this," and we choose to do the opposite anyway, we are willingly committing sin. God knows our heart, and we cannot use a prayer just to stay right with God. We cannot continually be in a relationship outside of marriage knowing it is sin and on a weekly basis, we ask God to forgive us while running right back into that sin. Yes, God does forgive, but He also knows our heart. God knows if our prayer is genuine. He knows if our prayer is just a means of being able to justify we are still going to heaven. God knows where our heart is, and if we die while we are choosing to walk back into our sin, in order to gratify the flesh, the outcome may not be what was expected. Now, if you do something out of habit then you are not willingly committing sin. In reading this book to this point, you may have gained knowledge in areas that you never knew prior, and if you were engaged in sin in those areas I have discussed, you were not willingly committing sin until you gained the knowledge about your sin. However, you are held responsible for your choice to walk in sin, once you gain the knowledge from this book, through the Word of God, or any other method God chooses to bring you the truth. When you begin that walk with the Lord and truly desire to know God, you are going to hear that voice and then you are accountable for the revelation which has been given to you. If you are a Christian or have been a Christian for some time and have never heard that voice, it may be because you have never desired that intimate relationship with the Lord. When God knows you really want to know Him, He will reveal Himself to you in one way or another, and then the Holy Spirit's job is to teach you all things and to remind you of truths. This includes those things which are habit. The Holy Spirit will continually correct you in order to break those bad habits.

John 14:26 (Amp) [26]But the Comforter (Counselor, Helper, Intercessor, Advocate, Strengthener, Standby), the Holy Spirit, Whom *the Father will send in My name [in My place, to represent Me and act on My behalf], He will teach you all things. And He will cause you to recall (will remind you of, bring to your remembrance) everything I have told you.*

When you begin to listen for that voice of the Holy Spirit, He will begin to teach you all things. He will begin to bring all truths to your mind because this is how the Holy Spirit works. God desires for us to know all truths not just some. To God, sin is sin, and it does not matter if we classify it as a big sin or little sin. You can die and go to hell for a little lie the same as you can go for murder, or you can be forgiven for a little sin the same as a big sin.

In order to see what willingly being in sin is and what it is not, let me share this story. One day, while I was traveling down interstate, I hear that voice that said, *"Jolene, you do not need to be going over the speed limit."* Of course, at this time in my life, I am sensitive to the Holy Spirit teaching me because I know that God desires my obedience in every area of my life. Therefore, I slow down and repent to the Lord saying, *"I'm sorry Father, you are right."* At that moment, I am forgiven; I am not in sin. To most, this would be a little sin; however, to God, sin is sin. As a society, we have been raised to believe it is okay if we go over the speed limit as long as it is only 5 miles over and in some places 10 miles over. However, why is it okay to go over? If the speed limit is set for "60", then in reality, that is what we are supposed to go. Most of us go over the limit because we know we will not be pulled over as long as we fall in a certain range. The speed limit is set due to what the highway department deems to be safe for that particular stretch of road. When we choose to go over, we are at a higher risk for a fatal accident, and God desires us to do what is right according to man's laws, unless contrary to His Word.

If, the Holy Spirit is trying to make you aware of something that you need to do or not do, it may very well be for your safety. God cannot keep me safe if I am not sensitive to that small voice. If, on the other hand, I think like most Americans, with the attitude I can go this fast because I will not get a ticket, later down the road I could be involved in a bad accident. I may be lucky enough that I did not die but later question God on why He allowed this to happen since I am a Christian. Perhaps, I was not listening to that small voice. Perhaps, I chose not to listen because I did not want to obey. Now when I share this, I always point out this was an area God dealt with me on obedience. If, He has not spoken to you about this, please do not take this as something you are required to do at this time. This is only an example to show how the Holy Spirit works in our lives. Remember, God begins cleaning up your life one area at a time, and there may be areas in your life that are of much greater importance right now. What God was trying to show me was that I was in sin by not obeying the speed limit, if in fact I willingly did this after hearing that small, quiet voice. By my obedience, I was immediately forgiven. Now, the next time I was traveling the same highway, again, the Holy Spirit spoke to me to slow down. I apologized and slowed down. Was I willingly committing that sin? No, when we have been doing something by habit for so many years, the habit will not be broken over night. Therefore, I automatically get behind the wheel and do what I do without even thinking about it over and over again. As long as each time I hear that voice I repent and slow down, gradually the old habit will be replaced with the new habit. After this, the Holy Spirit began showing me how to be a more courteous driver. I would repent and allow someone to cut in front of me instead of me cutting someone off. Here is what we need to see, if someone cuts you off in traffic and you are steadily cursing them out, it could be someone which has been dealt with by the Holy Spirit. If, they are listening to that voice, they have repented and were immediately forgiven, while you are in sin. When I used to hear my friends talk about their road rage that God was dealing with, I would share this. You may be perfectly fine that day, walking with God and in right-standing when someone like me cuts you off in traffic. God deals with me to be obedient, and I make it right while you lost it. You end up being in sin by your response to my mistake. Even though, I was the one who missed it first, you missed it right behind me because you allowed it to affect you. I repented and had a blessed day while satan kept you in defeat all day long. It is a thought because we never know where someone is at in their walk with God, and if satan can use that to start your day off wrong, then you are headed for destruction throughout your day!

What is sin and what is not sin? Sin is intentionally doing something or not doing something which we are commanded to do. We are not in sin when we do something by habit or something we were not aware was sin until we make that decision to do it anyway, after the Holy Spirit brought it before us.

Following the Shepherd

We desire to follow and allow Jesus to lead us to springs of living water.

Revelation 7:17 (NIV) [17]*For the Lamb at the center of the throne will be their shepherd; he will lead them to springs of living water. And God will wipe away every tear from their eyes."*

In order to find those springs of living water, which Revelation is referring, we must obey those things which Jesus commanded. There are the 10 commandments as well as commands which Jesus gave to all who consider themselves disciples. If we are wavering in any areas, in just one tiny area, we are in sin. Many of us today have based our salvation and our walk with the Lord on what man has told us, or our salvation is based on what a particular doctrine has said instead of receiving our beliefs and doctrines from God. We need to seek, for ourselves, to see if our beliefs and our way of thinking line up with what God's Word says. If not, we need to make that decision to seek God daily in order to know that we are going to heaven, and we are doing all that is commanded.

In my beginning walk with the Lord, I felt pressured to go forward to ask for salvation. I was getting married to a guy who was raised in church, and the family wanted me to be saved prior to our wedding. The preacher visited the house to speak to me one on one, and finally, I did go forward to receive salvation. However, it was not because I knew God. I did not have that deep, heartfelt relationship with the Father. Remember, Jesus told Peter in Matthew 16:17, blessed are you, Peter. Why was Peter blessed? No man, no doctrine, no preacher, no evangelist had revealed to Peter that Jesus was the Son of God. God in heaven revealed this to him. We should openly declare our salvation; however, we will never be saved unless God has revealed to us who He is. We will never have that deep, heartfelt relationship with God until it comes from the Father. People wonder why they do not feel the presence of God. They wonder why they do not hear His voice. Perhaps, it is because they have not submitted themselves to God in the right heart attitude to receive what He desires to give them. With me, I left the church that day feeling no different because I was no different. Prior to the day I walked forward, I was seeking God just like many today and continued to seek Him even after that day. I wanted to understand, and I wanted to know who He was. However, my heart was not right. My reasons for getting saved to begin with were not right. My salvation was due to the pressure which I felt from my future spouse and his family. By no means was this wrong because if they had not pushed me to begin with, I may never have found God. The wrong part here is that many today believe they are saved because of something similar happening to them, and they have never felt God in their lives. The point of this story is to see that many times our motivations for going forward at church or saying the sinner's prayer are not for the right reason. I had met my future spouse in the nightclub back during a time he was backslidden, and I was lost. My life during those days became one party after another, and there was no desire to change. Prior to us getting married, he had told me, the day we get married, our friends we hung out with were a thing of the past and partying was over. He had told me that we would be in church. Of course, I did not think he meant that, but he did. Therefore, when I went forward, my heart was not where it needed to be in order for me to receive salvation. I did not feel I needed God at that time in my life. However, a short time later, I did need God. You may be saying, we should not run to God out of a need, but I would have to disagree with you. Most people begin searching for God when they are in need. God desires to make us complete, and as His children, He wants us to run to Him when we come to that place of pain in our lives. Now, I will say that too many times, we run to God with a need, and after He seems to make everything right in our lives, we walk away feeling as though we no longer need Him. This will be discussed, but for now, my focus is to show you how to know if you are where you need to be in seeking God. We will never be able to follow if we are not being led by the Shepherd. Several months after I married, I was in the hospital facing a second miscarriage. The hospital was trying to do all they could to keep me from losing the baby. This story I will share in more depth later; however, the point is I came to that place where I needed God. God gave me a vision that night as I slept, and the next day, the baby died. I was very angry at God. I went home from the hospital, and while soaking in the bathtub, I cried out to God and told Him how it was not fair that He took my child. After all, I felt as if I was saved because I went forward at church. That is the first time I actually felt the presence of God in my life. To me, it was not that I thought I really needed God, I was just very angry with Him. The point is that I believed He existed, and He was responsible for my pain. Being an awesome God, He understands what we feel inside. He knew I just needed Him to love me, and that is what He did. Looking back, I believe I was seeking; however, my heart had not been right. During the loss of my baby, I was broken. In our brokenness, we can usually find God if we search deep. I realized God had given me the vision about my baby in my sleep that night, but I did not understand that vision for some time later.

Let me clarify our salvation or our walk with God. Our spiritual encounter needs to be revealed by the Father. We will never see victory in our lives until we know our Father. God cannot work in your life if your heart is not right. Our main focus in life before we can begin the life of a disciple should be to seek and find!

Deuteronomy 4:29 (NIV) [29] But if from there you seek the LORD your God, you will find him if you look for him with all your heart and with all your soul.

In Deuteronomy, it does not say you may find Him; it says you will find Him. However, it must be with all our heart and soul. Remember, God is an action God, and He desires action. Words can just be words and not mean anything if there is not action behind them. In order to seek God with all that is within us, we must get to know Him. Getting to know God is spending much time studying His Word. He left us a legacy, but He cannot make us read it. God knows if you really desire to seek Him. He will test you to see if you want it bad enough because He wants a people that are willing to die for Him! This is not necessarily a physical death but dying to self and following Jesus. Ask yourself, what are you doing for Christ? Jesus said, *"If you love me, you will obey what I commanded."* Do we even know what Jesus commanded us to do? If not, how can we say we know the Father and yet do not know everything we are to do?

John 14:15 (NIV) ¹⁵"If you love me, you will obey what I command."

Jesus said if we love Him, we will obey Him. It goes on in John 14:24 to say, we will obey His teachings. It does not say some of His teachings but "My teachings". I take that to mean everything that Jesus taught. These teachings, according to this Scripture, do not come from Jesus but from the Father who sent Him. Therefore, God spoke through Jesus everything He was to share with those who follow after Him.

John 14:24 (Amp) ²⁴Anyone who does not [really] love Me does not observe and obey My teaching. And the teaching which you hear and heed is not Mine, but [comes] from the Father Who sent Me.

Remember, Jesus is God's Word made flesh.

John 1:14 (NIV) ¹⁴The Word became flesh and made his dwelling among us. We have seen his glory, the glory of the One and Only, who came from the Father, full of grace and truth.

Therefore, we are not only to obey the 10 commandments, which were given in the Old Testament, but also everything that Jesus commanded and taught, as well. In order to obey, we must know our Father on an intimate level. We must get to the place where we have a deep love for the Father, Jesus, and the Holy Spirit. How can we do that if we know very little about the Trinity? If, we are living in the world and doing our own thing by continually satisfying the flesh, how can we claim to be living for Christ? Maybe, you were living the life of a Christian at one time, and perhaps, you walked away as I did. Perhaps, you find yourself backslidden today. Maybe, you are striving to find your way back just like I did so many times. If you are reading this, God sees your heart and sees that you have chosen to read and study in order to learn of Him. You may be striving to grow by spending time in His Word instead of reading something of the world. God knows if we desire to grow and to know Him. God will send people across our path, and the Holy Spirit will not stop convicting us. All of this is because God has such a great love for you and me. He just wants His children to come home. Throughout those 15 years that I was out in the world, God never ceased trying to get me home. The Holy Spirit did convict me time and time again, but sometimes we get so caught up in the things of the world, it is almost as if we are literally lost and cannot find our way back. This is how I felt, *"God, how do I get back to where I was; where do I begin?"* These were thoughts I had along with many conversations with my Father. It was a struggle to get back, but hallelujah, I made it home! The enemy had a good hold on me, and it began with one simple lie that I listened to and allowed to escalate. It says in 1 John, we are to test the spirits because they are not all from God.

1 John 4:1-2 (ESV) ¹Beloved, do not believe every spirit, but test the spirits to see whether they are from God, for many false prophets have gone out into the world. ²By this you know the Spirit of God: every spirit that confesses that Jesus Christ has come in the flesh is from God,

The first lie the enemy told me was that I did not need the church, and I could make it with just God and myself. Of course, I never thought the little voice I heard was from satan. I knew the church had made some mistakes and knew it was not the church that guaranteed your salvation; however, I did not test the spirit. I just listened as Eve did in the Garden of Eden. If you allow those false messages to come at you long enough, then you will entertain those thoughts and be deceived. I began to believe, *"Yes, I could walk with God and do not need the church."* Little did I know that opening the door to satan blinded me from the truth.

1 John 2:11 (Amp) ¹¹But he who hates (detests, despises) his brother [in Christ] is in darkness and walking (living) in the dark; he is straying and does not perceive or know where he is going, because the darkness has blinded his eyes.

When we fall into a trap and listen to a lie, we fall into darkness. God is love, and without that love, we hate, despise, detest, and judge. The door is open to suck us into the deceitfulness of satan all because we believed a lie. Just as Eve listened and entertained the thought, she then believed the lie. Besides the enemy taking every opportunity to bring us down, there are also many false prophets. We need to know if what we are listening to lines up with the Word of God, but that is not going to happen if we never study and read His Word to get it deep inside of us. I have met and ministered to many who have told me, the doctrine they have been brought up on never encouraged them to read the Scriptures. Therefore, their teachings of biblical truths came solely from leaders within that congregation. We need to know the voice we are listening to confesses, *"Jesus has come in the flesh and is the Son of God,"* then we know that spirit is from God. However, just because a church teaches Jesus, does not mean they teach the full gospel. Remember, we do not need some of the Word but all of the Word. It goes on to say, in 1 John, for us to love one another for God is love.

1 John 4:7 (ESV) ⁷Beloved, let us love one another, for love is from God, and whoever loves has been born of God and knows God.

Whoever loves is from God; they have been born of God and know God. Anyone who does not love does not know God. Love was made manifest in the flesh when God sent Jesus; therefore, this was God in the flesh, and God is love. God sent Jesus in order for us to live through Him and live in this God-kind of love.

1 John 4:8 (Amp) ⁸He who does not love has not become acquainted with God [does not and never did know Him], for God is love.

As Christians, we need to be careful about how we see God. Our desires should be one of seeking Him on a level where we come to know Him. If we do not know someone, how can we love them? If you have ever been married, think about those first days or even months, did you know your spouse? You knew that person enough to love them; otherwise, you would never have married them. Of course, sometimes there are other reasons for marrying, but in the normal sense, people get married because they feel a deep love for someone. Many times on down the road, we realize we never really knew who we married, and it ends in divorce. If prior to getting married, we would have found God and gotten to know Him, many of our marriages may not have ended in divorce. Have you ever heard the saying, until you can love yourself, you cannot love someone else? In a sense, this is true. If you are dealing with not liking yourself very much, it is hard to have that love in your heart to love someone else. However, you will never really love yourself to the degree you are capable until you can first love God. God is love; the world is not. There is a huge difference in the two kinds of love. The world's love is always looking out for what is in it for me, myself and I, while God's love is the complete opposite. God does not love like the world, and until we can learn to love like God, we will always fall short in our life. If, we desire to be able to love with that deep, heartfelt love, we must first seek the Father and learn from Him.

1 John 4:12 (Amp) [12]*No man has at any time [yet] seen God. But if we love one another, God abides (lives and remains) in us and His love (that love which is essentially His) is brought to completion (to its full maturity, runs its full course, is perfected) in us!*

When we learn to love, we know that God abides in us, and we abide in Him. However, if we say we love God and know God but we have hate for our brother, how can we say we love? If we hold grudges against others and unforgiveness is evident in our hearts, how can we say we love? He who does not love does not know God! We say we believe in Jesus, do we really know Him? Do we understand the plan that God desires to be completed in our lives? Do we understand how God feels when we disobey Him? Do we know how God hurts when He continually sees us not loving our brother or not sharing Jesus with someone He sends across our path? Do we know Jesus enough to believe in Him? Jesus is the son of God, love manifested in the flesh, do we know how Jesus feels? What moves Him? Do we understand how Jesus came to love us and care about our situations and concerns after walking in our shoes and feeling our pain? Do we really understand how painful it was for Jesus to endure our sin and suffer on the Cross at Calvary? Do we know what moves the Father? Do we know what grieves the Father? When we begin to know someone we are close to, we know what to do to put a smile on their face. We know the things to do to make them proud of us, and we know the things to do which makes them enjoy spending time with us. Do we know what puts a smile on our Father? Do we know what makes Him proud of us? Ask yourself, do you really know the Father? Do you really know Jesus? When we first come to the Lord, it is by faith. It is by faith that we ask Jesus into our heart, and it is by faith we believe He is the Son of God. Again, it is by faith we believe Jesus was sent by the Father in order to give us eternal life. Does it just stop there? No, we must strive to know the Father. We must seek to know Jesus, and we must pray. We must read His Word diligently because it contains everything we need to become who God desires us to be. When we ask Jesus into our heart, we will know if it is heartfelt because there will be a stirring and a desire deep within to want to seek Him. There will be a deep desire to want more of Him. If that desire is not there, I would question my salvation. I would hate to think I went to church one day, went forward and asked Jesus into my heart then came to church here and there, but I never really came to know who God is. If, we are never consistent because we put forth little to no effort in developing that relationship with God, how do we expect to know who Jesus is and understand God's purpose for our lives? Our lives will all come to an end one day, and it will be sad to know that we took a chance with our salvation. For those who took this chance, they may face God on judgment day with nothing to show for what they thought they believed to be true. There will be nothing to show for our walk with God other than a mere confession which we thought was faith but meant nothing because it was only words. The question should be, did we really believe what we asked for and if so, why did it stop there? Why do we continue to live in sin, knowingly living in sin day after day? I would hate to think I listened to a church sermon or person that was in the wrong spirit, and my Christianity was based on what someone had told me instead of what God wanted to show me. Today, God desires for you to seek Him. When you do begin to seek Him because you have that desire to know Him and be in His presence, what will happen? Seek and you shall find, ask and it shall be given, knock and the door will be opened.

Luke 11:9 (Amp) [9]*So I say to you, Ask and keep on asking and it shall be given you; seek and keep on seeking and you shall find; knock and keep on knocking and the door shall be opened to you.*

Notice that it says in Luke, to keep on, keep on, and do not stop! How many times, when we want something really bad, do we keep on and keep on until it manifest? Why do we quit so easily with God? The reason is because of unbelief. If, we believe that God is everything He says He is in the Scriptures, we would never stop. Remember, I shared when I came back after 15 years that I had made up my mind, *"God, this time I am not going anywhere until I feel you again in my life!"* I had struggled with this for 15 years. I had tried going back into the churches and walking the walk again, but I was only trying. The difference after 15 years was that I made up my mind I wanted Him back in my life, and I would not quit until He was there! It took me 3 months, going through the motions weekly at church, but it was well worth it! I continued to ask; I continued to seek, and I continued to knock. Do not stop! If, you want victory over your life and you want to know God, do not stop searching! If you want to have that deep, heartfelt relationship with our Creator, do not stop! The door will open just as it did for me. After you feel your relationship with God begin to grow, the Shepherd will lead you to springs of living water.

However, for some it may be hard to follow the Shepherd if you are not even sure the Scriptures are accurate. Recently, I was engaged in a conversation with someone who told me that we have no idea what part of the bible is true and what is not. This was based on the fact that it was written by man and not by God. If you feel that way, let me share something with you. The bible was inspired by God through men who were anointed by the Holy Spirit which is God's nature within.

1 John 3:9 (Amp) ⁹No one born (begotten) of God [deliberately, knowingly, and habitually] practices sin, or God's nature abides in him [His principle of life, the divine sperm, remains permanently within him]; and he cannot practice sinning because he is born (begotten) of God.

Even in the Old Testament, God's anointing was on the men of old, and their words were inspired by God. We see in Mark it speaks of David, who was inspired by the Holy Spirit.

Mark 12:36 (Amp) ³⁶David himself, [inspired] in the Holy Spirit, declared, The Lord said to my Lord, Sit at My right hand until I make Your enemies [a footstool] under Your feet.

Paul said in Thessalonians, we are to be imitators of him, and it goes further to say that his message was inspired by the Holy Spirit. Remember, if you are a child of God, the Holy Spirit should be in you; therefore, you should be imitators of Christ and imitators of those who are Disciples of Christ.

1 Thessalonians 1:6 (Amp) ⁶And you [set yourselves to] become imitators of us and [through us] of the Lord Himself, for you welcomed our message in [spite of] much persecution, with joy [inspired] by the Holy Spirit;

The words, which are inspired by the Holy Spirit, are to bring Jesus and the whole gospel to the world. Anytime a man or woman of God is bringing revelation, those words will line up with

303

what God's Word says. Those words brought should not be depreciated, meaning we should not decrease those words in value. We should not downgrade or devalue those words. The words brought forth are to either encourage us or give us warning.

1 Thessalonians 5:20 (Amp) [20]Do not spurn the gifts and utterances of the prophets [do not depreciate prophetic revelations nor despise inspired instruction or exhortation or warning].

If you have a hard time believing what is written, it is because you have never had that one on one heartfelt relationship with God. This very book, you are reading, was also inspired by God. The way it was formed was by the inspiration of God; however, the way it is presented has much of my personality which was given to me by God. We all have our own unique personalities which is our gift from God. When we line our lives up to begin serving Him, He desires for our personalities to come forth. After all, this is what makes each of us unique. Different people relate to different personalities. There may be people who can learn from me and others who cannot, but for the revelation given, it is inspired by God. For those whose eyes have been open to the truth, they can read and interpret that it is God's work within someone. For those who cannot see this, according to John, their eyes have been blinded. Many times, we are blinded by the truth due to our hearts being cold and unreceptive. If, you have a hard time understanding the Word or believing, you are not being open to the Father.

John 12:40 (Amp) [40]He has blinded their eyes and hardened and benumbed their [callous, degenerated] hearts [He has made their minds dull], to keep them from seeing with their eyes and understanding with their hearts and minds and repenting and turning to Me to heal them.

Again we see in Corinthians, that the god of this world, satan, has blinded those who are unbelievers. Those who have this revelation can see this. If you cannot see this, your heart has been hardened because of unbelief. Until you repent and ask God to reveal the light unto you, satan will continue to keep you in bondage.

2 Corinthians 4:4 (Amp) ⁴*For the god of this world has blinded the unbelievers' minds [that they should not discern the truth], preventing them from seeing the illuminating light of the Gospel of the glory of Christ (the Messiah), Who is the Image and Likeness of God*

Jesus said in John, those who believe in Him will also believe in the One who sent Him. It goes on to say when we look at Him, we will also see the One who sent Him. In other words, when we believe and see Jesus, we see Jesus in everything we do. As God's children, we can see Him working in our lives. We can see that our Father is at work in us because He is light, and we remain in the light when we trust and walk in faith with our Father. However, for those who cannot let go of those beliefs in which they have construed in their minds, they are blinded. When you trust in your own answers and your own way, you are blinded by the darkness, and there is no light within you. It goes on to say, those who reject Him and do not accept that the Word of God is inspired Words, will be condemned by those very Words they did not receive. In other words, if you reject words in the bible pertaining to a sin you are currently enveloped in, it will be that sin which will condemn you. This also holds true for any man or woman of God which brings inspired words that line up with God's Word.

John 12:44-50 (NIV) ⁴⁴*Then Jesus cried out, "When a man believes in me, he does not believe in me only, but in the one who sent me.* ⁴⁵*When he looks at me, he sees the one who sent me. ⁴⁶I have come into the world as a light, so that no one who believes in me should stay in darkness. ⁴⁷"As for the person who hears my words but does not keep them, I do not judge him. For I did not come to judge the world, but to save it. ⁴⁸There is a judge for the one who rejects me and does not accept my words; that very word which I spoke will condemn him at the last day. ⁴⁹For I did not speak of my own accord, but the Father who sent me commanded me what to say and how to say it. ⁵⁰I know that his command leads to eternal life. So whatever I say is just what the Father has told me to say."*

Even Jesus claimed He did not speak of His own accord, but God the Father commanded Him what to say and how to say it. Take this book or any spiritual book that you pick up to read, if it is inspired by God and lines up with the Word of God, that author will tell you nothing can be accomplished without Him who sent them. During my time spent on this book, there were times I would struggle with the words and then times when it went smooth. During one of those hard times, I had cried out to God wanting to know why all of a sudden I was struggling. God's reply, *"Jolene, you stopped letting me guide you through all truths, and you began trying to do it in you."* Wow, when I heard those words, I cried. I did not want this book to be me; I wanted it to be God. If we are struggling, it is not God.

If, you question the Scriptures, this is an area where satan will keep you bound in order for you never to know the truth. If, you are open to receiving the truth, your way of thinking must change. God is well pleased with those who have favor with Him. How do we have favor? We listen and obey. Stop trying to figure it out in you. Stop trying to reason with your mind. We do not need to try and find some kind of concrete evidence or scientific proof. If, we do not stop trying to be God, our eyes will never see the truth, and we will miss out on great revelation and insight into the depths of God.

Luke 2:14 (Amp) [14]*Glory to God in the highest [heaven], and on earth peace among men with whom He is well pleased [men of goodwill, of His favor].*

Listen to Isaiah, do we seek? Do we inquire and delight to know God's ways? Do we strive for righteousness in our lives and obey everything commanded? We need to delight in drawing near and seeking to find our God.

Isaiah 58:2 (Amp) [2]*Yet they seek, inquire for, and require Me daily and delight [externally] to know My ways, as [if they were in reality] a nation that did righteousness and forsook not the ordinance of their God. They ask of Me righteous judgments, they delight to draw near to God [in visible ways].*

If, you have never heard the voice of God speak to you or never felt that anointing come over you, which is the power of God, it may be easy to question, is all this real? However, I challenge you today not to stop, but continue your search and earnestly pray to God with everything within you in order to find that which you are seeking.

Making a Decision

Many times, I have heard people say they plan to come back to church but first there are things they need to clean up in their lives. Many people who do go to church say they plan to start reading their bible, but they have not been able to stop long enough to do so. Many people say they are going to start trying to pray and give time to God, but that time has not come. We need to stop making excuses! Our first decision to make is just to come to Jesus, and He literally wants us to come as we are. We need to get ourselves connected to a body of believers which are walking in the anointed Word of God. Many people think they cannot come to church or start praying and spending time with God because they know they are living in sin. Your guilt keeps you away; however, your guilt is not going to subside if you do not do something different. I have had some say, *"I'm not ready now because there are things I know I need to give up and change in my life before I can start living for God."* However, Jesus wants us to come to Him as we are. He did not die on the cross to save people who feel they are righteous and free of sin, and there is no such thing even though some may think they are free from sin. The Word says in Romans:

Romans 3:23 (Amp)[23]Since all have sinned and are falling short of the honor and glory which God bestows and receives.

All have sinned and come short of the glory of God, but Jesus died on the cross for all who are living in sin. He died for those who are beat down, depressed, alcoholics, drug addicts, living in sexual sin, and living with secrets due to shame. It is not about that person who thinks they are righteous and thinks they are going to heaven but do not "walk the walk" or "talk the talk." Maybe they make good money, have everything they want, and are just fine with their life the way it is. It does not matter, the only way to heaven is through one door and that door is Jesus Christ. There will come a day when those who have money and feel they do not need a God, they will find the treasures they have stored on earth, will not save them. For those who do not believe in God, the day will come that they will realize He is very real, and those things they trusted in will not save them. There will come a day when many, who did not seek God, will face great tragedies in their lives. Perhaps, when doctors can do nothing more or when money cannot buy what they need, the hand of God will come down upon them if they cry out for mercy. Perhaps, God will touch their lives to awaken them during times of hardship. At this point in their lives, they will realize they are not God, and there is a greater power which is more powerful than anything they have witnessed. Hopefully, that day will come for some, but many times, we have no warning when our time is coming near. For those who make excuses and know that their life is not right, their life can be cut short in an instance, and they could find themselves in hell and not heaven. They know they need God in their life but keep putting off today what they could do tomorrow. The same consequences can happen to those who do not believe there is a God as well as those who believe, as they continue to wait for tomorrow to get things right in their life. When life ends, it does not matter if we were believers and never took the time to make it right, or we were unbelievers and never took the time to search inside to find the truth. At this time in our lives, if we were wrong and missed it, there may be no second chance to get it right!

Galatians 5:1(Amp) [1]*IN [this] freedom Christ has made us free [and completely liberated us]; stand fast then, and do not be hampered and held ensnared and submit again to a yoke of slavery [which you have once put off].*

If you have been backslidden and you are trying to get back where you need to be, according to Galatians, we are warned not to be ensnared again to that yoke of slavery. We have discussed, if we are not free in Christ, we are slaves in bondage. In Galatians below, it tells us what happens to those who have fallen from grace and do not find their way back home.

Galatians 5:4(Amp) ⁴If you seek to be justified and declared righteous and to be given a right standing with God through the Law, you are brought to nothing and so separated (severed) from Christ. You have fallen away from grace (from God's gracious favor and unmerited blessing).

Those who have fallen will be judged according to the law. If we are judged according to the law, we are not in right standing with God. Remember, we cannot do any amount of works which will justify us to be in right standing with God. We are only saved through Christ and not by works. If you never make that decision to get your life right with God and repent of your sins, you will not be in right standing with our Father on judgment day.

1 Corinthians 9:24 (Amp) ²⁴Do you not know that in a race all the runners compete, but [only] one receives the prize? So run [your race] that you may lay hold [of the prize] and make it yours.

In 1 Corinthians, this is an example to show us how we are to run this race. This is not saying only one of us will receive a prize. Think about when there is really something you desire, and you just have to have it. You become persistent on doing whatever it takes to get that prize, and this is how we are to be in our walk with Christ. Jesus said come; that is it! We have to be diligent in our seeking. If we want to see the glory of God manifested in our lives, we need to be persistent in our efforts to seek and find God. It will not ever happen if we do not surround ourselves by others who believe. Notice, the psalmist said he hated being in the company of those who did evil and those who are wicked. We will not be able to draw close to God, if we do not make the decision to surround ourselves with those who believe.

310

Psalm 26:5 (Amp) ^{5}*I hate the company of evildoers and will not sit with the wicked.*

Today, if we have not made that decision to seek God and to get connected in order to grow, we need to do so. There is nothing out there that should keep us away from the most important decision of our life. Without Jesus, you are consumed in darkness. If, you wonder why your life is so messed up, ask yourself if it is easier to do a task in the light or the dark? I know I cannot do dishes in darkness, and I cannot fix my hair or put my makeup on in darkness. I cannot drive a car in darkness without some kind of light. Do you see what I am getting at?

John 8:12 (Amp) ^{12}*Once more Jesus addressed the crowd. He said, I am the Light of the world. He who follows Me will not be walking in the dark, but will have the Light which is Life.*

Our lives will remain a mess because without Jesus, there is no light and everything we are trying to do in reality is in total darkness. The light brings life. Are you ready to live a full life, a life full of light and not darkness? No one can make that decision for you. We are all running the race the bible speaks of if we are striving to gain insight and truth into the Kingdom of Heaven. However, some of us are just running in circles, and we never get anywhere, while others have that light shining before them to show the way. We have to make up our mind, we are going to serve God 100% no matter what. We cannot half way serve Him because we will only reap half of a life. Do you desire to have a full life which is full of good things? We are all to produce good fruit, but if you are in darkness, your fruit is spoiled. Fruit does not grow very well when it has no light nurturing it. Fruit needs to sprout forth vibrantly and will not do so without being nurtured. In

311

the natural sense, when we look at the effect the sunlight has on plant life, what do we see? The effect of sunlight or any light source is a form of energy. Photosynthesis is the making by light. It takes the energy carried by light to make and grow plant life. If you watch house plants, which are close to a window, they will begin to lean towards the light source; they follow the light. The same works for our spiritual bodies, if we are living in darkness, our spiritual man will wither and die. When we come into the light, we begin to thrive. In fact, did you know the word "thrive" means to succeed, prosper and increase? As we draw close to the light, which is Christ, this becomes our energy and fuel to be successful, prosperous, and increase in every aspect of our life. This is what fuels us to grow and thrive just the way God created and intended us to survive. Once we make the decision to seek that which is light, we must make that stand not to quit or become discouraged. We must make the decision that we will not allow anything the enemy or the world throws at us to keep us from running towards the light.

How do we do this? By first making the decision we are going to seek our Father. We must spend time in the Word and the presence of our Father. Being persistent always pays off. I cannot emphasize enough how important it is to study God's Word. If we want to learn how to play a new video game, what do we do? We keep practicing and practicing until we get good at it. If we go back to school to learn something to increase our wages, what do we do? We go to class, take notes, and we study because we want to be successful. Why would we not want to be successful Christians? God sent Jesus to die for us in order that we live and live more abundantly. Living a life of abundance would be having all we need and then some. The abundant life is living in perfect health, being happy, prosperous, full of joy, having peace, immersed in God's love, and successful in every area we

312

set forth our HANDS. Why would we not want to study to achieve the life that He has already given us? That life is there, and we just have to tap into it!

In making decisions, one other area needs to be addressed. This is an area which keeps many of us defeated. God cannot bless us when we continually act like the world. I received revelation which will help anyone who desires to be able to overcome those instances where we miss it. It is a matter of what decision you make when you hear that small voice, the Holy Spirit, who was sent to remind us of truth and teach us all things. We need to make the decision to either stop doing what we are doing wrong at that moment or do what He is telling us to do. When we hear His voice, we need to stop and ask ourselves, *"Is it worth disappointing my Father?"* Is this thing worth disappointing Him? I find myself in traffic, and someone cuts me off, then it is as if the "old me" wants to take over. The "old me" would catch up to them and cut them off, but I hear that voice, and the presence of God infiltrates me. I say to myself, *"Is cutting that person off worth it?"* Is it really worth it? This applies to all areas of our lives. When we go out into the world, satan is going to send those across our path to make us angry. He will send those to cause jealousy to emerge or those feelings of hate and selfishness. At that moment, we make a choice to do or not do what the Holy Spirit is saying. Here is the thing, when we stand before God, we will be reminded of all the thousands of times we did things such as:

•Cutting someone off in traffic
•Speaking harshly to a waiter/server in restaurant/drive through window
•Threw up to someone a past incident where they blew it, pointing out their faults
•Swore under your breath because someone made you angry

•Unspoken words but the thoughts were in your mind of those you felt did you wrong
•Sarcasm at those you felt were beneath you
•Criticism towards those you were jealous of

When the Lord reminds us of all these incidents, we are going to think, *"I do not even remember most of these."* The reason is that it is all so nominal. In fact, think back to the last time you cut someone off in traffic. Do you even remember the last time, much alone the details? Think about the last time you got angry with someone or cursed someone out. Do you even remember what it was about? I know many times, we go back and laugh at how foolish we acted once we come to our senses. My point, the Holy Spirit is going to speak to us when we find ourselves in these situations. Are you listening? If you do hear that voice, ask yourself if this is worth having to face your Father on judgment day? Wouldn't it be better to let that person cut you off and say, *"It's okay Lord; it did not hurt me."* In reality, these things do not hurt us. These little things do not cause us physical pain and especially if we do not allow it. We choose our moods. We choose to allow things to affect us, but they do not cost us anything or have any effect on our emotions, unless we allow it. We could even go a bit further, and say, *"Lord, forgive them, for they know not what they do!"* Wouldn't this be a better society if we all walked with this insight? Wouldn't there be more peace if we walked more like Jesus and not like the world? The world is so afraid that someone is going to get the best of them, and therefore, they stand by just waiting. The world is so afraid someone wants what they have, and they are afraid that someone will be better at something they are good at. Their beliefs cause people to think someone deliberately wants to show them up or hurt them in some way. In reality, the world's actions are only hurting themselves. As Christians, God will increase us. He will bless us and make us whole in every area of our lives. The only

314

thing we need to do is just love Him and obey. Let's make that decision today that we are not going to be like the world. We are going to choose God's way and not our way.

Where Do We Fit

If we claim we are saved, then we are God's children. If this is who we believe we are, then we need to wake up and look at our lives. Do our lives show Jesus lives in us? If Jesus does live in us, we would not be greedy, and we would not turn our head the other way. If Jesus lives in us, we would not commit adultery, and we would not knowingly lie in order to continue doing whatever it is we are doing in hopes of not getting caught. We need to look at our lives and be honest on what our lives speak about us. Do our lives say we are striving for the mark of the higher calling? When people look at us, who do they see? Do they see Jesus, or do they see someone selfish, rude, hateful, greedy, or dishonest? Before we begin to look at where we fit in the body of Christ, we need to ask ourselves these questions and be honest.

1) How much time do you spend reading God's Word each week? _____
2) How much do you strive to really come to know God?
   _____
3) Do you have bitterness towards your brothers? _____
4) Do you have unforgiveness towards anyone? _____
5) Do you believe that going to church and doing some ritual on occasions really cleanses you from your sins? _____
6) Do you believe that you can continue to commit adultery, live with hatred in your heart, cheat people, ignore helping those less fortunate, turn your head the other way if it meant having to get involved with something that would take your time, and continue to be greedy living day after day trying to have as much as possible, no matter who you hurt in the process and still make it to heaven? _____

315

If we desire to live that victorious life in Christ, then we must learn to walk this life in Christ and not the world.

Years ago when Jesus walked the earth, everyone knew who His followers were. Everyone knew who the Christians were and the unbelievers. The Christians stood out and were different than those of the world, but today, we cannot tell the difference. Those who claim to be Christians and claim to love Jesus, never witness to others about Him. They do not live differently than those in the world who do not even know Jesus.   However, we see those who are caught up in their own lives, trying to survive, are honest when they say they are not living right and do not believe they would go to heaven. The world is full of people who know they are not right and do not have a real relationship with God. These are the ones that need real Christians. They need Disciples of Christ who are not afraid to show them Jesus. Those who are striving to do their calling, which God has placed on their lives, need to realize the world is full of people who do not have the answers. The world is full of people that are anxious for someone to show them the way. They need someone to give them answers to their problems and solutions to their circumstances. The sad truth is they will receive any answers. They just need answers, and the world is all around them to give worldly wisdom and advice. It is quite evident how much our world is messed up, and those whose lives are shattered are primarily getting answers to their problems from the world.   You can turn on the TV any night or pick up a newspaper/magazine and the headlines are horrific with crime, rape, murder, suicide, depression, and poverty. The sad truth, those who God has called or have been chosen will not step up to the plate to give up some of their time to do that which He has called them to do.

316

The answers to life's solutions are in the Word of God, not the world. The truth is in the Word of God, and the truth will set God's people free. *(John 8:32 Amp)*

We need to step up and say, *"God, send me!"*

Isaiah 6:8 (Amp) ⁸Also I heard the voice of the Lord, saying, Whom shall I send? And who will go for Us? Then said I, Here am I; send me.

We need to show Jesus to those who are lost and suffering. We need to show them how the Father looks at them and how He loves them. We see below, John the Baptist said whoever does not obey the Son of God shall not see life. In order to see life, we must also obey.

John 3:36 (NIV) ³⁶Whoever believes in the Son has eternal life, but whoever rejects the Son will not see life, for God's wrath remains on him."

There are people who claim to be Christians everywhere that do not obey the Word of God. Obedience will be discussed in a later series; however, the point is that if we claim to be Christians, we should obey. If we believe we are saved and we are not obeying the commandments, how can we be sure we are even saved? If we are doing those things we know we are not to do and not doing those things God called us to do deliberately, how can we say that Christ is in us? How can we be sure of our salvation? Perhaps, you are reading this, and you know you are backslidden and need to get back right with God. The 15 years I spent in the world no longer growing, I knew I was not doing what I was called to do. I knew every day that I needed to get myself back to being right with God. Why did it take so long? I lived a lie, and my eyes were blinded to the truth. Where do we find the

317

truth? In the Word of God! The Truth will set us free, and we are only free when we are living under the grace of God, not under the law.

Why then do people think they are saved when they continue to live according to the flesh and according to the world, not the Word of God? I believe much of this is because of what people have been taught. Think back to when you were a child, there are many things our parents taught us that turned out to be wrong. Like for instance, they used to believe you smothered out a fever. Today, it has been found that putting on heavy blankets will only increase a fever, and it is better to have little to nothing on to keep a fever down. That is just one example. Today, there are many things that have been discovered scientifically which had been taught differently years ago. The same is true with religion. Not to say that it is anyone's fault, our parents learned from their parents and so forth. Beliefs go back many generations just as doctrines go back many generations. Many of us have beliefs that may not necessarily be correct, and the truth is we need to all be responsible for our own salvation. It needs to be something that we each seek in the Word of God, and we should not base our salvation on the words of a man or a particular doctrine. We need to know that Jesus lives in us, and the life we now live in the flesh, we live by faith knowing Jesus crucified himself for us.

Galatians 2:20 (Amp) [20]*I have been crucified with Christ [in Him I have shared His crucifixion]; it is no longer I who live, but Christ (the Messiah) lives in me; and the life I now live in the body I live by faith in (by adherence to and reliance on and complete trust in) the Son of God, Who loved me and gave Himself up for me.*

We need to have that deep, heartfelt feeling, knowing that God and Jesus are alive and are with us today. We need to know what that feeling is when the Holy Spirit comes down upon us, and when He gives us the anointing to have power to do all things in the name of Jesus. When we know that we are saved, there should be a desire within our heart that daily longs to know God. This is not just to know of Him but to know everything about Him.

Many people in the world today are looking for answers. Their lives are in torment, and they are engulfed in sin. They continue day after day to try the same things over and over again expecting a different result, only to be faced with more and more pain. Many have crossed my path, and I speak the Word. They listen and many times, the seed which is planted, the enemy consumes. We will look into the Word, in order to be able to recognize what category each of us fit in according to what Jesus shared with His disciples. This will help us possibly understand why we cannot connect with God, in order to be able to break through areas of our lives to reach that which may seem unreachable. The following parable, "The Parable of the Sower," is where Jesus taught the people, and then, He explained in more detail to His disciples in order for them to understand. We will examine the Scripture beginning with the explanation given to the disciples. The first type of person is one who hears the Word, and the enemy immediately takes away that which was planted.

Matthew 13:19-23(Amp)[19]While anyone is hearing the Word of the kingdom and does not grasp and comprehend it, the evil one comes and snatches away what was sown in his heart. This is what was sown along the roadside.

The seed which we sow represents the Word of God. Jesus described 4 types of people. The first type is someone who has a hardened heart. This person is someone who does not grasp or understand the Word, and the Word is rejected. They hear the

319

Word, but because of their heart being hardened, immediately the enemy comes and steals what was sown. Our enemy is satan. How does our heart become hardened? Many things can harden someone's heart. My heart was hardened from an early age. There was no God in our home, and there was no love in our home. There was a lot of pain which began from my earliest remembrances as a little girl. Many instances come to my mind when I think about my childhood, and of all those things that I remember, most were very painful. I remember very few happy times. When we are raised in a family with physical, mental, and emotional abuse, it is hard to have love within our heart. When we are living in a home where there is anger, fighting, and strife, we are absorbed into a world which is negative. When we grow up in this atmosphere, it is no wonder that our hearts are hardened. Let me share with you some of the effects of a hardened heart. These are some of the thoughts which go on inside the mind of the victim:

•I am not going to let that person get close to me.
•I will not open up and talk to anyone.
•Do not ask me to share anything with you because I have nothing to say.
•If you force me to talk, I am going to lie.
•I can just pretend that everything is okay, no one will know.
•I will not let you hurt me anymore.
•If, I act in the way they expect, no one will be able to see what is really on the inside.
•Pain, no there is no pain in my life, do you not see that I am always laughing and making jokes.

Do any of these speak to you? This was my life! I was always the center of attention with my friends, always laughing and joking around. I hid it very well from the outside world what went on in my home, along with what I felt deep inside. Around adults, regardless if it was family, neighbors, close contacts, or complete

320

strangers, there was no way anyone would have gotten me to open up. In front of a group of peers, where there were many who seemed to be excelling far beyond me, I was very quiet. Like I said earlier, I would take an "F" in class before I would get up in front of my classmates and read a report. Inside, I was hurting, and I felt inferior. I was very insecure, and I thought no one cared or loved me. To me, life did not matter. Maybe, that speaks to you. What did I do during these days? I began building those walls in order to keep anyone else from being able to get close to me. I feared being hurt by someone else, and I felt if you could not get close to me, you could not hurt me. I tried to control who and what I would allow to get next to me. However, even if I let you near, I did not open up! When we build walls in order to keep our pain in and not let anyone else close, we are enabling God from being able to reach us, as well.

If we see ourselves as the person who has hardened their heart, we have either built a wall or we have rejected God's Word. There are many who have hardened their hearts and may be unaware. Perhaps, we have a closed mind, or we believe we have already found what we need. Maybe, we think we are capable of making it without seeking "some God" that we cannot see. Maybe, we just do not believe that we even need any of that religious stuff. To a certain point, I could not agree with you more. Many have tried the church scene and have been disappointed because the church has become a social gathering. Many feel that they do not fit in the click within the churches, or they feel excluded. We will discuss this further, in another series, to examine the differences between religion and Christianity to a greater degree. For now, we need to look into why many in the world are without God. Many today have a false belief and have no desire to listen because they do not believe there is a God. Therefore, they do not want to hear what the Word says, and they refuse to believe there is a greater power. They look at the doctrine as being false. In order to get ahead and make it in this world, they believe fate falls in their own hands. Everyone at some point in their life will have a need that will be far greater than imaginable, and they will be unable to provide the answers or solution to have victory over their circumstance or situation. We will all see at some point, God does exist and does, in fact, answer prayers. We will come to recognize Jesus did die for all our sins in order that we may have life and have it more abundantly.

No amount of money can cure cancer or ease the pain of losing a child. No amount of money can take away depression, or no amount of education can solve every problem and situation that can occur in our life span. It does not matter how smart we think we are or how many years we have gone to school. The truth is, at some point in our life that which has been stored in our warehouse, to be able to live a good life, will not be sufficient. There is only one solution and answer to every problem, every situation that man can face today, and that is Jesus Christ.

The Second Type of Person

[20]*As for what was sown on thin (rocky) soil, this is he who hears the Word and at once welcomes and accepts it with joy;* [21]*Yet it has no real root in him, but is temporary (inconstant, lasts but a little while); and when affliction or trouble or persecution comes on account of the Word, at once he is caused to stumble [he is repelled and begins to distrust and desert Him Whom he ought to trust and obey] and he falls away.*

The second person Jesus describes is one who hears the Word and immediately receives it. This person may hear a dynamic message at church and be pumped up. They make the decision that they are going to get right with God and do what the message said. They are excited; however, there is no root. This person may go to church on occasions, or maybe, they go when they are seeking answers. They may have felt that the message they heard was an answer to prayer which was meant for them. However, they leave church and do nothing to retain the Word they heard. There is no growth because they do not read the Word. There is no root system because they do not spend time studying God's Word or seeking God in prayer. Since there is no root, as soon as temptations come and satan begins to attack, they begin to stumble. Next, the tests begin, and trials arise because of the Word they heard. They believed, and they listened. Persecution comes engulfing them from all directions. They stumble, and they fall because their roots are very shallow. The Word, which was received so intently, begins to fade very rapidly.

The Third Type Person

[22]*As for what was sown among thorns, this is he who hears the Word, but the cares of the world and the pleasure and delight and glamour and deceitfulness of riches choke and suffocate the Word, and it yields no fruit.*

The third person hears the Word because they go to church on a regular basis. However, this person's life is consumed in the world. The Word soon becomes forgotten because of the cares of the world. They believe in God and what the Word says, and at times, they strive to live by the Word. However, there are other things, which dominate what they do and where they go. The things which consume them may not be bad things, but they allow things to have priority over the Word. The things, which consume their lives, are the weeds and thorns which overshadow the Word. These individuals will never bear good fruit because they do not have priorities lined up with the Word of God. They are continually trying to do things their way and not Gods. They do not understand the concept of letting go of everything and letting God show them their path in life. They may even remain in church, struggling to be a victorious Christian. Their walk will never be fruitful, and they will never achieve that which God desires for them. Let's take a deeper look into who this third person is, the one who may be a Christian but is not fruitful. This person struggles in their walk with God. They allow the thorns and thistles to control their life. The thorns and thistles become anything they put before God or anything they allow to keep them in bondage. These things may be spending endless hours in front of the television, while their life or their family is a mess. It may be video games or countless hours on the computer which control their lives. Anything they allow to consume their time, instead of seeking those things above, becomes their thorns and thistles. Things in this world should be worked around our time with God, not the other way around. If our minds are being controlled to the things of this world, where we do not spend time seeking, studying, and growing with God, then those things become our idols. God desires great things for us, and He has chosen our paths. When we work God into our lives instead of working our lives into God's plan, we are allowing the weeds to choke out the Word which has been planted. The thorns and thistles in our lives will come in and choke the Word which we have within, and this is the enemies plan to keep us in bondage where we do not grow. The Word says we must die to self not live to satisfy our flesh. Paul said in 1 Corinthians…

1 Corinthians 15:31 (Amp) [31][I assure you] by the pride which I have in you in [your fellowship and union with] Christ Jesus our Lord, that I die daily [I face death every day and die to self].

We should die daily by putting off the old nature and walking according to the Spirit instead of the flesh. It should no longer be about our desires. It should no longer be the desires of the flesh, but instead, it should be God's desires and His will for our lives.

Galatians 5:24 (Amp) [24]*And those who belong to Christ Jesus (the Messiah) have crucified the flesh (the godless human nature) with its passions and appetites and desires.*

This third person will be unproductive, defeated, and very easily could fall. They continue to love God but do not understand why He is not blessing their life. They do not understand why they have so many problems and struggles in life. There may be an area of their life where sin holds them in bondage. There may be something they have a weakness in, and satan knows it. If the enemy knows, he will keep it in front of them in order to keep them defeated. If we remain consistent on surrounding ourselves around other believers, God is continually working on bringing us to a greater level of growth and revelation.

The Fourth Type Person
[23]*As for what was sown on good soil, this is he who hears the Word and grasps and comprehends it; he indeed bears fruit and yields in one case a hundred times as much as was sown, in another sixty times as much, and in another thirty.*

The fourth person is one who receives, understands, acts on and lives by the Word. These people have the revelation of how to let go and let God be in charge of their lives in every aspect. They will bear much fruit and produce good fruit. They will live a victorious life in Christ, and their life will represent service for God. They will be doing all in which He has called them to do, being obedient to His calling. Their life will be full, and blessings will begin to follow their every day walk, overflowing with abundance.

John 10:10(Amp) ¹⁰*I came that they may have and enjoy life, and have it in abundance (to the full, till it overflows).*

If you are a Christian who loves God and believes that Jesus is the Son of God, you need to study this parable Jesus taught. You need to look closely at where you fit in and where you desire to be. In order to begin seeing that victory rise up in our lives, we have to recognize where we are before we can strive to be in that preferred place.

Walking in Victory

Claim victory in your life today! Start walking in the truth, while speaking victory over your life, not defeat. What does the Word say about faith?

Hebrews 11:1-3(ESV ¹*Now faith is the assurance of things hoped for, the conviction of things not seen.* ²*For by it the people of old received their commendation.* ³*By faith we understand that the universe was created by the word of God, so that what is seen was not made out of things that are visible.*

We have to start believing those things which are not as though they were! Do we believe there is a God? Do we believe Jesus lived, and that He really died and rose again? Do we believe in the resurrection? We did not see any of this but only read about it! If you believe all of these things, which you have not seen, then this is faith. If you believe those things that are not as though they were, that is walking by faith. Faith is the

326

assurance of things hoped for but not seen. If we really believe something, it shows in what comes out of our mouth. If we really believe something, it shows by our everyday walk. What do we speak as Christians? Do we speak positive, faith-filled words? Or, do we speak defeat? We have to start walking in faith and watching what we say. What comes forth out of our mouth is really what is in our heart.

Luke 6:45 (NIV) [45]The good man brings good things out of the good stored up in his heart, and the evil man brings evil things out of the evil stored up in his heart. For out of the overflow of his heart his mouth speaks.

If we believe what God's Word says, then we should speak it forth. We should speak those positive things that God's Word says about us. When the enemy tries to attack us in areas where we are weak, we do not need to agree with him. There is a whole chapter, in another volume, which will speak on faith and how to walk in it. For today, we need to know that our words have great power, and we need to be aware of what we speak forth. Walking in victory takes faith. We believe we already have the victory through the blood of Jesus. It takes knowing that our words do make a difference, and it takes perseverance, which is standing on what we believe and not giving up. We must stand and not quit.

2 Thessalonians 2:13 (NIV) [13]But we ought always to thank God for you, brothers loved by the Lord, because from the beginning God chose you to be saved through the sanctifying work of the Spirit and through belief in the truth.

Of course, believing is never going to happen unless we spend time feeding our spirit man. We must read and study while also spending time in prayer and communion with God. It is not going to happen unless you bring your flesh into obedience to the Word of God. We have to line up our flesh to the Word and stop letting our flesh control what we do. Before we begin to look at how to walk in victory, let's first look at how we lost that victory which takes us back to the beginning.

From the beginning, we know that Adam and Eve lived a perfect life full of victory. However, once they sinned, everything they had ceased. Every single promise, every blessing, and their whole existence came to an end at that moment. They were cut off from everything which God had given them when they fell from grace. This is what God told Adam...

Genesis 3:17-18 (NIV) [17] *To Adam he said, "Because you listened to your wife and ate from the tree about which I commanded you, 'You must not eat of it,' "Cursed is the ground because of you; through painful toil you will eat of it all the days of your life.* [18]*It will produce thorns and thistles for you, and you will eat the plants of the field.*

This is the curse of the land today, but as God's children, this curse is not for us. This curse is for those who live according to the world and not the Word. This curse was for those who lived under the law. Today, if you are saved, you no longer have to put effort into your works and produce nothing in return. If you are living a victorious life in Christ, then your efforts you put forth in your work will and should prosper! If you are saying that your life is not prosperous and you are a Christian, then it is because satan is trying to keep you from the truth, so you cannot walk victoriously. I am here today to show you and tell you, this victorious life of a Christian can and will be yours. I can remember

328

a time in my life when I struggled to make ends meet. I never made enough money, and nothing seemed to prosper in my life. I lived like most Americans, paycheck to paycheck! After getting the concept that God wanted to bless us, during the time I was with my children's dad years ago, things began to change in our lives. He was offered a job that paid enough for me to quit work. We had medical/dental benefits for the whole family, and all our needs were met. I was a "stay at home" mom when my girls were little for many years! We had land given to us to put a house on and were prospering! Prior to that time, my life was like most of Americans today, living paycheck to paycheck. When God begins to prosper you, He also begins to teach you wisdom on how to spend your money. It is not that God does not want us to have nice things, but we have to go through a time where we are obedient with what He has given us before we start receiving more. After years of prospering and God teaching me how to make money, I never lost that gift. Even today at this time in my life, God is teaching me to be wise with what I have. My free spending has stopped, but it has not been a bad thing. God has been teaching me to recognize what is important to buy and what is not. When your life lines up with His will, all of a sudden, you find you want to spend more money on giving to His Kingdom. Not just in giving to the church, which we are required to do, but also to those who He sends across our path. I never know who I will be giving to, but He does. God knows I will be obedient when He tells me to give.

When we are not receiving the blessings in our life, which we are entitled to, as a child of God, the curses in our lives are not just about lacking in finances. When we have lack in our life, this lack may be spiritually, emotionally, and physically (in our bodies). Prior to Jesus shedding His blood, we were cursed with lack in all these areas. Today, we can be filled spiritually and emotionally with no lack. Today, we can be in total health where we are ailing in nothing. Our finances will start coming in as we draw close to God spiritually. I do not believe a person will ever quite get to the financial blessings if they do not reach the spiritual blessings first. God will not pour out material wealth on an individual who is not where he should be spiritually. The bible says the love of money is the root to all evil, but it does not say that money is the root. Until we can get to a place where we desire those things which are heavenly and pure, we could not handle the financial blessings because it would destroy us. In Matthew it says, for what profit is it if a man gains the world but loses his soul?

Matthew 16:26 (ESV) [26]*For what will it profit a man if he gains the whole world and forfeits his soul? Or what shall a man give in return for his soul?*

As a child of God, we are no longer under the curse; therefore, we should live in victory. We discussed above about the four types of people today, let's take a deeper look into the third and fourth. From all we have studied at this point, hopefully we are all seeking God. We should all be spending time in prayer and His Word. Perhaps, we are even seeking to be connected to a body of believers, at this time, in order to grow at a faster pace. We have to come to that place where we are more persistent and diligent in our seeking. When we are in that place with God, most of us are going to fall into either the third or fourth category. Therefore, we need to take a deeper look at both of these types.

The third person continues to walk in the curse that was placed on Adam and Eve. If, you fall into this category and desire the wisdom and knowledge to be able to walk like those in the fourth category, then the best way to achieve that is to look deeper into how that person walks.   The fourth type is one who understands the concept of living a Christian life, 7-days a week. They understand the importance of prayer, studying, and doing the calling that God has placed on their heart. They know when they walk according to the commandments in the Old Testament, as well as everything which Jesus taught in the New Testament, those thorns and thistles will begin to vanish. You may be in the third striving toward the fourth, which is a good thing as long as you remain diligent in your walk because eventually you will get there.

When we do get to that fourth category, there will still be trials. However, as we get stronger, we understand why those trials and tests are there. We understand that we do not walk them alone. The Holy Spirit is there with us in order to walk us through each and every trial. Remember, James said to count it all joy when we face temptations and trials. *(James 1:2)* With each test, we grow stronger. When Jesus walked on earth, He was tempted in every area. What happened when temptation came? He spoke Scriptures. He did not have to get angry or allow himself to be upset. Jesus did not have to worry or stress. He just spoke the word, *"It is written..."* The Scriptures say, we will face trials, but the growing process is learning how to deal with each situation we face. We will miss it, but that is okay. As long as we are open to hearing the Holy Spirit, He is going to let us know we missed it. Therefore, we need to ask for forgiveness and go on because even after we miss it, if we make it right with God, we will feel at peace. Many times, the Holy Spirit immediately begins to share revelation with me that explains why the path I just walked occurred in the first place. Why does He do this? He is trying to teach us lessons. The Holy Spirit will show us how satan was able to get through to us. He will show us why we reacted the way we did. Sometimes, He will encourage and give us reassurance that we did pretty well because we finally allowed His

Words to infiltrate us. *(John 14:26)* We may not have wanted to listen to the Holy Spirit in the beginning because we were upset, but if our heart is right, we cannot stay in that mindset. We then repent, and God forgives us. If you get by yourself with the Father, He is going to speak to you with greater wisdom. You will learn with each trial that you are not walking it alone, and there will be strength which comes as you endure the test knowing you have already won.

Let me say that if you are not the fourth type but desire to be in this category, and you find yourself struggling, stop struggling! Stop right now! It does not have to be a struggle to walk with God. You are only struggling within yourself, and God desires you to let go of something in order to receive more of Him. Just like the time when I was struggling with this book, it was about my flesh desiring to take over. When I realized this and let go, I allowed God to be in charge again. At that point, everything became peaceful again. Why would we not want peace all the time? Stop thinking that you have to achieve walking this overnight because you are only adding pressure to your life, and this is not God. If, you desire to be in this place with God, begin by taking the necessary steps to get there. Every day is a new day. We must have some type of goal in order to achieve this walk, and we must make a commitment to God. We need to decide, we are going to read the Word a little every day. We must make the commitment to pray and seek God a little every day, whether it is 5 or 10 minutes. This is the beginning to achieve that goal. Next, make a commitment that you are going to spend time with others on a weekly basis that are walking the walk, whether it is in church or some kind of small group ministry. We must spend time with others who believe like Christ. Those we should strive to spend quality time with should be those who are committed to God. Their Christian walk should show in their everyday life and not just on Sundays or whatever day they have church. If, you are at a place that you cannot get out to go to church due to sickness, no transportation, or whatever the reason, find a ministry on television and commit to watching it on a weekly basis. However, at some point, you need to be connected to a local ministry. Find one that makes home visits. I know I attend one in which we go into many homes on a weekly basis bringing the Word of God and praying for peace. If you are reading this and you are incarcerated in the prison system, there are many Christian agencies out there who would love to reach out to you. There are many churches with prison ministries, so be diligent in finding a source to get connected with a body of believers for your support system, and do not give up. Pray that God will lead you and others across your path that will bring light to your world, not darkness. We need to start with a goal, no matter how small and stick to it. As you become comfortable with spending time with God and praying, then increase your time. If you want to see God move in your life, you have to put forth effort. It will not happen if you stay where you are. It is important for us to continue to grow on a daily basis.

To walk in victory in our life, we know the number one key is drawing close to God, and we must be open enough to listen and obey. Our goal should be to strive to be that fourth person which Jesus taught in the parable. We should aim for that higher mark of Christianity. The higher mark is for all of God's children, but we must have that deep desire to want it. After salvation, our greatest aim should be to seek in order to find, and be persistent knowing our God will meet us if our heart is pure.

In the End

In the end, we will all have walked through our journeys in life. There will be some who will begin to question life and have a sense of dissatisfaction, while others will become satisfied no matter what road they travel. If we come to a place in our journey where we are searching for answers, only the truth in God's Word will set our feet on that course which was destined for each of us by our Creator, while we were yet in the womb. Even though, we must be thankful for the many blessings God has bestowed upon us, we must never get to a place of comfort that we stop striving to reach those different levels with our Creator. We have yet to arrive until Jesus returns, but while we are waiting, we must continue to reach for that deeper knowledge. With everything we gain, we must continually desire to pray, and we must seek God for wisdom and insight, only then will the pieces of the puzzle begin to line up for a clearer view of the "Big Picture" to the Kingdom of Heaven.

It is written... Those who choose the road to evil shall be cut off, while those who continually wait, hope, and look for the truth, only found in Jesus, shall inherit the earth. *(Psalm 37:9)* Where is your inheritance today? Where are you storing your treasures? We must never be content, but always know, there is so much more and continually look within ourselves for that God given faith to rise up, in order to run the race set before us enduring to the end. *(Hebrews 12:1)*

It is written... God might humble and test you, in order to do you good in the end. *(Deuteronomy 8:16)* Do we murmur and complain when faced with hardship, or do we walk forward boldly proclaiming Jesus to this dying world? Are we easily led astray due to circumstances, or do we strive and search deep within for the hidden answers and truth which God will reveal in order to see victory time and time again in our lives? What will your end be? Will you walk through this journey alone, or will you take comfort in knowing that God will never leave you or forsake you even in times of trouble? *(Hebrews 13:5)* Stand up and count it all joy when faced with hardship, for as we endure and walk through with confidence, we gain so much more, and our victories, gifts, and miracles will be evident as we gain a wealth of knowledge only given by the Father to those whose confidence rests in Jesus. *(James 1:2-4)*

It is written... In the last days, there will be those who seek to gratify their own unholy desires, and it is these who set up distinctions causing divisions, these are sensual creatures, worldly-minded, devoid of the Holy Spirit, and destitute of any higher spiritual life. *(Jude 1:18-19)* Are we led by our sensual desires or by a higher spiritual life, which can only be found through the Holy Spirit? We must search deep within in order to know we are continually filled with the presence of God, so that we do all which has been commanded of us up to our last days.

It is written... For the Lord delights in justice and forsakes not His saints; they are preserved forever, but the offspring of the wicked [in time] shall be cut off. (Psalm 37:28Amp) Through the journey of life, our search within must be one of knowing that we are in right-standing with our Creator, and we abhor from any and all wickedness. We must refrain from anger and turn from wrath, as it leads to evil; evil men will be cut off, but those who place their hope and trust in the Lord will inherit the land. *(Psalm 37:8-9)*

It is written... Misfortune pursues the sinner, but prosperity is the reward of the righteous. (Proverbs 13:21NIV) In our search, we must be mindful of the calamity which falls beside us and desire that God tests our hearts, in order that we remain pure and righteous in His sight.

Many wake up towards the end of their days, and they have regrets because their life was one spent of satisfying the sinful nature and leaving God behind. We only have one journey, and we all are on a course either uniquely designed by God or by the enemy. My prayer for every person who has read this book is that you truly seek God for direction from this point forward, and you never stop striving to learn of Him, to learn of Christ. Every journey in this life can be one that ends with fulfillment, knowing you ran the race which was set before you, and you endured to the end. Paul said in 2 Timothy 2:15, we should study and be eager and do our utmost to present ourselves to God approved, correctly analyzing and dividing the Word of Truth. As Paul came close to the end of his life, in 2 Timothy 4:7-8, he stated that he had fought the good fight and finished the race holding firmly to the faith. For Paul's obedience and devotion to serving God, as a true Disciple of Christ, his crown of righteousness was laid up in heaven, not only for him, but for all those who have loved and yearned for the return of Christ.

Father, I thank you and pray for every individual who reads these words. I pray that You will cultivate every seed planted and manifest who You are, in a way that they receive Your Words of Truth and begin their journey in life searching deep within, in Jesus name. Amen.

References

Chapter 5 – The Journey through Adolescence

1. APA: *research: statistics on top new year's resolutions.* (n.d.). Retrieved from
http://www.proactivechange.com/resolutions/statistics.htm

The Sinner's Prayer

Heavenly Father, I come before you and I acknowledge that Jesus Christ is Your only begotten Son and that He came to earth in the flesh, died on the cross in order to take away all of my sins and the sins of the world. I believe that Jesus then rose from the dead on the third day, in order to give all who call upon His name, eternal life.

Jesus, I confess all of the sinful things which I have done in my life, and I ask that You forgive me and wash away all my sins by Your precious blood, which you shed for me and all of mankind on the cross at Calvary. I accept You Lord Jesus, right now, as my personal Lord and Savior, and I ask that You come into my life and live with me for eternity.

Amen!